FIRST BOOK
OF
SANSKRIT

FIRST BOOK
OF
SANSKRIT

BEING A TREATISE ON GRAMMAR WITH EXERCISES

BY

SIR RAMKRISHNA GOPAL BHANDARKAR
M.A.., PH.D., LL.D., K.C.I.E., & c., &c.,

ENLARGED AND REVISED BY

SHRIDHAR R. BHANDARKAR, M.A.

GYAN

Published by

Gyan Publishing House
5, Ansari Road
Daryaganj, New Delhi-110002
Phone: 011-47034999, 9811692060
E-mail: books@gyanbooks.com

Distribution Network
gyanbooks.com
India, USA, Canada, UK, Australia, France

ISBN : 978-81-212-2556-4 (HB)
First Published, 1883

2nd Impression 2021

Printed at: Gyan Press, Delhi.

First Book of Sanskrit
Author: Sir Ramkrishna Gopal Bhandarkar

अथ

मार्गोपदेशिका

संस्कृतं जिज्ञासूनां

अनेकपण्डितपरिषद्भिर्धर्मशास्त्राचार्यतत्त्वमीमांसाचार्येति

भारतवर्षराजाधिराजेन च राजपुरुषविशेषे-

त्युपपदैर्भूषितनाम्ना

भाण्डारकरकुलोत्पन्नेन गोपालसूनुना

रामकृष्णेन

विरचिता ।

तज्ज्येष्ठसूनुना मास्तर आव् आर्तेत्युपपदधारिणा

श्रीधरेण प्रपञ्चिता च ।

PREFACE TO THE FIRST EDITION

The study of Sanskrit has but recently risen in the estimation of the educated natives of this Presidency and of our educational authorities. The old Sanskrit College of Poona owed its existence and continuance rather to a spirit of conciliation and toleration in our rulers than to their conviction of the utility of Sanskrit as a branch of general education. The modern critical and progressive spirit was not brought to bear upon it. The old Śāstris were allowed to carry all things in their own way. After about thirty years since its establishment, the authorities began to exercise active interference, until at length the College was abolished and a new system inaugurated, which, to be complete and effective, requires, in my humble opinion, a partial restoration of the old institution.

This newly-awakened and more enlightened zeal in favour of Sanskrit cannot last, or produce extensive results, unless books are prepared to facilitate the general study of that language. I have heard students complain that they find Sanskrit more difficult than Latin, and many have actually left the study of their own classical tongue for that of its foreign rival. I do not know if this complaint has a foundation in the structure of the two languages; but this, at least, I am sure of, that Sanskrit would be considerably more easy than it is, if there were men educated in our English Colleges to teach it, and if books specially adapted for beginners were available. It was with the view of supplying, in some measure, this latter desideratum that this little book was prepared about a year and a half ago. Its plan was originally sketched out by

Dr. Haug, though in a few places I found it necessary to deviate from it. The book is intended principally for boys; but, for the benefit of young men whose minds have already undergone some culture, I have added a great deal of matter, especially in foot-notes, which perhaps ought not to be introduced into a book written merely for children. In preparing the book I found nothing so difficult as composing from about forty to fifty sentences, Sanskrit and English, for each lesson, since my choice of words and grammatical forms was considerably limited by the conditions. of that lesson. I have, however, done what I could, and in several places, especially at the end, have put in such sentences, occurring in original Sanskrit works, as I remembered. It is attempted to teach nearly all the declensions, some irregularities only being omitted, four conjugations of verbs, two tenses end one mood, passive forms, and some of the more important verbal derivatives.

Poona, March 1864 R. G. B.

PREFACE TO THE SECOND EDITION

One of my aims in giving to this book its peculiar form was to enable the intelligent student to go through it without assistance. I am now happy to learn that this object it remarkably fulfils. To increase its efficacy in this respect, such explanations as seemed to be called for have been added in the shape of foot-notes, and a few other improvements and modifications been made.

Ratnagiri, 16th November 1866. R. G. B.

PREFACE TO THE FIFTH EDITION

It has come to my knowledge that, in some of the schools, in which this book is taught, the teachers consider it to be their only duty to get their pupils to translate mechanically from and into Sanskrit the sentences given in each lesson. They pay little or no attention to the grammatical portion. In others, such books as the common *Rūpāvali* are put into the hands of the pupils, and they are made to learn by heart the declensional forms given in these. This shows a misconception of the object of this book, which is evidently to teach grammar, and to teach it not for its own sake, but in its connection with the language, not in a manner simply to overburden the pupil's memory, but in a manner to awaken and encourage thought. The sentences are intended to serve as exercises in the rules and forms and should be used as such. The teacher should see that the pupil thoroughly understands the rules and knows the forms, and, in going over the sentences, get him frequently to explain the grammar of the words occurring therein, and such other points. Repeated exercise is what the teacher should particularly attend to. To help him in this portion of his work, and to enable the pupil to digest what he has learnt into a connected whole, I have in certain places given examination questions, and brought together the results of the lessons that precede. Another improvement is a General Glossary of all the words contained in the book, which will be found at the end.

I am very glad to hear from my friend, the Curator of the Government Book Depot, that this book is used in various parts of India, and that the demand for copies is daily increasing and extending over a wider area. The improvements made in this edition will, I earnestly hope, increase its usefulness and render it still more acceptable.

Bombay, 9th September 1871. R. G. B.

PREFACE TO THE EIGHTH EDITION

A new lesson on the Potential Mood has been added in the present edition. All the conjugational tenses and moods of the first group of conjugations have thus been brought together in the same book.

Poona, 17th May 1888. S. R. B.

PREFACE TO THE TWELFTH EDITION

It has long been the intention of the author of this book to add to the sentences for exercise given in the various lessons. Time and the opportunity offering themselves, this intention has been carried out in the present edition.

There seems to be a feeling among some teachers that the introduction of rules regarding grammatical forms makes the acquisition of a language very difficult to beginner and that it would be much easier to acquire a language, if, instead of rules, ready-made grammatical forms of model words were set before the student to learn off by heart. But in a language, like Sanskrit in which a great many words in common use have peculiarities of their own, such model words would carry a student but a little way. And a scientific study of the grammar of a dead language, which is not learned for use in practical life, is certainly to be preferred to a mere empiric study; while, in the case of Sanskrit, it has, as remarked by the author in the Preface to the Third Edition of his Second Book, a very high educational value. The great mission of Sanskrit has been to communicate a powerful impetus to the philological thought of Europe and supply it with correct principles and sound basis and thus to bring Comparative Philology and the Science of Language into existence as branches of human knowledge. It is the knowledge of the scientific grammar of the language as elaborated by the great Indian Grammarians which has led to these results and not the transparency of Sanskrit, as thought by some scholars, since Sanskrit is no more transparent than, for instance, Greek, and, but for the labours of the Indian Grammarians, would have been as opaque as that language was up to the discovery of Sanskrit. And such a knowledge alone will enable our students to understand those results and to carry on similar investigations, at least as regards the Vernaculars of the Country. And, as observed by the author in the place above indicated, grammar learnt scientifically is more easily and longer remembered than when learnt empirically. For these reasons a scientific study of the grammar of Sanskrit cannot be begun too early; but, if anybody for any reason whatever prefers the empiric method, he may follow it even in using this book. He has simply to confine his attention to the model words and ready-made forms given there. Those too, who object to the introduction, in the first lessons, of the rules about *guṇa* and about the change of the final vowel of roots of the first conjugation on the ground of difficulty to beginners, ought not to forget what the author stated thirty-two years ago in the Preface to the First Edition, *viz.*, that the matter given in foot-notes is specially intended for young men whose minds have already undergone some culture; and they will see that the student, who finds it difficult to master those two or three rules, can without any inconvenience whatsoever disregard them altogether until he is well advanced in his study of the book.

Bombay, 24th April 1896. S. R. B.

PREFACE TO THE NINETEENTH EDITION

At the suggestion of some teachers the *saṁdhi* rules and rules relating to Syntax occurring in the foot-notes are in this edition gathered together, for convenience of reference, in an Appendix placed before the Glossaries.

Bombay, 1st November 1914. S. R. B.

PREFACE THE TWENTY-EIGHTH EDITION

The diacritical marks used in the previous editions of this book were those that had been in vogue when the first edition was published in 1864. Oriental Societies in India and elsewhere have since adopted a practically uniform system for transliterating the Sanskrit and allied alphabets; and finding it desirable that students should be familiar with it from the commencement of their study of Sanskrit, I hav introduced in this edition the diacritical marks adopted in that system.

A. S. BHANDARKAR.

उपोद्घातः ।

संस्कृतभाषागहनं प्रविविक्षूणां मार्गोपदेशिकेयं पाठावलिर्ग्रथ्यते । अस्यां चैकैकस्मिन् पाठे पूर्वं प्रकृतिप्रत्ययाङ्गकार्यादीनि प्रदर्श्य पश्चाद्यथासंभवं सुप्तिङ्कृदन्तानां रूपाणि वाक्येषु प्रयुज्योदाहरिष्यामि । तानि च वाक्यान्याङ्ग्लभाषया विद्यार्थिनो विपरिणमयेयुः । तथैवाङ्ग्लवाक्यानि पाठान्ते लेखिष्यमाणानि संस्कृतरूपं प्रापयेयुः । इत्थमल्पायासेनैव यान्यत्र विभक्त्यादिरूपाण्युपनिभन्त्स्यन्ते तान्यध्येतुः स्मृतौ दृढमवगाढानि भविष्यन्ति । संस्कृतवाक्येषु व्युत्पत्तिस्तद्रचनायां चाल्पमपि पाटवं समासादितं च भविष्यति ।

संस्कृतं जिज्ञासूनामीप्सितसिद्धिकृत्सु रघुवंशादिकाव्येषु सत्सु किमर्थोऽयं यत्न इति चेदुच्यते । काचिदप्यपरिचितपूर्वा भाषा तस्या व्याकरणमनधीत्य न सम्यग् ज्ञायते । एतदेवाभिप्रेत्य व्याकरणप्रयोजनेषु लघ्वसंदेहाविति प्रयोजनद्वयं कात्यायनः परिसंचख्यौ भाष्यकृच्चेन्द्रबृहस्पत्याख्यायिकामुदाजहार । ननु तर्हि सहैव काव्येन लघुकौमुदी तत्सदृशोऽन्यो वा व्याकरणग्रन्थोऽप्यधीयतां किं पुनरनया पाठावल्येति चेन्न । तादृशानां ग्रन्थानां

बालकैः प्रौढवयस्कैरपि पुरुषैः संस्कृतमजानद्भिर्दुरव-
बोधतया तेषामध्ययने महान् कालक्षेपो भवति गरीयांश्च
परिश्रमोऽपेक्ष्यते । न तथेद्दशस्य ग्रन्थस्य । तस्य सरलान्व-
यिवाक्यवत्त्वात्तद्गतव्याकरणसिद्धान्तानामपि वैशद्येना-
भिहितत्वात् । एतल्लक्षणस्य ग्रन्थस्याभावात्संप्रति कति-
पये नवविद्यार्थिनः संस्कृताध्ययनात्पराजयन्ते तन्मा
भूदितीयं पाठावलिर्यथामति विरच्यते ॥

TABLE OF CONTENTS

Notes

Notes

FIRST BOOK OF SANSKṚT.

ALPHABET.

Vowels.

अ *a*, आ *ā*, इ *i*, ई *ī*, उ *u*, ऊ *ū*, ऋ *ṛ*, ॠ *ṛ*, ऌ *ḷ*,
ए *e*, ऐ *ai*, ओ *o*, औ *au*,

ं (Anusvāra) *ṁ*   : (Visarga) *ḥ*.

Consonants.

Gutturals	क् *k*,	ख् *kh*,	ग् *g*,	घ् *gh*,	ङ् *ṅ*,
Palatals	च् *c*,	छ् *ch*,	ज् *j*,	झ् *jh*,	ञ् *ñ*,
Linguals	ट् *ṭ*,	ठ् *ṭh*,	ड् *ḍ*,	ढ् *ḍh*,	ण् *ṇ*,
Dentals	त् *t*,	थ् *th*,	द् *d*,	ध् *dh*,	न् *n*,
Labials	प् *p*,	फ् *ph*,	ब् *b*,	भ् *bh*,	म् *m*,

Semi-vowels {
Palatal य् *y*,
Lingual र् *r*,
Dental ल् *l*,
Dental and Labial व् *v*,

Sibilants ... {
Palatal श् *s'*,
Lingual ष् *ṣ*,
Dental स् *s*,

Aspirate..................ह् *h*.

The last three letters of each of the first five classes together with the semi-vowels and the aspirate, are called *soft consonants*.

The rest are called *surds* or *hard consonants*.

The vowel letters assume the following forms when added to consonants :—

The addition of अ is to be known by the obliteration of the nether stroke; and for आ, इ, ई, उ, ऊ, ऋ, ॠ, ऌ, ए, ऐ, ओ, औ, we have ा, ि, ी, ु, ू, ृ, ॄ, ॢ, े, ै, ो, ौ, respectively, as in the following instances, in which these vowels are added on to क्—क ka, का kā, कि ki, की kī, कु ku, कू kū, कृ kṛ, कॄ kṝ, कॢ kḷ, के ke, कै kai, को ko, कौ kau.

The principal conjunct consonants are these :—

क्क k-ka	ग्र्य g-r-ya	ट्ट ṭ-ṭa	त्प t-pa
क्त k-ta	ग्ल g-la	ट्य ṭ-ya	त्प्र t-p-ra
क्त्व k-t-va	ग्व g-va	ठ्य ṭh-ya	त्फ t-pha
क्न k-na	घ्न gh-na	ठ्र ṭh-ra	त्म t-ma
क्म k-ma	घ्य gh-ya	ड्ग ḍ-ga	त्य t-ya
क्य k-ya	घ्र gh-ra	ड्म ḍ-ma	त्र t-ra
क्र k-ra	घ्व gh-va	ड्य ḍ-ya	त्र्य t-r-ya
क्ल k-la	ङ्क ṅ-ka	ड्व ḍ-va	त्व t-va
क्व k-va	ङ्क्त ṅ-k-ta	ढ्य ḍh-ya	त्स t-sa
क्ष k-ṣa	च्च c-ca	ण्ण ṇ-ṇa	त्स्न t-s-na
क्ष्ण k-ṣ-ṇa	च्छ c-cha	ण्म ṇ-ma	त्स्य t-s-ya
क्ष्म k-ṣ-ma	च्छ्र c-ch-ra	ण्य ṇ-ya	द्ग d-ga
क्ष्य k-ṣ-ya	च्छ्व c-ch-va	ण्व ṇ-va	द्द d-da
क्ष्व k-ṣ-va	च्म c-ma	त्त t-ta	द्ध d-dha
ख्य kh-ya	च्य c-ya	त्त्र t-t-ra	द्ब d-ba
ग्ध g-dha	ज्ज j-ja	त्थ t-tha	द्ब्र d-b-ra
ग्न g-na	ज्र j-ra	थ्य th-ya	द्भ d-bha
ग्र g-ra	ज्व j-va'	त्न t-na	द्म d-ma

द्य d-ya
द्र d-ra
द्र्य ḍ-r-ya
द्व d-va
द्व्य d-v-ya
द्व्र d-v-ra
ध्न dh-na
ध्म dh-ma
ध्य dh-ya
ध्र dh-ra
ध्व dh-va
न्न n-na
न्म n-ma
न्य n-ya
न्व n-va
प्त p-ta
प्त्य p-t-ya
प्न p-na
प्म p-ma
प्य p-ya
प्र p-ra
प्ल p-la

प्स p-sa
ब्ज b-ja
ब्द b-da
ब्ध b-dha
ब्य b-ya
ब्र b-ra
भ्ण bh-ṇa
भ्न bh-na
भ्य bh-ya
भ्र bh-ra
भ्व bh-va
म्म m-ma
म्य m-ya
म्र m-ra
म्ल m-la
म्व m-va
य्व y-va
र्ण्य r-ṇ-ya
र्ध्व r-dh-va
ल्क l-ka
ल्ग l-ga
ल्प l-pa

ल्म l-ma
ल्य l-ya
ल्ल l-la
ल्व l-va
व्य v-ya
व्र v-ra
श्च ś-ca
श्न ś-na
श्म ś-ma
श्य ś-ya
श्र ś-ra
श्ल ś-la
श्व ś-va
ष्क ṣ-ka
ष्क्र ṣ-k-ra
ष्ट ṣ-ṭa
ष्ट्य ṣ-ṭ-ya
ष्ट्र ṣ-ṭ-ra
ष्ट्व ṣ-ṭ-va
ष्ठ ṣ-ṭha
ष्ठ्य ṣ-ṭh-ya
ष्ण ṣ-ṇa

ष्प ṣ-pa
ष्प्र ṣ-p-ra
ष्म ṣ-ma
ष्य ṣ-ya
ष्व ṣ-va
स्क s-ka
स्ख s-kha
स्त s-ta
स्थ s-tha
स्न s-na
स्प्र s-p-ra
स्फ s-pha
स्म s-ma
स्य s-ya
स्र s-ra
ह्ण h-ṇa
ह्न h-na
ह्म h-ma
ह्य h-ya
ह्र h-ra
ह्ल h-la
ह्व h-va

LESSON I.

VERBS.

*Parasmaipada**—Present tense.

SINGULAR TERMINATION.

1st Pers. मि, 2nd Pers. सि, 3rd Pers. ति.

Roots of the First Conjugation.

गम् [गच्छ †] to go	बुध् (बोध्) to know or understand	रक्ष् to protect
नी (नय् ‡) to lead, to carry	भू (भव्) to be, to become	वद् to speak
पत् to fall		वस् to dwell
		सृ (सर्) to move

* There are two sets of conjugational terminations in Sanskṛt, *Parasmaipada* and *Ātmanepada*. Some roots take exclusively the former, and some the latter; while there are others which take either.

† The substitutes and other changes which some roots undergo before the conjugational sign (such as that mentioned in rule, p. 5) are shown within rectangular brackets

‡ The final vowel and the penultimate short of roots take their *guṇa* substitute before the अ (see rule, p. 5) of the first conjugation. The *guṇa* of इ or ई is ए, of उ or ऊ is ओ, of ऋ or ॠ is अर्, and of ऌ is अल्.

Thus नी becomes ने to which अ is to be joined, and then the termination ति. In Sanskṛt, two vowels cannot come together without coalescing, and the rule to be observed in the present case is, that the preceding ए, ओ, ऐ and औ become अय्, अव्, आय् and आव् respectively; and then the following vowel is added on to them; ने+अ=नय्+अ=नय; and with ति, नयति. Similarly, भू+अ=भो+अ=भव्+अ=भव; and with ति, भवति. The forms, which roots assume in consequence of such vowel changes, are enclosed within circular brackets.

* *Roots of the Second Conjugation*—अस् to be, अद् to eat.

अ is added on to the roots of the first conjugation before the terminations. In the second conjugation the terminations are applied directly.

Before the terminations of the first person beginning with म् and व् the preceding अ is lengthened.

वदामि ।	सरसि ।	गच्छति ।	भवति ।
रक्षसि ।	नयामि ।	अद्मि ।	अत्ति । †
पतति ।	वससि ।	नयति ।	अस्ति ।
बोधसि ।	सरामि ।	बोधामि ।	

1st Conjugation

चर् to go, to walk
दह् to burn
पच् to cook
जीव् to live
नम् to bow to, to salute
त्यज् to abandon

(Thou) speakest.	(I) dwell.	(He) moves.
(He) speaks.	(Thou) fallest.	(I) become.
(Thou) goest.	(Thou) walkest.	(Thou) eatest.
(I) go.	(He) knows.	(I) am.
(He) dwells.	(Thou) leadest.	(Thou) art.‡

---

* As the Second Conjugation is very difficult, only two roots are given in this book. It is fully treated of in the Second Book.

† Before hard consonants, the preceding consonants, except nasals, substitute the first (*i. e.*, hard unaspirate) letter of their class; as ककुभ्+प्रान्त = ककुप्प्रान्त, and वृक्षाद् + पतति = वृक्षात्पतति.

‡ अस् loses its final before सि.

(He) lives.	(Thou) burnest.	(He) cooks.
(He) abandons.	(I) protect.	(I) abandon.
(Thou) bowest.	(He) walks.	
(I) cook.	(I) live.	

LESSON II.

PLURAL TERMINATIONS.

1st Pers. मस्, 2nd Pers. थ, 3rd Pers. * अन्ति.

4th Conjugation	*6th Conjugation*
नश् to perish	इष् [इच्छ्] to wish
नृत् to dance	प्रच्छ् [पृच्छ्] to ask
पुष् to nourish	मुच् [मुञ्च्] to leave, to release
मुह् to be silly, to lose sense, to faint	विश् to enter
	सृज् to abandon, to create
लुभ् to covet	स्पृश् to touch

In the fourth conjugation य, and in the sixth अ, are added on to the roots before the terminations. †

The अ of the root अस् is dropped before the plural and dual terminations.

वदामः । ‡	नयामः ।	स्थ ।
गच्छन्ति ।	भवथ ।	अदन्ति ।
बोधथ ।	वसन्ति ।	दहामः ।

* The preceding अ is dropped before a termination with an initial अ.

† In these conjugations the vowels do not take their *guṇa* substitute as in the first.

‡ At the end of words स्, whether followed by any letter or not, and र्, followed by a hard consonant or by nothing, are changed to a *visarga*.

सन्ति ।	नश्यन्ति ।	स्पृशामः ।
जीवथ ।	नृत्यथ ।	सृजथ ।
नमन्ति ।	मुह्यामः ।	इच्छन्ति ।
पुष्यामः ।	लुभ्यन्ति ।	पृच्छथ ।

मुञ्चामः । विशन्ति ।

1st Conj.	*4th Conj.*	*6th Conj.*
जि (जय्) to conquer	अस् to throw	क्षिप् to throw
दृश् [पश्य्] to see	कुस् to embrace	तुद् to inflict pain on
धाव् to run	तुष् to be pleased or satisfied	दिश् to show
पा [पिब्] to drink	लुट् to wallow	सिच् [सिञ्च्] to sprinkle
यज् to worship	शुष् to dry	
वह् to bear, to blow, to flow.		
स्मृ (स्मर्) to remember		
हृ (हर्) to take away, to remove		

(You) speak.	(You) live.	(We) drink.
(We) go.	(They) nourish.	(You) worship.
(They) know.	(We) perish.	(They) bear.
(You) lead.	(They) dance.	(We) remember.
(They) become.	(You) are silly.	(You) throw.
(We) dwell.	(We) covet.	(They) embrace.
(You) eat.	(They) touch.	(We) are satisfied.
(We) are.	(We) conquer.	(They) dry.
(They) burn.	(You) take away.	(You) wallow.
(We) live.	(They) see.	(You) sprinkle.
(They) inflict pain.	(We) throw.	

LESSON III

DUAL TERMINATIONS.

1st Pers. वस्, 2nd Pers. थस्, 3rd Pers. तस्.

* *Roots of the Tenth Conjugation.*

कथ् to tell	चिन्त् to contemplate	प्रथ् to publish
गण् to count	चुर् (चोर्) to steal	प्री [प्रीण्] to please
घुष् (घोष्) to proclaim	पीड् to give pain to, to afflict	रच् to arrange
		स्पृह् to desire

Roots of the tenth conjugation take अय before the terminations.

चोरयावः ।	घोषयथः ।	नमथः ।
पीडयथः ।	स्पृहयावः ।	स्तः ।
कथयतः ।	चिन्तयतः ।	स्मरावः ।
गणयावः ।	प्रीणयथः ।	जयथः ।
प्रथयावः ।	गच्छतः ।	नश्यतः ।
रचयतः ।	नयावः ।	नृत्यावः ।
अद्धः ।	विशतः ।	इच्छतः ।

---

* Roots of the 10th conjugation are, as a general rule, both *Parasmaipadi* and *Ātmanepadi*.

† Before अय the final vowels and the penultimate अ (except in some cases, as कथ्, गण्, रच्, प्रथ्, &c.) take their *vṛddhi* substitute; the *vṛddhi* of अ is आ; of इ, ई or ए is ऐ; of उ, ऊ or ओ is औ; of ऋ or ॠ is आर्; and of ऌ is आल्. The penultimate short vowel (except in some cases, as स्पृह्, मृग्, &c.) takes its *guṇa* substitute. Thus, चि becomes चै, which with अय is चायय, and with ति, चाययति; तड्+अय=ताड्+अय=ताडय, and with ति, ताडयति; घुष्+अय=घोष्+अय=घोषय, and with ति, घोषयति.

1st Conj.	*4th Conj.*	*6th Conj.*
अट् { to wander, to ramble	कुप् to be angry	उञ्छ् to glean
चल् to go, to move	क्षुभ् to be agitated	कृष् to plough
जल्प् to prate; prattle	श्लिष् to embrace	स्फुर् to throb
निन्द् to censure		
शंस् to praise or tell		

10th Conj.

पूज् to adore, वर्ण् to extol or describe, सान्त्व्, to appease.

(You two) steal.
(They ,,) give pain.
(We ,,) tell.
(You ,,) count.
(They ,,) see.
(We ,,) arrange.
(You ,,) desire.
(They ,,) proclaim.
(We ,,) contemplate.
(You ,,) publish.
(They ,,) please.
(We ,,) censure.

(You two) are angry.
(They ,,) plough.
(We ,,) adore.
(You ,,) ramble.
(They ,,) are agitated.
(We ,,) glean.
(They ,,) extol.
(We ,,) embrace.
(You ,,) prate.
(They ,,) appease.
(We ,,) praise.

(You two) speak.
(They ,,) become.
(You ,,) cook.
(We ,,) understand.
(They ,,) eat.
(We ,,) are satisfied.
(You ,,) covet.
(They ,,) wallow.
(We ,,) touch.
(You ,,) ask.

LESSON IV.

Present Tense Generally.

1st Conj.	*4th Conj.*
क्षि (क्षय्) to waste away	मद् [माद्] to be mad, to err
द्रु (द्रव्) to water, to be wet	शम् [शाम्] to be or become calm, cool or tranquil
रुह् (रोह्) to grow	श्रम् [श्राम्] to be weary
स्था [तिष्ठ्] to stand	
ह्वे (ह्वय्) to call	

10th Conj.

क्षल् (क्षाल्) to wash off | **तुल् (तोल्)** to weigh
तड् (ताड्) to beat | **भूष्** to adorn

वदसि ।	मुह्यति ।	ताडयसि ।	हरतः ।
वसथ ।	इच्छामि ।	रोहन्ति ।	जयसि ।
बोधामः ।	मुञ्चथ ।	पूजयति ।	पिबन्ति ।
रक्षति ।	स्पृशति ।	तिष्ठामि ।	पश्यावः ।
पतामि ।	स्मरथ ।	स्पृहयथ ।	ह्वयति ।
नयन्ति ।	वहतः ।	क्षालयति ।	पीडयन्ति ।
अत्थः ।	सिञ्चति ।	क्षयतः ।	यजामः ।
सन्ति ।	लुभ्यन्ति ।	अद्मि ।	श्राम्यामि ।
नश्यसि ।	तुष्यामि ।	जीवामः ।	घोषयथ ।
नृत्यति ।	अस्यथः ।	त्यजथ ।	गणयति ।
विशामः ।	कथयामि ।	पचन्ति ।	कृषामः ।
पृच्छथः ।	शंसथ ।	पुष्यामि ।	द्रवन्ति ।

चिन्तयति ।

(He) nourishes.	(He) is silly.	(It) wastes away.
(I) dance.	(They) are satisfied	(Thou) tellest.
(You) covet.	(I) conquer.	(He) weighs.
(He) enters.	(You) go.	(They) steal.
(Thou) wishest.	(Thou) art weary.	(You) arrange.
(I) adore.	(I) wish.	(He) proclaims.
(Thou) givest pain	(We two) drink.	(I) remember.
(It) grows.	(You) burn.	(They two) dwell.
(We) call.	(They) wash off.	(We) take.

(You) tell.	(He) steals.	(They) beat.
(Thou) touchest.	(We two) are.	(We two) cook.
(They) desire.	(Thou) pleasest.	(You) adore.
(You two) go.	(I) enter.	

GENERAL RESULTS AND EXAMINATION

PRESENT TENSE

1st Conjugation

	Sing.	*Du.*	*Pl.*
1st pers.	बोधामि	बोधावः	बोधामः
2nd pers.	बोधसि	बोधथः	बोधथ
3rd pers.	बोधति	बोधतः	बोधन्ति

4th Conjugation

1st pers.	पुष्यामि	पुष्यावः	पुष्यामः
2nd pers.	पुष्यसि	पुष्यथः	पुष्यथ
3rd pers.	पुष्यति	पुष्यतः	पुष्यन्ति

6th Conjugation

1st pers.	विशामि	विशावः	विशामः
2nd pers.	विशसि	विशथः	विशथ
3rd pers.	विशति	विशतः	विशन्ति

10th Conjugation

1st pers.	चोरयामि	चोरयावः	चोरयामः
2nd pers.	चोरयसि	चोरयथः	चोरयथ
3rd pers.	चोरयति	चोरयतः	चोरयन्ति

1. What are the

   a Gutturals,
   b Palatals,
   c Linguals,
   d Dentals,
   e Labials,
   f Semi-vowels,
   g Soft consonants,
   h Hard consonant ?

2. Give the *Guṇa* and *Vṛddhi* of

   (*a*) इ,
   (*b*) उ,
   (*c*) ऋ,
   (*d*) ऌ.

3. What are the characteristics of the

   (*a*) First conjugation,
   (*b*) Fourth „ ,
   (*c*) Sixth „ ,
   (*d*) Tenth „ ,
   (*e*) Second „ .

4. Repeat the terminations of the Present Tense.

5. What change does the preceding अ undergo before व् and म् of the 1st person ?

6. To what syllables are ए, ओ, ऐ and औ changed, when followed by a vowel ? Give instances.

7. Explain the change a consonant undergoes when followed by a hard consonant. Give instances.

8. What are final स् and र् changed to ? Under what circumstances does the latter undergo the change ?

9. Give the forms of the Present Tense of—[As many roots as are necessary to impress the forms thoroughly on the pupil's memory should be put under this question by the teacher.]

Prepositions (उपसर्ग).

Prepositions (उपसर्ग) when prefixed to verbs modify the original sense of the roots. The following are the principal of these :—

अति beyond; अतिक्राम्यति goes over or beyond, transgresses.

अधि { over, about, upon; अधिगच्छति goes over or on *i. e.*, knows or gets.

अनु after, like; अनुसरति, अनुगच्छति goes after, follows.

अभि to, unto, near to; अभिगच्छति goes to, or near to.

अव down, off, from; अवतरति goes down, descends.

आ { bounding or limiting, reversing to, as far as; आगच्छति comes, आरोहति grows to, ascends.

उद् { up, above, superior; उत्पतति falls up, jumps; उद्गच्छति goes up, rises.

उप near, less, next to; उपगच्छति approaches.

नि in, down; निषीदति sits down.

परा opposite, or opposed to; पराजयते defeats.

प्रति reverted, again; प्रतिभाषते speaks in return, replies.

प्र forth, before; प्रयाति goes forth.

वि privation, apart, away; विश्लिष्यति separates.

सम् being conjoined with; *संगच्छते becomes united unites.

---

*म् at the end of a word or particle, followed by a consonant in general, is changed to an *anusvāra* optionally, and necessarily when it is followed by श्, ष्, स्, र्, or ह्. When it is not changed to an *anusvāra*, it is changed to the nasal of the class to which the following letter belongs and to a nasal य्, व्, ल्, when followed by य्, व्, ल्, respectively.

LESSON V.

NOMINATIVE CASE.

1. Nouns ending in अ.

Terminations.

	Singular	*Dual*	*Plural*
Masculine	स्	औ	अस्
Neuter	म्	ई	आनि
	नृपः	नृपौ*	नृपाः†
	फलम्	फले‡	फलानि

SUBSTANTIVES.

(*Masculine*).

अनल fire	नर a man	मेघ a cloud
अश्व a horse	नृप a king	राम name of a person
ईश्वर God	पवन wind	वृक्ष a tree
कूर्म a tortoise	पुत्र a son	समुद्र the see
जन people, a man;	बुध a wise man	सूद a cook
जीव life, an animal	मूर्ख a fool	हस्त the hand

* If ए, ऐ, ओ or औ follow अ or आ, the vowel which takes the place of both is ऐ in the first two cases, and औ in the last two.

† When any vowel, short or long, except the last four, is followed by the same vowel, short or long, the substitute for both is the same vowel lengthened; दैत्य+अरि=दैत्यारि; कवि+ईश=कवीश; &c.

Note *p. 6 is not applicable in the case of the forms of the Nom. and Acc.

‡ If अ or आ is followed by इ, उ, ऋ, or ऌ, short or long, the corresponding *guṇa* letter is substituted for both.

(*Neuter*)

कमल a lotus	दुःख misery	पर्ण a leaf	मुख the mouth
गृह a house	धन wealth	फल fruit	सुख happiness
जल water	नेत्र the eye	मित्र a friend	हृदय the heart

SENTENCES

नृपो*जयति ।	सुखं§ प्रीणयति ।	कूर्मः सरति ।
अश्वा†वुत्पततः ।	जीवो मुह्यति ।	फले पततः ।
जना‡वदन्ति ।	हस्तौ हरतः ।	धनं नश्यति ।
बालःस्पृहयति ।	मुखानि द्रवन्ति ।	नरा गच्छन्ति ।
गृहाणि‖रक्षन्ति ।	दुःखं पीडयति ।	कमले नृत्यतः ।
नेत्रे पश्यतः ।	रामः पूजयति ।	मित्राणि कथयन्ति ।
मेघः सिञ्चति ।	पुत्रौ तुष्यतः ।	
बुधौ मुञ्चतः ।	जलं शुष्यति ।	सूदो विशति ।
पवनो हरति ।	मूर्खौ कुप्यतः ।	समुद्रः शाम्यति ।

* When a *visarga* is preceded by अ and followed by अ, or a soft consonant, it is changed to उ, which, with the preceding अ, becomes ओ (see the last note, p. 14).

† See note ‡, page 4.

‡ *Visarga* preceded by आ and followed by a vowel or a soft consonant is dropped. It is also dropped when preceded by अ and followed by any vowel except अ. The two vowels, thus brought together by the dropping of *visarga*, do not coalesce ; *e. g.*, नरा इमे for नराः इमे; बुध इच्छति for बुधः इच्छति.

‖ न् coming after ऋ, ॠ, or ष् in the same word is changed to ण्. This change takes place even if a vowel, a semi-vowel (ल् excepted), the aspirate ह्, or a letter of the guttural or labial class comes between ऋ, ॠ, or ष् and न्. This change does not take place when न् ends a word ; as नरान्.

§ See note, page 13.

Kings protect.
(Two) children wallow.
(A) son pleases.
Horses gallop.
Winds bear.
God creates.
Trees grow.
(The two) tortoises move.
Animals perish.
(The) hand throws.
Fire burns.
(An) eye throbs.
(The two) seas are agitated.
(A) wise man is calm.
Fools prate.
(A) friend asks.
Leaves fall.
(The) heart is satisfied.
Cooks cook.
People censure.
(A) man tells.
(A) lotus adorns.
(The) mouth speaks.

2. Nouns ending in इ.

Terminations

	Singular	*Dual*	*Plural*
Masculine	स्	(none)	अस्

In the dual the vowel इ is lengthened, and before अस् of the plural it takes the *guṇa* substitute.

	हरिः	हरी	(हरे + अस् =) हरयः
Neuter	(none)	ई	इ

Before the terminations beginning with a vowel न् is added on to nouns in इ of the neuter gender. इ is lengthened before the nominative and accusative plural terminations.

वारि वारिणी वारीणि

SUBSTANTIVES.

(*Masculine*).

अग्नि fire
अरि an enemy
असि a sword
उदधि ocean
ऋषि a sage
कपि a monkey

कवि a poet
गिरि a mountain
धूर्जटि the god Śiva
नृपति a king
पवि Indra's thunderbolt
पाणि the hand
यति an ascetic
व्याधि sickness or disease
हरि the name of a man, or the god Indra

न not (indeclinable).* **वारि** *n.* water.

SENTENCES

उदधिः क्षुभ्यति ।
कपयः क्षिपन्ति ।
ऋषी चिन्तयतः ।
अरिः पीडयति ।
पाणी हरतः ।
नृपति†र्यजति ।
वारीणि शुष्यन्ति ।
अग्निर्दहति ।
कवयः शंसन्ति ।
वारि नास्ति ।
गिरिर्वहति ।
व्याधयो नश्यन्ति ।
पविःपतति ।
असयः पतन्ति ।
यती चिन्तयतः ।

‡ Śiva protects.
|| Sages are tranquil.
Monkeys run.
(A) poet describes.
Kings lead.
(The two) fires become cool.
Disease afflicts.
Ascetics do not desire.
(The) sword falls.
(The two) enemies conquer.
Hari becomes angry.
(The) hand sprinkles.
(The) mountain § stands

---

* Words which do not take case-terminations, *i. e.*, are not inflected, are *indeclinable*.

† स् or *visarga* preceded by any vowel except अ or आ, and followed by a vowel or a soft consonant, is changed to र्.

‡ र् followed by र् is dropped, and the preceding vowel (except ऋ), if short, is made long.

|| *Visarga* followed by श्, ष्, or स् is either retained or changed to श्, ष्, or स् respectively.

§ *Visarga* followed by च् or छ् is changed to श्; by त or थ् to स्; and by ट् or ठ् to ष्; as हरिश्चरति for हरिः चरति; रामस्तरति : रामष्टीकते.

LESSON VI

ACCUSATIVE CASE.

1. Nouns ending in अ.

Terminations.

	Singular	*Dual*	*Plural*
Masc.	म्	औ	आन्
	बुधम्	बुधौ	बुधान्

Neuter—same as the nominative.

The accusative forms of neuter nouns are always the same as those of the nominative.

SUBSTANTIVES.

(*Masculine*).

अगद medicine	पुरुष a man	व्याघ्र a tiger
ओदन cooked rice	प्राज्ञ a wise man	व्याध a hunter
किंकर a servant	बिडाल a cat	शठ a rogue
कोश a treasure	ब्राह्मण Brāhmaṇa	शर an arrow
गज an elephant	भार a burden	शिष्य a pupil
ग्राम a village	मोक्ष absolution	सिंह a lion
जनक father	योध a warrior	सूर्य the sun
देह the body	वेद Veda (Hindu sacred scriptures)	स्तेन a thief
पाद the food		स्वर्ग heaven

(*Neuter*).

अरण्य a forest	नगर a town	वस्त्र cloth
तत्त्व reality, truth	पाप sin, evil	विष poison
तृण grass	पुस्तक a book	सुवर्ण gold
धान्य corn	मांस flesh	

Roots :—*10th Conj.*

दण्ड् to punish ; भक्ष् to eat ; मार्ग् to seek.

SENTENCES.

ईश्वरं जनः पूजयति ।
नृपः शठान् दण्डयति ।
रामो*ऽश्वमारोहति ।
व्याघ्रो मांसमत्ति ।
हरिर्हस्तौ क्षालयति ।
योधः शरान् क्षिपति ।
धनं लुभ्यति ।
स्तेनो धान्यं चोरयति ।
नगरं †गच्छामि ।
पापं वदसि ।
स्मरसि मित्राणि ।
बुधो मोक्षमिच्छति ।
व्याधयो नरान् पीडयन्ति ।
जलं पिबथ ।

कविर्बुधौ शंसति ।
पुत्रो जनकं सान्त्वयति ।
पुस्तकं मार्गयामि ।
सुवर्णं तोलयामः ।
ग्रामानटावः ।
फले भक्षयामि ।
कमलानि पश्यति ।
भारं वहति किंकरः ।
प्रज्ञान् वर्णयन्ति जनाः ।
वस्त्रे त्यजति मूर्खः ।
तृणा‡न्यत्त्यश्वः ।
यतिर्देहं मुञ्चति ।
बिडालां‖स्ताडयति पुरुषः ।
गृहं प्रविशामः ।

---

* When ए or ओ at the end of a word or grammatical form is followed by अ, the latter merges into the former, *i. e.*, it is neither pronounced nor written. In its place the mark ऽ is generally put.

† Verbs implying motion govern the accusative, and sometimes the dative, of the place to which the motion is directed.

‡ When इ, उ, ऋ, and ऌ, short or long, are followed by a dissimilar vowel, य, व्, र्, and ल् are respectively substituted for them.

‖ A final न्, when followed by च्, छ्, त्, थ् and ट्, ठ् is changed to an *anusvāra* and *visarga*. The *visarga* is, in the present case, further changed to स् (see foot note §, p. 17).

Rāma sees tigers.
Horses bear (the) treasure.
(A) wise man ascends (to) Heaven.
Lions devour elephants.
(He) counts (the) fruits.
(The) ascetic goes to (a) forest.
(The) warrior discharges (two) arrows.
God protects men.
(We) enter (two) villages.
(A) son pleases (his) father.
Men eat tortoises.
Monkeys ascend trees.
(He) asks (the) servants.
(They) wash (their) feet.

(Two) fools drink poison.
Kings punish thieves.
(They) arrange (the) books.
(You) eat cooked rice.
(His) friends remember Rāma.
People praise (their) kings.
Wise men lead people.
(I) understand (the) truth.
(The) *Vedas* praise (the) sun.
(The) father calls (his two) children.
Fools censure wise men.
(The) king speaks (to the) warrior.

2. Nouns ending in इ.

Terminations.

	Singular	*Dual*	*Plural*
Masc.	म्	[none]	न्

The ending इ is lengthened in the dual and before the न् of the plural.

हरिम् हरी हरीन्

SUBSTANTIVES (*Masculine*).

अतिथि a guest
अधिपति a master
अलि a bee
कलि a strife, a quarrel
किरि a boar
बलि an oblation (food)
भिक्षुक a beggar
मणि a jewel
रवि the sun
राशि a heap
वायस a crow
विधि fate.
व्रीहि rice of various kinds (a grain of)
सारथि a charioteer

क्षल् *10th Conj. with* प्र, to wash
गण् *10th Conj.* to care for, to mind
दा [यच्छ्] *1st Conj.* to give, to offer
नन्द् *1st Conj. with* अभि, to rejoice in, to like
नी *1st conj. with* आ, to bring
सृ *1st conj. with* अनु, to follow
अपि (indeclinable) even

SENTENCES.

वायसो बलिं भक्षयति ।
नृपतिररीञ्ज्* जयति ।
हरिं पीडयति व्याधिः ।
मेघो वारि सिञ्चति ।
कमलमलीन् प्रीणयति ।
रामो रविं नमति ।
पाणी प्रक्षालयामः ।
असीन्वहन्ति योधाः ।
कपिं मुञ्चामि ।
नृपतिं वर्णयन्ति कवयः ।
मणिं चोरयति स्तेनः ।

अधिपतीन्किंकरा अनुसरन्ति ।
उदधिं गच्छावः ।
ऋषी नमामः ।
व्याघ्रः किरीनत्ति ।
सारथीनाह्वयामः ।
ईश्वरो विधिं जयति ।
राशिं नयतः ।
व्रीहीनुञ्छति भिक्षुकः ।
गिरी†आरोहन्ति ।
कविं जनः पूजयति ।

---

*When स् or a consonant of the dental class is compounded with श् or a consonant of the palatal class, a letter of the latter class is substituted for the former, and in this order, *viz.*, श् for स्, च् for त्, ज् for द् &c. The same happens when dentals are combined with linguals, ष् being substituted for स, ट् for त्, ड् for थ्, &c.

†There are a few cases in which two vowels, though coming together, do not coalesce. The rule applicable in the present case is, that when the dual of a noun or a verb ends in ई, ऊ, or ए, these vowels do not combine with another following them

यतिं पृच्छन्ति शिष्याः ।
व्याधिं न गणयामि ।

अतिथीन्पूजयन्ति ब्राह्मणाः ।
कलींश्चाभिनन्दति बुधः ।

Poets praise sages (*Ṛṣis*).
Rāma salutes poets.
(An) ascetic goes to (the) mountain.
(I) strike (two) monkeys.
Hari brings heaps.
(He) touches (the) hand.
Medicines remove diseases
(The) hunter sees (two) boars.
Hari beats (his) enemy.

(A) warrior throws (a) sword.
(I) desire jewels.
(He) rambles (over) seas.
(The) man enters fire (pyre).
(He) asks (two) charioteers.
People please (the) kings.
Even kings bow to ascetics.
Horses drink water.
Men offer oblations.

LESSON VII.

Instrumental Case.

Nouns ending in अ and इ.

Terminations.

		Singular	Dual	Plural
Masc.	अ	इन	भ्याम्	ऐस्
	इ	ना	भ्याम्	भिस्

The preceding अ is lengthened before भ्याम्

Singular	Dual	Plural
दण्डेन	दण्डाभ्याम्	दण्डैः
मणिना	मणिभ्याम्	मणिभिः

Neuter { Nouns ending in अ are in all except the first two cases declined exactly like the corresponding masculine.

	Singular	Dual	Plural
इ	आ	भ्याम्	भिस्
	वारिणा*	वारिभ्याम्	वारिभिः

---

* See the rules p. 16, and note ‖, p. 15.

SUBSTANTIVES.

(*Masculine*).

अलंकार an ornament.
आतप sun (sunshine)
इन्द्र god of thunder
उपहार a present
कर the hand
कासार a lake
कौशिक a descendant of **कुशिक**
दण्ड a stick
देव God, a god
नद a river
नाविक a sailor
पत्ति a foot-soldier
बाण an arrow
मन्त्र Vedic verse
यजमान a sacrificer
यत्न effort
रथ a chariot
रावण king of Lankā or Ceylon, the great enemy of Rāma
विधि sacret precept
श्लोक a verse

(*Neuter*)

अन्न food
अर्घ्य materials of worship
इन्धन fuel
खनित्र a spade
गोत्र family, race
चक्र a wheel
नख a nail
पुण्य merit
यन्त्र a machine
रत्न a jewel
शरीर the body
शास्त्र a science
शीर्ष the head
सूक्त a Vedic hymn

ADJECTIVES.

खञ्ज lame
प्रभूत many, much, plentiful.

Note :—Adjectives agree with the substantives they qualify in number, gender and case.

ROOTS.

1st conj.

खन् to dig
गम् *with* **अव**, to know
चल् to move
नम् *with* **अव**, to become bent, to bend down
राज् *with* **वि**, to shine, to appear beautiful
हृ *with* **प्र**, to strike

दॄ (**दार्**) *10th* conj.* to tear.

INDECLINABLE

सह with

---

* **दॄ**, to tear, belongs to the 9th conj. but may be practically regarded as belonging to this conj. also

SENTENCES

पुरुषःस्तेनं दण्डेन ताडयति।

शरीरमलंकारैर्भूषयति।

नाविका नदेन समुद्रं प्रविशन्ति।

योधो बाणैररिं जयति।

पादेन खञ्जः। [हरिः।

पुत्रैः *सह ग्रामं गच्छति

चक्राभ्यां चलति रथः।

खनित्रेण खनति।

रामोऽर्घ्येण†ऋषिं पूजयति।

कवयः श्लोकैर्नृपं वर्णयन्ति।

बुधाःसुखेन जीवन्ति।

नेत्राभ्यां पश्यति जनः।

वारिणा हस्तौ क्षालयति।

पाणिभ्यां स्पृशति शीर्षम्।

सिंहो नखैर्गजान् दारयति।

अग्निना गृहं दहति।

बुधः शास्त्रै‡स्तत्त्वमवगच्छति।

पत्तिभिर्गच्छति योधः।

पादाभ्यां धावन्ति बालाः।

पुण्येन हरिं पश्यति।

करेणाह्वयति रामं हरिः।

रामःकपिभिर्जयति रावणम्।

गोत्रेण कौशिकोऽस्मि।

दुःखेन मुह्यति जीवः।

इन्धनैः पचत्योदनम्।

Rāma adorns (his) body with jewels.

Man speaks with (his) mouth.

Men nourish (their) bodies with food.

---

* सह governs the instrumental.

† ऋ (short) after any vowel except the last four is optionally not combined, and the preceding vowel, if long, is made short.

‡ See note §, page 17.

(They) bear loads by (their) heads.
Hari pleases (the) sage with efforts.
Kings are pleased with presents.
Chariots move by (means of) machines.
(The) Brāhmaṇas invoke (a) god with (two) hymns.
(He) worships God according to (by) (the) sacred precept.
(He) praises Rāma by (two) verses.
(The) man strikes (his) enemy with (a) sword.
Rāma goes with (the) charioteer.
(A) lake appears beautiful by (means of) lotuses.
People are not pleased even with many jewels.
(We) go to (a) village in (by) (a) chariot.
(He) pleases (the) gods with oblations.
(A) tiger lives on (by) flesh.
(He) contemplates God in (by) his mind.
Indra strikes mountains with (his) thunderbolt.
Trees grow by (means of) water.
Monkeys are satisfied with fruits.
Spring adorns trees with leaves.
Lakes get dry on account of (by) (the) sun.
(The) head bends down with (the) burden.

LESSON VIII.

DATIVE AND ABLATIVE CASES.

Terminations.

			Singular	*Dual*	*Plural*
Nouns ending in अ	Masc.	Dat.	य	भ्याम्	भ्यस्
		Abl.	आत्	भ्याम्	भ्यस्
	Neuter—same as the masculine.				

Before य and भ्याम् the preceding अ is lengthened, and before भ्यस् becomes ए.

		Singular	Dual	Plural
		रामाय	रामाभ्याम्	रामेभ्यः
		रामात्	रामाभ्याम्	रामेभ्यः

Nouns ending in इ } Masc. and Neut. { Dat. ए भ्याम् भ्यस्; Abl. अस् भ्याम् भ्यस्

	Singular	Dual	Plural
Dat.	हरे* + ए = हरये	हरिभ्याम्	हरिभ्यः
Abl.	हरे + अस् = हरेः†	हरिभ्याम्	हरिभ्यः
Dat.	वारिणे	वारिभ्याम्	वारिभ्यः
Abl.	वारिणः	वारिभ्याम्	वारिभ्यः

SUBSTANTIVES.

(*Masculine*).

अश्वपति name of a man
आचार्य preceptor, tutor
कृषीवल a husbandman
कृष्ण name of a person
क्रोध anger
क्रोश two miles
तिल sesamum
द्वीप an island, continent
निष्क a golden coin
पर्वत a mountain
पाप a sinner; *adj.* sinful
प्रासाद a palace
भृत्य a servant
माष a kind of pulse
मोदक sweetmeat
याचक a mendicant
लोक people, world
वध killing
वराह a hog
विनय modesty
शिखर the top, summit
सार्थ a caravan, a crowd
सेनापति a general, commander of an army
सैनिक a soldier

* The ending इ or उ of masculine nouns takes its *guṇa* substitute before the terminations of the Dative, Ablative, and Genitive singular.

† The अ of अस् is dropped after the preceding ए or ओ.

(*Neuter*).

अज्ञान ignorance
आकाश sky
आसन a seat
उद्यान a garden
कल्याण welfare, good
कुसुम a flower
क्षेत्र a field
जाड्य sluggishness
ज्ञान knowledge
तारक a star
पद a step
पल्वल a small pond, a puddle
भोजन dinner
मौन silence
योजन eight miles
राज्य kingdom
वन a forest, wood
शत a hundred
सिंहासन a throne
स्वकृत्य one's duty

AN ADJECTIVE.

मूक silent.

ROOTS.

1st Conjugation.

गम् *with* अधि, to obtain; *with* प्रति and आ, to return
दा *with* प्रति, to exchange
भज् to worship
भू *with* उद्, to be produced, to result
स्था [तिष्ठ्] *with* उद्, to get up, rise

दिश् *with* उप, *6th Conj.* to teach, to advise

धृ *10th Conj.* to hold, to wear, to owe*

INDECLINABLES.

नमस्† bow! | विना without | स्वस्ति! hail;

---

* धृ in this sense governs the dative of the person to whom something is owing.

† नमः and स्वस्ति govern a dative, and विना an accusative, instrumental, or ablative.

SENTENCES

हरिर्ब्राह्मणेभ्यो निष्कान् यच्छति ।

मनुष्यो ग्रामाय गच्छति ।

कल्याणाय हरिं भजति ।

फलेभ्यो गच्छामि ।

हरये* नृपतिः कुप्यति ।

मोदकेभ्यो बालः स्पृहयति ।

नगराद् † गच्छति ।

अश्वात्पतति ।

अतिथिभ्योऽन्नं यच्छति ।

तिलेभ्यः प्रतियच्छति माषान् ।

आसनेभ्य उत्तिष्ठन्त्याचार्याः ।

वधाद्विनारिर्न शाम्यति ।

रवेर्लोकः सुखमधिगच्छति ।

प्रासादा‡ज्जनं पश्यति नृपः ।

शिष्याय शास्त्रमुपदिशति ।

कालेभ्यो दुःखान्युद्भवन्ति ।

शिखरात्पतन्ति गजाः ।

द्वीपाद्द्वीपमटति सार्थः ।

भृत्यं क्रोधाद्रामस्ताडयति ।

नगरं वनाद्योजनम् ।

नमो देवेभ्यः ।

स्वस्ति हरये ।

पल्वलेभ्यो वराहा उत्तिष्ठन्ति ।

विनयः सुखाय भवति ।

निष्कान् धारयति रामाय हरिः ।

---

* Verbs implying anger, malice, rivalry, and jealousy (*i. e.*, having the sense of क्रुध्, द्रुह्, ईर्ष्या, and असूया) govern the dative of the person or thing against whom or which the feeling is directed. स्पृह् also governs the dative of the object of wish.

† The preceding consonant (except a nasal) takes the third consonant of its class as its substitute when compounded with a soft consonant or the initial vowel of a word.

‡ See rule in note*, page 21.

Rāma goes home for dinner.
Fruits fall from trees.
(I) give money to mendicants.
Hari owes (a) hundred to Aśvapati.
(A) wise man worships God for absolution.
(The) general leads*(his) soldiers from village to village.
Brāhmaṇas obtain wealth from kings.
(The) mountain is two coss (*krośa*) from (the) sea.
Hari goes to (the) garden for flowers.
Misery results from sin.
(The) gods throw sinners from heaven.
Rāma errs from his duties.
(He) brings rice from (two) heaps.
Pupils get knowledge from (their) preceptors.
Kings protect (their) kingdoms from (their) enemies.
(The) king speaks to (his) general from (his) throne.
From sluggishness (he) does not move even (a) step.
Through modesty (he) stands silent.
(I) return from (the) garden.
(The) husbandmen plough (the) field for corn.
(The) son gets wealth from (his) father.
Fools prate through ignorance.
(The) hogs drink water from (the) lake.
Stars fall from (the) sky.
Hail to (the) poets!

---

* There are some roots that govern two accusatives; नी, प्रच्छ् and याच् are instances. The synonyms of these also govern two.

LESSON IX

GENITIVE, LOCATIVE, AND VOCATIVE CASES.

Terminations.

			Singular	*Dual*	*Plural*
Nouns ending in अ	Masc.	Gen.	स्य	ओस्	नाम्
		Loc.	इ	ओस्	सु

Neuter—same as the masculine.

The preceding short vowel becomes long before नाम्. The final अ becomes ए before ओस् and सु.

			Singular	*Dual*	*Plural*
Nouns ending in इ	Masc.	Gen.	अस्	ओस्	नाम्
		Loc.	औ	ओस्	सु

The preceding इ is dropped before औ.

The vocative singular of nouns ending in अ is the same as the crude, and that of nouns ending in इ is formed by simply changing the इ to ए. The dual and plural of the vocative are in all cases the same as those of the corresponding nominative.

Gen.	रामस्य	रामयोः	रामाणाम्
Loc.	रामे	रामयोः	रामेषु
Voc.	राम	रामौ	रामाः
Gen.	हरेः*	हर्योः	हरीणाम्
Loc.	हरौ	हर्योः	हरिषु
Voc.	हरे	हरी	हरयः

* See notes * and †, page 26.

Nouns ending in इ	Neuter		*Singular*	*Dual*	*Plural*
		Gen.	अस्	ओस्	नाम्
		Loc.	इ	ओस्	सु

The Vocative singular is वारे or वारि.

Gen.	वारिण:	वारिणो:	वारीणाम्
Loc.	वारिणि	वारिणो:	वारिषु
Voc.	वारे or वारि	वारिणी	वारीणि

SUBSTANTIVES.

(*Masculine*).

अवकाश room, space
आचार conduct
खड्ग a sword
ग्रीष्म summer
चन्द्र the moon
दीप a lamp
धनपति god of wealth, Kubera
धनिक a rich man
धर्म duty, virtue
निधि a store
पराक्रम exploit
पालक a protector
प्रकाश light.
प्रसाद favour, grace
यक्ष servant of Kubera
वर्ण colour, caste
वास residence
वीर a warrior
वृष a bullock
श्वापद a beast of prey
सुमन्त्र name of Rāma's charioteer

(*Neuter*).

औषध medicine
कारण cause
घृत ghee
चरित the manner of leading life
चित्त mind
प्रमाण evidence, authority
युद्ध battle
यूथ a herd
लाङ्गूल tail
वचन saying
वैर enmity
सौन्दर्य beauty
हर्म्य a mansion
हिम snow

ADJECTIVES.

आह्लादक delighting
गर्ह्य censurable
चण्ड hot, fierce
दीर्घ long
प्रथम first
प्रशस्य praiseworthy
लवण salt
श्रेष्ठ best, superior

ROOTS, &c.

क्षम् [क्षाम्] *4th Conj.* to forgive, to pardon

रुह् *with* प्र, to grow

विश् *with* उप, to sit

क्व *ind.* where ?

नराणां पालको नृपः ।
समुद्रस्य जलं लवणम् ।
देवस्य प्रसादेन जीवामि ।
शास्त्राणां तत्त्वं प्राज्ञो बोधति ।
वीरयोर्युद्धं भवति ।
वारीणां निधिरुदधिः ।
आसनेषूपविशन्ति ।
गिरेः शिखराद्वृक्षः पतति ।
कासारे कमलान्युद्भवन्ति ।
गजानां यूथं चरति ।
ग्रीष्मे सूर्यस्य प्रकाशश्चण्डो भवति ।
वर्णानां ब्राह्मणः श्रेष्ठः ।
ऋषीणां वचनं प्रमाणम् ।
शठानां चरितं गर्ह्यम् ।
कवयो लोकेषु वीराणां पराक्रमान् प्रथयन्ति ।

हरे, पुस्तकं क्वास्ति ।
नगरे जना वसन्ति ।
रामस्य पुत्रा ग्रामं गच्छन्ति ।
वनेषु श्वापदाः सन्ति ।
आचार्याः शिष्याणां धर्मं कथयन्ति ।
मनुष्याणामगदेन व्याधयो नश्यन्ति ।
रामस्य सारथिः सुमन्त्रो वनं रथं* नयति ।
चन्द्रस्य प्रकाशो जनानामाह्लादको भवति ।
गिरिषु वसन्ति सिंहाः ।
अरीणां सैनिकान् नृपतिर्जयति ।
योधस्य पाणौ खड्गोऽस्ति ।
धूर्जटौ यतीनां चित्तमस्ति ।

* See note*, page 29.

(The) conduct of (the two) sons of Hari is praiseworthy
(There) are lamps in (the) houses.
(The) *yakṣas* are (the) servants of (the) god of wealth.
(The) tails of monkeys are long.
Among poets Kālidāsa is (the) first.
(The) man's servant goes to (a) village.
Kings reside in palaces.
Rich man dwell in mansions.
Rāma is (the) best of men.
(The) water of (the) lakes is salt.
(There) is snow on (the) tops of (the) mountains.
(A) thief steals (the) wealth of (a) Brāhmaṇa.
(I) am pleased at (the) beauty of (the) gardens.
(He) brings (a) leaf of (the) tree.
(I) throw ghee into (the) fire.
(The) enmity of (the) sailors is (the) cause of (the) battle.
(There) is no medicine for (of) (a) fool.
By modesty, O Hari, are people pleased.
Clouds move in (the) sky.
(The) residence of ascetics is in forests.
(There) are many jewels in (the) ocean.
Flowers adorn (the) trees in (the) garden.
(A) wise man does not give room to anger in (his) mind.
God pardons (the) sins of sinners.
Lotuses grow in water.

General Results and Examination.

नृप *m.*

	Sing.	*Du.*	*Pl.*
Nom.	नृपः	नृपौ	नृपाः
Acc.	नृपम्	नृपौ	नृपान्
Instr.	नृपेण	नृपाभ्याम्	नृपैः
Dat.	नृपाय	नृपाभ्याम्	नृपेभ्यः
Abl.	नृपात्	नृपाभ्याम्	नृपेभ्यः
Gen.	नृपस्य	नृपयोः	नृपाणाम्
Loc.	नृपे	नृपयोः	नृपेषु
Voc.	नृप	नृपौ	नृपाः

कलि *m.*

	Sing.	*Du.*	*Pl.*
Nom.	कलिः	कली	कलयः
Acc.	कलिम्	कली	कलीन्
Instr.	कलिना	कलिभ्याम्	कलिभिः
Dat.	कलये	कलिभ्याम्	कलिभ्यः
Abl.	कलेः	कलिभ्याम्	कलिभ्यः
Gen.	कलेः	कल्योः	कलीनाम्
Loc.	कलौ	कल्योः	कलिषु
Voc.	कले	कली	कलयः

वन *n.*

	Sing.	*Du.*	*Pl.*
Nom.	वनम्	वने	वनानि
Acc.	वनम्	वने	वनानि
Instr.	वनेन	वनाभ्याम्	वनैः
Dat.	वनाय	वनाभ्याम्	वनेभ्यः
Abl.	वनात्	वनाभ्याम्	वनेभ्यः
Gen.	वनस्य	वनयोः	वनानाम्
Loc.	वने	वनयोः	वनेषु
Voc.	वन	वने	वनानि

सुरभि *adj. m. f. n.*

n.

Nom.	सुरभि	सुरभिणी	सुरभीणि
Acc.	सुरभि	सुरभिणी	सुरभीणि
Instr.	सुरभिणा	सुरभिभ्याम्	सुरभिभिः
Dat.	सुरभिणे	सुरभिभ्याम्	सुरभिभ्यः
Abl.	सुरभिणः	सुरभिभ्याम्	सुरभिभ्यः
Gen.	सुरभिणः	सुरभिणोः	सुरभीणाम्
Loc.	सुरभिणि	सुरभिणोः	सुरभिषु
Voc.	सुरभि or सुरभे	सुरभिणी	सुरभीणि

1. State and explain the rules of *Saṁdhi* of the following with instances :—

a. Similar vowels except the last four.

b. अ or आ followed by इ, उ, ऋ, or ऌ, short or long.

c. अ or आ followed by ए, ऐ, ओ, or औ.

d. इ, उ, ऋ, or ऌ, short or long, followed by any dissimilar vowel.

e. ए or ओ followed by अ.

f. The ending ई, ऊ, or ए of dual nouns followed by a vowel, and ऋ after any vowel except the last four.

g. म् at the end of a word.

h. स् and the dentals with श् and the palatals.

i. स् and the dentals with ष् and the linguals.

k. Any consonant of the five classes, except a nasal, followed by a soft consonant or the initial vowel of a word.

l. र् followed by र्.

2. When is न् changed ण् ?

3. Under what circumstances is *visarga* changed to ओ, र्, or स्, श् and ष्, and when is it dropped ?

4. When is final न् changed to an *anusvāra and visarga* ?

5. What cases do the following verbs and particles govern :—

a. Verbs implying motion.

b. Verbs implying anger, malice, rivalry and jealousy.

c. धृ in the sense of *to owe*, and स्पृह्.

d. सह, नमः, स्वस्ति and विना.

6. Mention any roots governing two accusatives.

7. Decline the nouns—[Put in as many as may be necessary, of the masculine and neuter genders, ending in अ or इ] .

Some of the important Indeclinables.

अव्ययानि ।

अतः hence	कथम् in what man-	तदा then
अत्र here	कदा when ? [ner ?	पुनर् again [first
अद्य to-day	किंतु but	पुरा formerly, at
अधुना now	कुतः whence ?	यतः whence (*rela-*
अपि even	कुत्र or क्व where ?	*tive*). [*tive*)
इति so, thus [ner	च* and	यत्र where (*rela-*
इत्थम् in this man-	चिरम् long (*time*)	यथा in which
इव like, as	ततः thence	manner (*rela-*
एव only	तत्र there [ner	*tive*). [*tive*)
एवम् thus	तथा in that man-	यदा when (*rela-*

*See note *, page 27.

वा* or
वृथा in vain
श्वस् to-morrow
सदा always
सर्वत्र everywhere
सुष्ठु well
हे O!
ह्यस् yesterday

LESSON X.

Atmanepada Terminations—*Present Tense.*

SINGULAR.

1st pers.	2nd pers.	3rd pers.
इ	से	ते
वन्दे	वन्दसे	वन्दते

ROOTS.

† *1st Conj.*

ईक्ष् to see, to take into account, to care for; (*with* अप, to expect; *with* प्र, to see; and *with* परि, to examine)
कम्प् to shake
काश् *with* प्र, to shine
भाष् to speak
मुद् (मोद्) to rejoice
यत् to strive
रभ् *with* आ, to begin, to be engaged in
रम् to sport, to be diverted
रुच् (रोच्) to please, to be liked
लभ् to get
वन्द् to salute
वृत् (वर्त्) to be
वृध् (वर्ध्) to increase
वेप् to tremble, to quake
शंस् *with* आ, to hope
शङ्क् to suspect
शिक्ष् to learn
शुभ् (शोभ्) to be splendid, to become, to behave
श्लाघ् to panegyrize, to praise, to extol
सह् to endure
सेव् to serve

---

*च or वा is used after each of the parts of speech joined together, or once only, that is, after them all; हरिश्च गोविन्दश्च or हरिर्गोविन्दश्च जल्पतः.

† The conjugational peculiarities formerly mentioned should be remembered in conjugating these roots.

4th Conj.

जन् [जा] to be produced, to result
युध् to fight

6th Conj.

मृ [* म्रिय्] to die
विद् [विन्द्] to obtain

10th Conj.

धीर् *with* अव, to disregard, to despise
† मृग् to seek
सूद् *with* नि [निषूद्] to destroy

SUBSTANTIVES, &C.

अध्ययन *n.* study
अर्चन *n.* worship
असंख्येय *adj.* innumerable
असत्य *n.* a lie, falsehood
अस्त्र *n.* a miraculous weapon
आध्यात्मिक *adj.* spiritual
उद्गम *m.* coming to birth, appearance
उद्यम *m.* exertion, industry
कट *m.* a mat
क्लेश *m.* pain, distress
दण्ड *m.* punishment
दुराचार *m.* bad conduct
ध्यान *n.* contemplation
नारायण *m.* name of a man
नाश *m.* ruin. loss
न्याय *m.* a school of philosophy
पारितोषिक *n.* a reward
प्रबल *adj.* strong
प्रायस् *ind.* generally
बिम्ब *n.* a disc
भक्त *m.* a devotee
भय *n.* fear
मणिकार *m.* a jeweller
मास *m.* a month
लाभ *m.* acquisition, obtaining.
वात *m.* wind
विश्वामित्र *m.* name of a sage
शासन *n.* an order
शुक्लपक्ष *m.* bright half (of a month)
सदाचार *m.* good conduct
स्नेह *m.* affection, friendship
स्वास्थ्य *n.* tranquility, peace

* Roots of the *6th Conj.* ending in short ऋ substitute, for the ऋ, रि, which with the following अ of the conjugational sign becomes रिय; *e.g.*, दृ and पृ make द्रियते and प्रियते.

† The vowel does not take the *guṇa* substitute in this instance. The root is Ātmanepadi only, see page 8, note*.

SENTENCES.

देवं वन्दे ।
भयं शङ्कसे ।
भयाद्वेपते हृदयम् ।
सूर्यः प्रकाशते ।
व्याघ्रो म्रियते ।
असत्यं भाषसे ।
हरेरुद्यमं श्लाघे ।
पुस्तकानि मृगयसे ।
वीरोऽरिं निषूदयते ।
मोदको बालकाय * रोचते ।
कटः कुत्र वर्तते ।
मणीन्परीक्षते मणिकारः ।
पुत्रस्य लाभेन मोदते ।
बुधो मोक्षं लभते ।

हे राम सुष्ठु शोभसे विनयेन ।
ज्ञानात्सुखं जायते ।
नारायणे रामस्य स्नेहो वर्धते ।
जनानां कल्याणाय नृपो यतते ।
आचार्यं शिष्यः सेवते ।
विश्वामित्रादस्त्राणि शिक्षते रामः ।
सदाचारेण मनुष्यः स्वास्थ्यं [लभते ।
पुत्रस्य दुराचारात्सुखं नाशं- [से ।
देवानामर्चनमारभे ।
प्रबलेनापि वातेन पर्वतो न कम्पते ।
ईश्वरस्य ध्याने रमे ।

(I) begin (the) study of *Nyāya*.
(Thou) endurest pain.
Kṛṣṇa sports with children.
(The) tree shakes.
(Thou) servest (the) king.
(I) obtain wealth.
(He) salutes *Ṛṣis*.

(A) warrior fights with (his) enemies.
(Thou) expectest (a) reward.
(I) rejoice at (the) welfare of friends.
(The) rogue despises (the) king's orders.
(I) see (a) monkey.

---

* रुच् and other verbs having the same sense govern the dative of the person or thing pleased or satisfied.

Rāma shines by (his) innumerable virtues.

From fear of God, (he) does not speak (a) lie.

The disc of (the) moon increases in (the) bright half of (the) month.

(*A*) sinner suspects even friends.

(A) tree looks beautiful by (the) appearance of fruits.

From sin results spiritual ruin.

(He) seeks jewels.

Generally (a) man strives for wealth.

(A) devotee likes (the) worship of God.

(I) tremble from fear of punishment.

(I) learn duty from (my) preceptor.

(The) poet panegyrizes (the) king.

(I) die by (the) arrows of (my) enemies.

LESSON XI.

Dual and Plural.

	1st pers.	2nd pers.	3rd pers.
Dual	वहे	इथे	इते
Plural	महे	ध्वे	*अन्ते

As in the Parasmaipada, the preceding अ is lengthened before the व् and म् of the Ātmanepada terminations.

Dual	वन्दावहे	वन्देथे	वन्देते
Plural	वन्दामहे	वन्दध्वे	वन्दन्ते

Roots.

1st Conj.

कत्थ् to praise, to flatter

क्षम् to forgive

गल्भ् *with* प्र, to swagger

डी (डय्) to fly

† भिक्ष् to beg

याच् to beg

स्पन्द् to throb

स्मि (स्मय्) to smile *with* वि, to wonder, to be dismayed.

स्वाद् to taste

* See note*, page 6.

† See note*, page 29.

4th Conj.	*10th Conj.*
रुध् *with* **अनु**, to obey	**वाद्** *with* **अभि**, to salute, to respect

SUBSTANTIVES, &c.

अपराध *m.* a fault
अभ्युदय *m.* rise, prosperity
आम्र *n.* a mango (fruit)
आराधन *n.* propitiation, pleasing
उद्योग *m.* application, exertion
उपालम्भ *m.* a taunt
कपट *n.* fraud, deceit
गात्र *n.* a limb
गान *n.* singing
गायक *m.* a songster
गुण *m.* merit, quality, virtue
चातुर्य *n.* skill
तण्डुल *m.* rice
दिवा *ind.* by day
द्रव्य *n.* money
नयन *n.* the eye
निर्देश *m.* direction
नृत्य *n.* dancing, a dance
भङ्ग *m.* violation, breaking
भोग *m.* enjoyment sensual enjoyment
मयूर *m.* a peacock
वचनीय *n.* censure, anything censurable
वसन्त *m.* spring
वाक्य *n.* sentence, words.
वातायन *n.* window
विविध *adj.* various
विहग *m* a bird
वैयात्य *n.* rudeness, impudence
शस्त्र *n.* a weapon
शुक *m.* a parrot
संगीत *n.* singing
संसार *m.* this world, worldly existence
सत्य *adj.* true
स्वीय *adj.* one's own
हितकर *adj.* beneficial

SENTENCES

मोदकान् स्वादन्ते ब्राह्मणाः।
धनिकं द्रव्यं याचेते भिक्षुकौ।
स्वीयान् गुणान् कत्थेथे।
उद्योगाद्धनं लभध्वे।
वृथा प्रगल्भध्वे।
बुधा मोक्षं विन्दन्ते।
कपटं शङ्केथे।

मित्राणामभ्युदये नरा मोद-
मुनीनभिवादयावहे । [न्ते
मूर्खाणां वैयात्यं न सहामहे ।
वृक्षेषु कुसुमानि वर्तन्ते ।
आचार्यस्य निर्देशमनुरुध्य-
ध्वे । [महे ।
भृत्यानामपराधान् क्षमा-
रामस्य नयने स्पन्देते ।
आकाशे विहगा डयन्ते ।
कृष्णस्य चातुर्येण विस्म-
यन्ते जनाः । [भामहे ।
देवस्याराधनाय गानमार-

दिवा तारकाणि न प्रका-
शन्ते ।
पापा न वचनीयमीक्षन्ते ।
सत्यं हितकरं च वाक्यं
भाषन्ते प्राज्ञाः ।
शासनस्य भङ्गं न क्षमन्ते
नृपतयः ।
गायकात्संगीतं शिक्षावहे ।
मोक्षाय यतन्ते बुधाः ।
वातेन वृक्षा कम्पन्ते ।
देवान् भोगान् भिक्षन्ते
नराः ।

(We) get fruits in spring.
(You) speak lies.
Mountains shake.
Stars shine.
(You) learn dancing.
Nārāyaṇa's (two) friends strive for (his) welfare.
(We two) serve (the) king.
(You two) taste mangoes.
(We) see (a) peacock on (the) top of (the) palace.

Tigers do not eat (taste) grass and leaves of trees.
(We two) salute (the) *Ṛṣis*.
Misery and happiness are born of (the) world.
(You two) fight without cause.
(Two) children sport in (the) garden.
(We two) expect good from Hari.

(You) two forgive (the) faults of (your) friends.

(They) extol (the) merits of wise men.

Distresses result from sin.

Men die.

Beggars beg for rice.

Parrots fly at (the) window.

Men obtain (the) fruit of (their) efforts.

(The) limbs of (the) fool grow (increase), but not (his) knowledge.

(We two) endure (the) taunts of (our) enemies.

Warriors destroy (their) enemies with various weapons

LESSON XII.

PASSIVE AND IMPERSONAL FORMS.

These* are made up by adding य to the root†, and then appending the Ātmanepada terminations :—

त्यज् + य + ते = त्यज्यते, त्यज्यसे, त्यज्ये, &c.

If a root ends in ऋ which is not preceded by a conjunct consonant, रि is substituted for it before the य of the passive ; as कृ becomes क्रि.

The final इ or उ of a root is lengthened before य ; as जि becomes जी.

---

* There is no conjugational distinction in the case of passive forms; that is, they are formed in the same manner from all roots, subject, however, to certain peculiarities of the roots themselves. Several roots, therefore, belonging to conjugations which, as being complicated, have not been introduced into this book, are given in the text. The student, of course, will not be able to make up their active forms.

† The original roots, and not the substitutes which some roots take before the conjugational sign, as गच्छ् for गम्, तिष्ठ for स्था, &c

Roots.

अर्थ् *with* प्र, to request	दिश् *with* आ, to command	रुद् to cry
कृ to do	पठ् *1st conj. Par.* to learn	श्रु to hear
ज्ञा to know	पा [पी] to drink	स्था [स्थी] to stand
दा* [दी] to give		हन् to kill

Substantives

आदेश *m.* a command
काष्ठ *n.* wood
चाप *m.* a bow
छात्र *m.* a scholar, a pupil
ध्वनि *m.* a sound
पौर *m.* an inhabitant of a city, a citizen
प्राज्ञ *m.* an intelligent man

Sentences.

निष्का ब्राह्मणेभ्यो दीयन्ते।
नृपतेरादेशः क्रियते।
अग्निना काष्ठं दह्यते।
शठौ पुरुषैस्ताड्येते †।
आचार्यैर्धर्म उपदिश्यते।
भृत्यैः सेव्यसे।
मित्रैस्त्यज्ये।
जनैर्दृश्यामहे।
व्याधिभिः पीड्यध्वे।
प्रेक्ष्यसे जनेन।
पुत्रैः पूज्येथे।
धान्यस्य राशयो नीयन्ते।
तत्त्वं बुध्यते प्राज्ञैः।
नृपेणारयो जीयन्ते।

---

* The forms which some roots assume before the passive य are here enclosed within rectangular brackets.

† Those roots of the tenth conjugation, whose vowels take a *guṇa* or *vṛddhi* substitute in the active voice, undergo the same change before the य of the passive; as चुर्, चोरयति act.; चोर्यते pass., not चुर्यते.

बालकै*रुद्यते ।

सारथी हन्येते ।

ऋषयो जनेन वन्द्यन्ते ।

सूर्येण प्रकाश्यते ।

ईश्वरेण भूयते ।

लोकैः प्रशस्यध्वे † ।

शिष्यैर्नम्यावहे ।

मोदकाः स्वाद्यन्ते बालैः ।

छात्रैः श्लोकाः पठ्यन्ते ।

ओदनः पच्यते सूदैः ।

देवो वन्द्यते ।

(An) enemy is killed with (an) arrow.

(The) child's hands are washed with water.

(Thou) art extolled by poets.

(You) are sought by men.

(I) am served by servants.

(We) are protected by God.

(You two) are known by people.

Elephants are mounted.

(We two) are requested by (the) citizens.

(The) world is abandoned by ascetics.

(The) body is nourished with food.

(The two) horses are being taken away by thieves.

Water is being sprinkled on (the) trees.

Heaps of corn are being arranged.

Kṛṣṇa's body is adorned with ornaments.

(The) virtues of wise men are celebrated by poets.

(A) sound is heard.

Thieves are punished by kings.

Fruits (two) are eaten by Hari.

Arrows (two) are discharged.

(You) are commanded by (the) King.

---

* See notes † and ‡, p. 17.

† If roots have a penultimate न् or *anusvāra*, it is dropped before य, except in certain cases.

Happiness is always wished for by men.	(The) gods are pleased by (means of) good conduct.
(The) waters of (the) sea are not drunk.	(The) soldiers are being counted by (the) general.

GENERAL RESULTS AND EXAMINATION.

स्मि Ātm. 'to smile.'

PRESENT TENSE.

	Singular	*Dual*	*Plural*
1st pers.	स्मये	स्मयावहे	स्मयामहे
2nd Pers.	स्मयसे	स्मयेथे	स्मयध्वे
3rd Pers.	स्मयते	स्मयेते	स्मयन्ते

Passive—श्रु 'to hear.'

1st Pers.	श्रूये	श्रूयावहे	श्रूयामहे
2nd Pers.	श्रूयसे	श्रूयेथे	श्रूयध्वे
3rd Pers.	श्रूयते	श्रूयेते	श्रूयन्ते

1. What form does the final ऋ (short) take in the 6th Conjugation? In what other case does it assume the same form?

2. What modification does the final short vowel undergo before the य of the Passive? What substitute does the आ of स्था, दा and पा 'to drink' take in the same circumstances, and how are roots of the tenth conjugation dealt with?

3. Give the Present Tense or वृध्, मृ *6th Conj.* [and any number of other Ātmanepadi roots necessary].

4. What case do रुच् and other roots having the same sense govern? Give an instance.

5. Repeat the Passive forms of गम्, दृश्, स्था [and any number of other roots, Parasmaipadi and Ātmanepadi, the teacher may deem necessary.]

6. Explain the use of च and वा.

LESSON XIII.

Feminine Nouns ending in आ and ई.

Nominative and Accusative Cases.

Terminations.

		Singular	Dual	Plural
Nouns ending in आ	Nom.	(*none*)	ई	अस्
	Acc.	आम्	ई	अस्
	Nom.	रमा	रमे	रमाः
	Acc.	रमाम्	रमे	रमाः
Nouns ending in ई	Nom.	(*none*)	औ	अस्
	Acc.	म्	औ	इस्
	Nom.	नदी	नद्यौ*	नद्यः
	Acc.	नदीम्	नद्यौ	नदीः

Substantives, &c.

(*Feminine*).

अरुन्धती name of the wife of Vasiṣṭha, a great sage.
आज्ञा a command
कथा a story
कन्या a daughter, a girl
कला an art
कुमारी a virgin
क्षमा forgiveness
गङ्गा the Ganges
जननी mother
नटी an actress
नदी river

---

* See *saṁdhi rule*‡, p. 19.

नारी a woman
पत्नी wife
पृथ्वी the earth
प्रजा subjects; progeny
प्रमदा a young woman
भार्या wife
मही the earth
माला a garland, a wreath
रजनी night
लज्जा shame
लता a creeping plant
ललना a woman
वापी a well
शोभा beauty
सखी a female friend
सहचरी a female companion or mate

आत्मीय *adj.* one's own
आधार *m.* support
आरम्भ *m.* beginning
उपवन *n.* a garden
कण्ठ *m.* neck
गमन *n.* departure
जनक *m.* father of Sītā, the wife of Rāma
नाटक *n.* play, a drama
नारद *m.* name of a heavenly *Ṛṣi*
प्रसाद *m.* a palace, and तल *n.* surface ; प्रसादतल *n.* the upper surface or terrace of a palace
बल *n.* an army
भर *m.* weight
भूषण *n.* an ornament
विश्व* *n.* the universe
सूत्रधार *m.* the manager or chief actor in a play
हरिण *m.* a deer

Roots

गम् *with* सम् *Ātm.* to join; to go or flow together
चर् *with* आ, to practise, to do
तन्त्र् *10th Conj. Ātm.* to tend, to take care of
तृ (तर्) *1st Conj. Parasm.* to cross, to surmount ; *with* अव to descend
नी *with* परि, to marry; *with* अप, to take off, to remove
वृध् *with* सम्, to increase to flourish
शुच् *1st Conj. Parasm.* to bewail
हृ to captivate

---

* This is declined like a pronoun.

SENTENCES.

वसिष्ठस्य पत्न्यरुन्धती ।

नार्यो हर्म्याणां वातायनेभ्यः पश्यन्ति ।

कृष्णः कलाः शिक्षते । [णयति ।

रामो जनकस्य कन्यां परि-

गङ्गा समुद्रं गच्छति ।

क्षमा वीरस्य भूषणम् ।

नारायणो जननीमाह्वयति ।

उपवने नृपस्य कन्ये रमेते ।

लते स्पृशति ।

चन्द्रेण रजनी शोभते ।

नद्यौ संगच्छेते ।

कुमारी सख्यौ भाषते ।

वराहाः सहचरीः शोचन्ति ।

लज्जां त्यजति मूर्खः ।

नटी सूत्रधारस्य भार्या ।

प्रजा नृपतिना रक्ष्यन्ते ।

उद्यानस्य शोभां पश्यति ।

ललनाः प्रासादतलमारोह-

नृपस्याज्ञे*अनुरुध्येते । [न्ति ।

ब्राह्मणा महीमटन्ति ।

रामस्य कथाः श्रूयन्ते ।

वने प्रमदे दृश्येते ।

वापी नगरात्क्रोशौ ।

नृपतेर्बलस्य भरेण पृथ्वी कम्पते ।

कुसुमानां मालाः कण्ठादपनीयन्ते ।

Nārada descends from Heaven to (the) earth.

Krṣna tells stories of kings.

Young women play in (the) garden.

(He) wears (two) wreaths of flowers on (his) neck.

Rāma's wife salutes Arundhatī.

(We) see (two) virgins.

(The) deer's mates follow (the) deer.

---

*See note †, p. 21.

There are (two) wells in (the) village.

(The) chief actor (of a play) calls (the) actress.

Hari goes to (the) river.

Rāma's (two) mothers bewail (his) departure to (a) forest.

Women go to (the) wells.

Subjects obey (the) king's orders.

(The) daughters of Hari learn dancing.

(The) arts flourish by industry.

(The) wise always practise forgiveness.

(The) beauty of (the) universe captivates (the) mind.

(The) mother rejoices at (the) welfare of (the) children.

In (the) beginning of (the) play, (the) manager calls (his) wife.

Men protect women.

(The) stars beautify (the) night.

Shame is conquered by impudence.

Creepers seek (the) support of trees.

(The) woman leaves (her female) friend through anger.

(The) king tends (his) subjects as his own progeny.

LESSON XIV.

Instrumental, Dative and Ablative Cases.

Terminations.

		Singular	*Dual*	*Plural*
Nouns in आ and ई	Instr.	आ	भ्याम्	भिस्
	Dat.	ए	भ्याम्	भ्यस्
	Abl.	अस्	भ्याम्	भ्यस्

The ending आ is changed to ए before the Instr. sing. termination.

Nouns ending in आ take the augment या, and those in ई, the augment आ, before the terminations of the Dat., Abl., Gen., and Loc. singulars; माला+या+ए= मालायै, नदी+आ+ए+=नद्यै.

Or the following may be regarded as the singular terminations :—

	Dat.	Abl.	Gen.	Loc.
Nouns in	आ—यै	यास्	यास्	याम्
———	ई—ऐ	आस्	आस्	आम्

Instr.	मालया	मालाभ्याम्	मालाभिः
Dat.	मालायै	मालाभ्याम्	मालाभ्यः
Abl.	मालायाः	मालाभ्याम्	मालाभ्यः
Instr.	नद्या	नदीभ्याम्	नदीभिः
Dat.	नद्यै	नदीभ्याम्	नदीभ्यः
Abl.	नद्याः	नदीभ्याम्	नदीभ्यः

SUBSTANTIVES, &C.

(*Feminine*)

अवन्ती name of a town, Ujjain
कान्ता a female beloved; wife
कौशाम्बी name of a town
क्रीडा sport, play
चिन्ता anxiety
जरा old age,
दासी a maid, a maid-servant
देवता deity
पञ्चवटी name of a place
पाठशाला a school
पुरी a town
पूजा worship
प्रभा light
महिषी a crowned queen
वाचा speech
व्यथा pain
सीता Rāma's wife

अनुराग *m.* love

करभक *m.* the young (of an elephant)

कलह *m.* a strife, a quarrel

गीत *n.* a song

जरठ *m.* an old man

दूत *m.* a messenger

नाग *m.* an elephant

पल्लव *m. n.* a sprout

मौक्तिक *n.* a pearl

रक्त *adj.* red

विरूप *adj.* deformed

संदेश *m.* a message

स्वस्थ *adj.* tranquil

हित *adj.* beneficial; *n.* benefit

ROOTS.

गम् *with* निर्, to depart

दा *with* प्र, to give

द्युत् (द्योत्) *1st Conj. Ātm.* to shine

पत् *with* उद्, to rise up, to fly up

वृ *with* परि, to surround*

वृत् *with* नि, to return

स्था *with* प्र, *Ātm.* to set out, to start

हि *with* प्र, to send

ह्लाद् *10th Conj. with* आ, to delight

SENTENCES.

देवताभ्यो बलिं यच्छति ।
चित्तस्य व्यथया रामो मुह्य-
कान्तायै संदेशः प्रहीयते । [ति ।
अवन्त्या आगच्छति । [चन्ते ।
कृष्णस्य पत्न्यै फलानि † रो-
दास्या सेव्यते महिषी ।
जरया क्षीयते शरीरम् । [दः ।
मणीनां प्रभाभिर्द्योतते प्रासा
लज्जया प्रविशति गृहम् ।

देवस्य पूजायाः सुखं लभते ।
प्रजाभ्यो हितमिच्छन्ति नृपतयः ।
कौशाम्ब्या निवर्तते दूतः ।
क्रीडायै प्रविशत्युद्यानम् ।
सखीभिः परिव्रियते सीता ।
सहचरीभ्यामनुगम्यते नागः ।
पञ्चवट्या निर्गच्छति रामः ।

---

* Here the passive forms only of this and हि are used.

† See note*, p. 39.

लताभ्यां शोभते वृक्षः ।

गङ्गायाः पुरी क्रोशौ ।

वापीभ्यो जलं वहति ।

बालकाः पाठशालाभ्य
आगच्छन्ति । [णाम् ।

चिन्तया वर्धते चित्तं नरा-
यथा कलहस्तथानुरागोऽपि

वाचाया उद्भवति ।

हरिः कन्याभ्यो मौक्तिकानां मालाः प्रयच्छति ।

स्वस्थेन चित्तेन श्रूयते महिष्या नृपतेः संदेशः ।

गजस्य करभकः सीतया पल्लवैः पुष्यते ।

Hari appeases (his) friend by (his) speech.

(The) city is surrounded by rivers.

From forgiveness (a) man obtains tranquillity of mind.

Wise man go to Heaven from (the) earth.

Vasiṣṭha comes with Arundhatī.

Rāma gives ornaments to (his) daughters.

(He) adorns (his) body with garlands.

(The) queen gets angry with (her) maid.

(He) derives pleasure from (the) old man's stories.

Rice is cooked by Nārāyaṇas's wife.

By (the) king's command (I) go to Avantī.

(The) mother likes (her) children though deformed.

(The two) warriors start from (the two) towns with weapons.

(The) sky is adorned by (the) red light of (the) sun.

(The) happiness of(the)people is increased by arts.

Men desire (the) acquisition of happiness from deities.

(An) offering is made by (two) virgins.

Pain results from anxiety.

Sītā learns songs from (her female) friends.

Soldiers come out of (the) town by order of (the) general.

(The) children delight (the) heart of (their) father by (their) sport.

(He) brings flowers for (the) worship of (the) gods.

(A) reward is given by (the) queen to (her) maid,

(The) bird rises up into (the) sky from (the) earth.

LESSON XV

GENITIVE, LOCATIVE AND VOCATIVE CASES

Terminations.

		Singular	*Dual*	*Plural*
Nouns ending in आ and ई	Gen.	अस्	ओस्	नाम्
	Loc.	आम्	ओस्	सु

After ई, सु becomes षु. Third final आ is changed to ए before ओस्. The Vocative singular of nouns ending in आ is made up by changing the final vowel to ए, as हे रमे; and of nouns ending in ई by shortening the vowel, as हे नदि. The dual and plural forms are the same as those of the corresponding nominative. (See rule, page 30).

Gen.	मालायाः	मालयोः	मालानाम्
Loc.	मालायाम्	मालयोः	मालासु
Voc.	माले	माले	मालाः
Gen.	नद्याः	नद्योः	नदीनाम्
Loc.	नद्याम्	नद्योः	नदीषु
Voc.	नदि	नद्यौ	नद्यः

WORDS.

अतीव *ind.* very
अनुष्ठान *n.* performance, execution
अयोध्या *f.* name of a city
अवचय *m.* gathering, collecting
इन्द्राणी *f.* the wife of Indra
उज्जयिनी *f.* name of a town, Ujjain
उदक *n.* water
काम *m.* desire
कौमुदी *f.* moonlight
गोदावरी *f.* name of a river
चकोर *m.* a species of bird
छाया *f.* shade
जयन्त *m.* name of Indra's son
तीर *n.* bank, shore
तृष्णा *f.* thirst, greed
दक्ष *adj.* diligent
दण्डका *f.* name of a forest
दशरथ *m.* the name of a king, the father of the hero Rāma
देश *m.* a country
निरतिशय *adj.* unsurpassed, full, perfect
निशा *f.* night
निशाचर *m.* an evil spirit, a wicked person
परम *adj.* very great
पुण्य *adj.* holy
प्रतिष्ठापन *n.* establishment, establishing
प्रवर्तन *n.* inciting, establishing
प्रवाह *m.* flow current.
प्रावीण्य *n.* proficiency
प्रिय *adj.* beloved
बाहुल्य *n.* multiplicity
मण्डप *m.* a bower
मत्स्य *m.* a fish
माधुर्य *n.* sweetness
मानव *m.* a human being, a man
रथ्या *f.* street
वचन *n.* advice, request
वल्लभ *m.* a lover, husband
वाणी *f.* speech
विवाह *m.* marriage
शकुन्तला *f.* name of a woman
शिला *f.* stone
शूद्रक *m.* name of a king
श्रद्धा *f.* confidence
संघात *m.* a collection
संभार *m.* preparation; *plur.* preparations, requisites.
संमार्जन *n.* sweeping
सदैव (सदा + एव) *ind.* always
स्निग्ध *adj.* affectionate

अर्ह् *1st Conj. Parasm.* to deserve
ऋध् *4th Conj. Parasm. with* सम्, to prosper
क्रीड् *1st Conj. Parasm.* to play
चर् to stalk abroad

फल् *1st Conj. Parasm.* to fructify, to be fulfilled
रुध् *with* नि *pass.* to be checked
हृ *with* वि, to divert one's self, to amuse, play

SENTENCES

अवन्त्यां शूद्रको वसति। गङ्गायां प्रभूतं जलं वर्तते। प्रजानां धर्मे प्रवर्तनं नृपैः क्रियते। उज्जयिन्यां शिवस्य पूजासु नृत्यन्ति नार्यः। सखि गच्छामि नद्यास्तीरम्। गोदावर्या जले गजौ विहरतः। ग्रीष्मे नदीनामुदकेषु नृपाः प्रमदाभिः क्रीडन्ति। लतानां मण्डपं प्रविशन्ति ललनाः। वाप्यां कमलानि प्ररोहन्ति। वृक्षाणां छायासु शिलाया-मुपविशति। [शंसति। कृष्णो भार्याया विनयं

चन्द्रो निशाया वल्लभः। कन्ययोर्विवाहस्य संभार क्रियते। [रामः जनन्योराज्ञामनुरुध्यते प्रिये पुत्रो ग्रामं गच्छति। सख्योः परमः स्नेहः शकु-न्तलायाः। [हरति। कौमुद्याः शोभा चित्तं बुधानां वाण्यां सदैव माधुर्यं वर्तते। कान्ताया वचनं क्रियते रामेण। दास्योर्वचनेषु महिष्या निर-तिशया*श्रद्धा। पाठशालानां प्रतिष्ठापनेन जनेषु ज्ञानं वर्धते।

---

*आ and ई are the feminine terminations in Sanskrt. Adjectives ending in अ generally, though not invariably, take the first.

रथ्यानां संमार्जनं क्रियते पौरैः ।

अयोध्याया नृपो दशरथः ।

जरायामपि मानवानां तृष्णा न शाम्यति ।

देवतानां पूजया कामाः फलन्ति नराणाम् ।

(There) are trees on (the) banks of (the) Ganges.

Jayanta is (the) son of Indrānī. [city.

Rāma's friends live in (the)

(The) *cakora* is delighted in moonlight.

(He) brings (a) flower of (the) creeper.

Hari praises (the) merits of (his) daughters.

(There) are fishes in rivers.

(I) see chariots in (the) streets of Ayodhyā.

Śakuntalā deserves (the) love of (her) friends.

(There) is sweetness in Rāma's speech. [Sītā?

Where are (the) sons of

(There) are evil spirits in Dandakā. [earth.

(There) are islands on (the)

(I) see men under (the) shade of (the) tree.

Generally evil spirits stalk abroad in (the) night.

(The) heart of (the) mother is very affectionate towards (her) daughter.

(The) waters of (the) Ganges are holy.

By order of (the) Queen (the) rogue is punished.

(A) country prospers by (a) multiplicity of arts.

(The) current of (the) river is checked by (a) collection of stones.

(The) maid servant brings (the) requisites of worship.

(I) go to (the) garden for gathering (the) flowers of (the) creepers.

(He) is diligent in (the) execution of (the) king's orders.

GENERAL RESULTS AND EXAMINATION.

शाला *f*. an establishment.'

	Singular	*Dual*	*Plural*
Nom.	शाला	शाले	शालाः
Acc.	शालाम्	शाले	शालाः
Instr.	शालया	शालाभ्याम्	शालाभिः
Dat.	शालायै	शालाभ्याम्	शालाभ्यः
Abl.	शालायाः	शालाभ्याम्	शालाभ्यः
Gen.	शालायाः	शालयोः	शालानाम्
Loc.	शालायाम्	शालयोः	शालासु
Voc.	शाले	शाले	शालाः

दासी *f*.

Nom.	दासी	दास्यौ	दास्यः
Acc.	दासीम्	दास्यौ	दासीः
Instr.	दास्या	दासीभ्याम्	दासीभिः
Dat.	दास्यै	दासीभ्याम्	दासीभ्यः
Abl.	दास्याः	दासीभ्याम्	दासीभ्यः
Gen.	दास्याः	दास्योः	दासीनाम्
Loc.	दास्याम्	दास्योः	दासीषु
Voc.	दासि	दास्यौ	दास्यः

1 Decline सहचरी, प्रमदा, &c, &c.

2 What are the feminine terminations in Sanskrt? How is the feminine of adjectives ending in अ generally formed?

LESSON XVI.

IMPERFECT, OR FIRST PRETERITE TENSE.

Parasmaipada.

Terminations.

	1st pers.	2nd pers.	3rd pers.
Singular	अम्*	स्	त्
Dual	व	तम्	ताम्

अ is prefixed to roots in this tense.

Singular	अबोधम्	अबोधः	अबोधत्
Dual	अबोधाव	अबोधतम्	अबोधताम्

The conjugational signs are added on to the roots before the terminations of the imperfect.

The terminations त् and स् take the augment ई in the case of the root अस् 'to be' and अ in the case of अद् 'to eat'; as आसीत्, आदत्.

WORDS.

अज *m.* goat
असारता *f.* worthlessness
आशा *f.* hope
गोष्ठ *m. n.* a cow-pen
ग्रन्थ *m.* a work, a book
तनय *m.* a son
पुरतस् *ind.* in front, in the presence (of)
महिष *m.* a buffalo
मुष्टि *m.* a handful
शनैस् *ind.* slowly
संकट *n.* difficulty, perplexity
सभा *f.* court, assembly
समराङ्गण *n.* field of battle
सेना *f.* an army

गै *1st Conj. Parasm.* to sing.

---

* See page 6, note *.

SENTENCES.

रामो रावणमजयत् ।
सीता गोदावर्यास्तीरम-
गच्छत् ।
गङ्गाया जलमपिबम् ।
योधोऽरौ शरानक्षिपत् ।
ललने छायायामुपाविशता-
पुत्राणां धर्ममकथयः । [म् ।
सीतां वनेऽत्यजाव ।
संकटेभ्यो जनमरक्षः ।
गिरेः शिखरादजावपतताम् ।
रथं समराङ्गणमनयम् ।
हरिरश्वमारोहत् ।
भिक्षुकेभ्यो निष्कानय-
देवानयजाव । [च्छम् ।
अरण्ये महिषानपश्यम् ।

स्तेनौ धनिकस्य धनमचोर-
यताम् ।
दशरथस्तनयमाह्वयत् ।
ईश्वरस्य प्रसादेन हरेः क्ले-
शोऽनश्यत् । [मवसम् ।
पुरा भार्यया सहोज्जयिन्या-
शिष्यावाचार्यमनमताम् ।
अवन्त्यामभवः ।
अयोध्यायामासीः ।
अग्निर्वनमदहत् ।
संसारस्यासारतामबोधम् ।
नृपस्य पुरतोऽसत्यमवद-
* च्छठः । [च्छम् ।
तदा मूर्खोऽस्मीत्यवाग-

(The) water of (the) lake dried.

(The) general led (his) army to (the) battle-field.

(His two) friends remembered Rāma.

(Thou) wert pleased with Rāma's conduct.

(We two) appeased (the) sages.

God created (the) earth.

Men (two) entered (a) garden.

(1) censured Hari.

(You two) dwelt in (a) forest.

---

* When a word or form ending in any of the first four consonants of a class is followed by श्, the श् is optionally changed to छ्, when it is itself followed by a vowel, a semi-vowel or a nasal.

(The) caravan rambled from town*to town.

(I) published (the) work.

(You two) took away fruits from Hari's garden.

(Thou) toldst Rāma (a) story.†

(Two) tigers ran to (the) cow-pen.

Kṛṣṇa washed (his) feet.

(The) warrior protected (the) women from (the) enemy.

(The) tortoise moved slowly.

(I) then lived without (any) hope of prosperity.

(We two) cooked rice for dinner.

(The) queen sang in (the) court of (the) king,

With handfuls of corn (the) girl fed (the) deer.

(Thou) abandonedst (thy) wife without (any) fault.

(You two) burnt (the) village without cause.

(He) fell from (the) top of (the) tree and perished.

(The) child danced with joy.

LESSON XVII.

IMPERFECT TENSE (*Continued*).

Parasmaipada Plural and Ātmanepada Singular

Terminations

	1st pers.	2nd pers.	3rd pers.
Parasm. Pl.	म	त	अन्
	अगच्छाम	अगच्छत	अगच्छन्

---

* If the word नगर be used here, the following *saṁdhi* or phonetic rule should be borne in memory:—A consonant at the end of a word or grammatical form followed by a nasal is changed to the nasal of its class optionally; as एतद्+मुरारि=एतन्मुरारि or एतद्मुरारि. This change is necessary, when the nasal belongs to a nominal termination, as चित्+मय=चिन्मय.

† कथ् sometimes governs two accusatives, or the indirect object may be in the dative or genitive case.

	1st pers.	2nd pers.	3rd pers.
Ātm. Sing.	इ	थास्	त
	अलभे	अलभथाः	अलभत

Roots beginning with a vowel take the augment आ, instead of अ, which with the following इ or ई becomes ऐ, with उ or ऊ becomes औ, and with ऋ becomes आर्, as आ+ईक्ष+त=ऐक्षत.

WORDS.

आशीर्वाद *m.* a blessing
उज्ज्वलम् *adv.* brightly
गोप *m.* a herdsman
ग्रथन *n.* wreathing
चन्द्रापीड *m.* name of a prince
चित्रकूट *m.* name of a mountain
देवी *f.* a woman of distinction; a goddess
धार्तराष्ट्र *m.* son of धृतराष्ट्र, cousin of पाण्डु

नृशंस *adj.* wicked
पञ्जर *m.* a cage
पण्डित *m.* a learned man
पाण्डव *m.* son of पाण्डु, a king
बलि *m.* name of a king
मदिरा *f.* wine
माणवक *m.* name of an individual
मारुत *m.* wind, or the deity that presides over it

मार्ग *m.* a road
राक्षस *m.* a wicked person, an evil spirit
लव *m.* name of a son of Rāma
वसुधा *f.* the earth
विराव *m.* a cry
शव *n.* a dead body
शृगाल *m.* a jackal
संचलन *n.* moving to and fro
स्थान *n.* a place

सृज् *with* अति, to give

SENTENCES.

पाण्डवानां धार्तराष्ट्रैः सह युद्धान्यभवन्।
आचार्या धर्ममुपादिशन्।

रामः सीतया सह गोदावर्यास्तीरेऽरमत।
उद्यमेन धनमलभथाः।

व्याघ्रस्य विरावेण नार्या हृदयमवेपत ।

मित्रस्य कल्याणायायते ।

गोपा अजान् ग्राम*मनयन् ।

पुरुषमताडयत ।

शृगालोऽम्रियत ।

नृपस्य सभां पण्डिताः प्राविशन् ।

शवमस्पृशत ।

प्रासादे नार्योऽनृत्यन् ।

माणवकं मार्गमपृच्छाम* ।

क्लेशो रामेणासह्यत ।

देवीमभाषे ।

नृशंसो राक्षसोऽहन्यत ।

नृपतेः शासनमवाधीरयथाः ।

लवस्य विनयेनर्षयोऽतुष्यन् ।

हरिणा जनकोऽसेव्यत ।

चित्रकूटस्य शिखरेऽवसाम ।

शृगालं व्याघ्रं चैक्षे ।

वित्तस्य नाशेनामुह्यन् ।

प्रभूतं धनं नृपेण ब्राह्मणेभ्योऽत्यसृज्यत ।

चन्द्रापीडस्य बलस्य संचलनेन मह्यकम्पत ।

पञ्जराद्विहगममुञ्चाम ।

(We) sat in (the) shade of (a) tree.

(He) forgave (the) faults of (his) servants.

(The) Brāhmaṇas fell into (the) waters of (the) Ganges.

Horses ran to (the) battle-field.

Rāma obeyed (the) commands of (his) father.

Hari learned music from Nārāyaṇa.

(I) tasted (the) fruits of (a) mango-tree.

Messengers went to Ayodhyā.

(Thou) spokest (a) lie.

---

* See note *, page 29.

Kṛṣṇa rejoiced at (his) friend's prosperity.

(You) lived at Kauśāmbī then.

(He) wondered at Rāma's exploits.

(Thou) foughtest with (an) enemy.

(The) rogue was beaten by (the) king's order.

(You) counted (the) *niṣkas*.

(A) blessing from (the) *Ṛṣi* was wished for by Rāma.

By favour of (the) gods, (you) conquered (your) enemies.

(We) drank water in place of wine.

(You) took away (the) books hence to (your) house.

(The) sun shone brightly yesterday.

(The) house was entered into at night by (a) thief.

(We) saw (the) general and (his) army

(They) bore away (the) king from the battle-field.

(They) discharged* arrows at (their) enemies.

(I) began to wreathe (the wreathing of) (a) garland of flowers.

LESSON XVIII.

Imperfect Tense (*Continued*).

Atmanepada Terminations (*Continued*).

	1st pers.	2nd pers.	3rd pers.
Dual	वहि	इथाम्	इताम्
Plural	महि	ध्वम्	अन्त
	अलभावहि	अलभेथाम्	अलभेताम्
	अलभामहि	अलभध्वम्	अलभन्त

* Use मुच्

ध्वंस् *1st Conj. Ātm.* to perish.

मन् *with* अव, to disregard.

मन्त्र् *with* नि *10th Conj. Ātm.* to invite

मृश् *6th Conj. Parasm.* with वि, to test, to examine.

रम् to feel happy

लज्ज् *6th conj. Ātm.* to feel shame

स्पर्ध् *1st conj. Ātm.* to rival

स्रंस् *1st conj. Ātm.* to drop down

हस् *with* वि *1st conj. Parasm.* to laugh in contempt

WORDS.

अनिष्ट *n.* evil, calamity

अवधीरणा *f.* a repulse, repulsion

असुर *m.* (*in pl.*) demons, the enemies of gods

आरोपण *n.* planting, sowing

उपदेश *m.* advice, counsel

कबरी *f.* a braid of hair

कार्य *n.* action, work

गन्धर्व *m.* an individual of a class of celestial beings

ग्रहण *n.* capture

चोर *m.* a thief

जाल *n.* a net

ज्योत्स्ना *f.* moonlight

त्याग *m.* leaving

दर्शन *n.* sight

दुष्कृत *n.* a wicked action

नायक *m.* a leader

परम् *ind.* however, but

पान्थ *m.* a traveller

प्राची *f.* the east

प्राश्निक *m.* an examiner

बल *n.* strength

बीज *n.* seed

भूप *m.* a king

रमण *m.* a lover, husband

वीर्य *n.* heroism, bravery, valour

सचिव *m.* minister

समूह *m.* a multitude, a crowd

पाण्डवा राज्यमविन्दन्त ।

आचार्यांञ्* शिष्या अभ्यवादयन्त ।

सचिवा भूपमभाषन्त ।

नार्यौः कबर्याः पुष्पे अस्रंसेताम् ।

जनेन व्यहस्यध्वम् ।

रथ्यायां जनानां समूहमैक्षामहि ।

रामस्य दुःखान्यध्वंसन्त ।

मित्राणां त्यागे नालज्जेथाम् ।

वृक्षेभ्यः शुका उड्डयन्त ।

मृगावहन्येतां व्याधैः ।

जनानां सुखायायतामहि ।

देवैः सहासुरा अस्पर्धन्त ।

रमणैः सह ज्योत्स्नायामरमन्त नार्यः ।

उज्जयिन्याः कदा न्यवर्तध्वमिति जनैर†पृच्छ्यामहि ।

वातेन वृक्षा अकम्पन्त ।

अरीणां पराजयेनामोदन्त सेनापतयः ।

गृहं प्राविशंश्चोराः परं नालभन्त धनम् ।

कन्या अवन्दन्त जनकम् ।

आचार्यादस्त्राण्यशिक्षामहि ।

वीर्येण विद्यायाश्च बलेन प्राकाशन्त ।

बीजस्यारोपणमारभन्त कृषीवलाः ।

नारायणस्य दुष्कृतानि नारोचन्त जनकाय ।

उद्यमा‡द्धरेर्धनान्यवर्धन्त ।

नानिष्टमाशङ्कामहि ।

धनस्य राशयो ब्राह्मणेभ्योऽदीयन्त ।

---

* See rule in note*, p. 21.

† प्रच्छ् becomes पृच्छ् in the passive.

‡ ह preceded by any of the first four letters of a class is changed to the fourth letter of that class optionally.

Monkeys fought with *Rākṣasas* (evil spirits).

(We two) spoke to (the) learned men at Kāśī.

(They) endured (the) taunt with calmness.

Stars (two) shone in (the) east.

(You) were praised by [men.

(You two) were commanded by Rāma.

(We) invited (the) *Ṛṣis* for dinner.

When did (the) messengers return from Ayodhyā?

(We) did not expect favour from Hari.

(We) got books at school.

(The two) examiners examined (the two) girls in dancing

(We two) rejoiced at (the) sight of (our) mother.

(You two) did not begin (the) work.

(We two) saluted (the) *Ṛṣi*.

(They two) suspected a repulse from (the) king.

(We) were born of (a) family of *Gandharvas*.

(The) birds disregarded (the) advice of (their) leader, and fell into (the) net.

(The) faults of (the) Brāhmaṇas were forgiven by (the) king.

(You two) shook with fear at (the) sight of (the) tiger.

(You) strove for (the) captue of (the) elephant.

(The two) children did not feel happy without (their) mother.

Rāma's virtues were praised by poets.

By application (they) obtained much wealth.

(They two) sought (their) daughter in (the) forest.

Two mangoes were tasted by (the two) travellers.

GENERAL RESULTS AND EXAMINATION.

नी

	Singular	Dual	Plural
1st pers.	अनयम्	अनयाव	अनयाम
2nd pers.	अनयः	अनयतम्	अनयत
3rd pers.	अनयत्	अनयताम्	अनयन्

द्युत्

1st pers.	अद्योते	अद्योतावहि	अद्योतामहि
2nd pers.	अद्योतथाः	अद्योतेथाम्	अद्योतध्वम्
3rd pers.	अद्योतत	अद्योतेताम्	अद्योतन्त

1. Give the forms of the Imperfect of अस्, अद्, ईक्ष्, मृग्, सृज्, रुच्, मन्त्र्, *with* नि, इष्, शिक्ष्, जीव्, डी, मृ, जन्, वृत्, &c., &c.

1. What change does a final consonant undergo when compounded with the following nasal ? When is the change necessary ?

3, What change does ह् undergo when it follows any of the first four letters of a class ?

4. When is a श् changed to छ् ?

LESSON XIX.

MASCULINE AND NEUTER NOUNS ENDING IN उ AND ऊ

Nouns of the masculine gender ending in उ are declined like those ending in इ, with this difference that where इ, ई, ए or य् occurs in the latter. उ, ऊ, ओ or व् should be substituted respectively in the former.

Nouns of the neuter gender ending in उ or ऋ are declined like वारि, ऊ or ॠ being substituted for इ, ऊ or ॠ for ई, and ओ or अर् for ए.

(*Masculine*).

गुरु *m.*

	Singular	*Dual*	*Plural*
Nom.	गुरुः	गुरू	गुरवः
Acc.	गुरुम्	गुरू	गुरून्
Instr.	गुरुणा	गुरुभ्याम्	गुरुभिः
Dat.	गुरवे	गुरुभ्याम्	गुरुभ्यः

(*Neuter*).

मधु *n.*

Nom. & Acc.	मधु	मधुनी	मधूनि
Instr.	मधुना	मधुभ्याम्	मधुभिः
Dat.	मधुने	मधुभ्याम्	मधुभ्यः

कर्तृ 'doer' *n.*

Nom. & Acc.	कर्तृ	कर्तृणी	कर्तॄणि
Instr.	कर्तृणा	कर्तृभ्याम्	कर्तृभिः
Dat.	कर्तृणे	कर्तृभ्याम्	कर्तृभ्यः

Masculine nouns ending in ऋ change it to आर् before the terminations of the nominative and of the singular and dual of the accusative. A few nouns, such as पितृ, भ्रातृ, जामातृ, देवृ, नृ and सव्येष्टृ change the final ऋ to अर्. The nominative singular of all ends in आ, र् and the termination स् being dropped.

Terminations of the First Four Cases

	Singular	*Dual*	*Plural*
Nom.	स्	औ	अस्
Acc.	अम्	औ	न्
Instr.	आ	भ्याम्	भिस्
Dat.	ए	भ्याम्	भ्यस्

Before न् the preceding ऋ is lengthened

नेतृ *m.* 'leader.'

Nom.	नेता	नेतारौ	नेतारः
Acc.	नेतारम्	नेतारौ	नेतॄन्
Instr.	नेत्रा	नेतृभ्याम्	नेतृभिः
Dat.	नेत्रे	नेतृभ्याम्	नेतृभ्यः

Nom.	भ्राता	भ्रातरौ	भ्रातरः
Acc.	भ्रातरम्	भ्रातरौ	भ्रातॄन्
Instr.	भ्रात्रा	भ्रातृभ्याम्	भ्रातृभिः
Dat.	भ्रात्रे	भ्रातृभ्याम्	भ्रातृभ्यः

SUBSTANTIVES, &c.

(*Masculine*)

इषु an arrow
ऋतुपर्ण name of a king
कपोल cheek.
गुरु a preceptor, a venerable person
जामातृ a son-in-law
तडाग a tank
तरु a tree
त्वष्टृ the architect of the gods'
दुर्जन a wicked person
देवृ husband's brother
धातृ the Creator
नृ a man
परशु an axe
परशुराम a *Brāhmaṇa* hero, who exterminated the worrior caste
पांसु dust
पितृ father
प्रभु a lord
बाहु an arm

बिन्दु a drop
भर्तृ husband, master
भीम name of one of the sons of Pāṇḍu
भ्रमर a bee
मनु the Hindu legislator

Masc. & Neuter.
कर्तृ doer, author
गन्तृ goer
दातृ giver, donor
द्रष्टृ seer
द्वेष्टृ hater

लक्ष्मण brother of Rāma
वायु wind
विघ्न an obstacle
विमार्ग a wrong path
विष्णु the god Viṣṇu
रक्षितृ defender, Protector

Neuter.
अग्र the tip
अश्रु a tear
तालु the palate

शत्रु an enemy
शम्भु the god Śiva
शिशु an infant, a child
सव्येष्टृ a charioteer
मधु honey
राष्ट्र a country, nation
वसु wealth

Feminine.
अमरावती Indra's capital
जिह्वा tongue

ADJECTIVES.

क्षुधित hungry
श्याम dark

INDECLINABLES.

अनेकशस् frequently
तु but (not used at the beginning of a sentence).

ROOTS.

इष् *4th Conj. Parasm. with* अनु, to search for
गम् *with* अनु, to go after, to follow
गल् *1st Conj. Parasm.* to drop
छिद् *pass.* to be cut off
नी with प्र, to compose, to write
भृ *1st Conj. Parasm. and Ātm.* to fill; भ्रियते *pass.*
मन् *with* अनु, to consent to, to agree to
मा *with* निर्, to produce, to create; निर्मीयते *pass.*
वाञ्छ् *1st Conj. Parasm.* to desire

अ prefixed to words beginning with a a consonant and अन् to those beginning with a vowel, express negation.

SENTENCES.

शम्भुर्जयति ।
बाहू स्फुरतः ।
वायुना तरवः कम्पन्ते ।
भ्रमरा मधु पिबन्ति ।
नरो वसूनि वाञ्छन्ति ।
इन्द्रः शत्रूनजयत् ।
योधोऽराविषू क्षिपति ।
चातको जलस्य बिन्दुमपि न लभते ।
विष्णवे पूजा रोचते ।
प्रभुभिर्भृत्या आदिश्यन्त ।
विश्वस्य कर्तारं नमामि ।
गुरुभ्यः शिष्यस्याविनयं कथयामि । [च्छत् ।
सीता लक्ष्मणं देवरमन्वग-

कन्याया भर्तारं जामातरं वदन्ति ।
भर्त्रे संदेशः प्रहीयते ।
नार्याः कपोलयोर्नयनाभ्यामश्रूणि गलन्ति ।
त्वष्ट्रामरावती निरमीयत ।
पितरो वन्द्यन्ते पुत्रैः ।
रामो जनकस्य जामाता ।
पाण्डवा द्रुह्यून् युद्धेऽजयन् ।
भर्तारमनुसरति किंकरः ।
मनुना धर्मः प्राणीयत ।
धात्रा प्रजाः सृज्यन्ते ।
तडागस्य जलं मार्गे गन्तृभिरपीयत ।
याचका दातारं नालभन्त ।

Rāma gives sweetmeat to children.

(The) sky is filled with dust.

Paraśurāma struck (his) enemies with (an) axe.

Drops of water fall from (the) clouds.

(The) king called (the) defenders of (the) town.

(A) child obeys (his) father.

(The) lord of Avantī spoke to (his) ministers.

Hari touched (his) palate with (his) tongue.

Women went to (the) garden with (their) husband.

(The) *Ṛṣis* were the seers [of *mantras*.

People adore Viṣṇu.

Ṛtuparṇa spoke to (his) charioteers.

Rāma went to (the) forest with (his) brother Lakṣmaṇa.

Rāvaṇa's heads were cut off* by Rāma with arrows.

(A) work is frequently not begun by men for fear of obstacles.

With (his) arms, Bhīma fought with (his) enemy.

(The) gods punish (the) doers of evil.

Those who go (the goers) by (the) wrong path are censured by men.

Virtue is (the) protector of (a) country (nation) from ruin.

Honey dwells on (the) tip of (the) tongue of (a) wicked person, but in (his) heart poison.

Trees delight travellers by (their) shade.

Rāma's departure to (a) forest with Viśvāmitra was consented to by (his) father.

(The) wind is scattering (the) dark clouds.

People praise (the) givers of food to (the) hungry.

Sītā's husband and (her) husband's brother searched for Sītā.

---

*छ् following a vowel is changed to च्छ्. This change takes place optionally when the vowel is long and at the end of a word or grammatical form; but after मा (negative particle) and आ (preposition) it is necessary.

LESSON XX.

NOUNS ENDING IN ऋ AND ॠ—MASC. & NEUT.—

(*Continued*).

			Singular	*Dual*	*Plural*
Nouns in ऋ	Masc.	Abl.	(none)	भ्याम्	भ्यस्
		Gen.	(none)	ओस्	नाम्
		Loc.	इ	ओस्	सु

The singular of the ablative and genitive cases is formed by substituting उर् for ऋ. Before the इ of the locative singular, ऋ takes अर् as its substitute, and before नाम् it is lengthened. This latter change is optional in the case of नृ. The vocative singular is made up by puting अर् for ऋ, and the dual and plural are the same as those of the nominative.*

(*Masculine*).

	Singular	*Dual*	*Plural*
Abl.	नेतुः	नेतृभ्याम्	नेतृभ्यः
Gen.	नेतुः	नेत्रोः	नेतॄणाम्
Loc.	नेतरि	नेत्रोः	नेतृषु
Voc.	नेतर्	नेतारौ	नेतारः

(*Neuter*).

Abl.	कर्तृणः	कर्तृभ्याम्	कर्तृभ्यः
Gen.	कर्तृणः	कर्तृणोः	कर्तॄणाम्
Loc.	कर्तृणि	कर्तृणोः	कर्तृषु
Voc.	कर्तर् or कर्तृ	कर्तृणी	कर्तॄणि

* See rule, page 30.

(*Masculine*).

	Singular	*Dual*	*Plural*
Abl.	गुरोः	गुरुभ्याम्	गुरुभ्यः
Gen.	गुरोः	गुर्वोः	गुरूणाम्
Loc.	गुरौ	गुर्वोः	गुरुषु
Voc.	गुरो	गुरू	गुरवः

(*Neuter*).

Abl.	मधुनः	मधुभ्याम्	मधुभ्यः
Gen.	मधुनः	मधुनोः	मधूनाम्
Loc.	मधुनि	मधुनोः	मधुषु
Voc.	मधो or मधु	मधुनी	मधूनि

WORDS.

अनुज्ञा *f.* permission

अप्रिय *adj.* unpalatable, disliked

अर्जुन *m.* name of one of the sons or Pāṇḍu

अलङ्घनीय *adj.* that cannot be transgressed

अलम् *ind.* enough, away with (used with the instrumental)

अवस्तु *n.* not a thing; an unreal thing

अवस्त्वारोप *m,* ascribing something that is not real

आदर *m.* respect

आरोप *m.* ascribing

आर्य *m.* a respectable person; name of the remote ancestors of the Hindus

इच्छा *f* wish

इन्दु *m.* the moon

उत्कण्ठा *f,* anxiety, longing

उत्साह *m.* happiness cheerfulness, energy

कर्ण *m.* name of a hero

कलङ्क *m.* a stain, a spot

कारुण्य *n.* compassion, kindness

कुरु *m.* name of a country (*in pl*)

कृतज्ञता *f.* gratitude

कृपा *f.* favour

ज्ञाति *m.* a relation

तनु *adj.* small, little.

तूल *m.* cotton

द्विज m. one of the first three classes or castes

नप्तृ *m.* a grandson

निर्बन्ध *m.* importunity

निशित *adj.* sharp

पथ्य *n.* a wholesome thing, what is wholesome

पशु *m.* beast

पात *m.* fall, falling

पितृव्य *m.* paternal uncle

बन्धु *m.* a relation

भारतवर्षीय *m.* a native of Bhāratavarṣa or India

भूत *n.* a creature, an animal

भ्रातृ *m.* a brother

मद *m.* intoxication, insolence

मुख्य *adj.* chief

मृग *m.* deer

मृत्यु *m.* death

रघु *m.* (*in the plural*) the descendants of a king named रघु

रमा *f.* name of a woman

लक्ष्मी *f.* wife of Viṣṇu; goddess of wealth

लङ्घ् *1st Conj. Ātm.* to transgress, to overcome

वक्तृ *m.n.* a speaker

वस्तु *n.* a thing, a real thing

वार्ता *f.* intelligence, news, account

विभव *m.* wealth, riches

वैकुण्ठ *n.* name of the celestial abode of the god Viṣṇu

श्रोतृ *m.n.* a hearer

साधु *m.* a sage, a man of piety *adj.* good

स्रष्टृ *m.n.* a creator

SENTENCES.

तरोः पुष्पाण्यपतन् ।

शम्भोः कृपया कल्याणं भवति ।

गुरूणामादेशाननुरुध्यामहे ।

साधवो मृत्योर्भयं न गणयन्ति ।

पितरि रामस्य परम आदरः ।

विश्वस्य स्रष्टुरिच्छाऽलङ्घनीया ।

द्वेष्टृणामुत्साहं न सहते ।
इन्दौ कलङ्को दृश्यते ।
रामो बन्धुषु स्नेहेन वर्तते ।
मधुनि माधुर्यमस्ति ।
नृषु द्विजः श्रेष्ठः ।
दातृभ्यो धनं लभन्ते ।
कुरुभ्यो दूत आगच्छत् ।
पितृव्यः पितुर्भ्राता ।
वस्तुन्यवस्त्वारोपोऽज्ञानम् ।
बाह्वोर्बलेन पृथ्वीमजयत् ।
भीमस्य भ्रातर्यर्जुने कर्णो बाणानमुञ्चत ।
तूलस्य राशावग्नेरिव मृदुनि मृगस्य शरीरे निशितस्य बाणस्य पातः ।
तनुषु विभवेषु ज्ञातिभिस्त्यज्यन्ते नराः ।
पशुष्वपि कृतज्ञता दृश्यते ।
श्रोतॄणां निर्बन्धात्कथामारभत ।
अप्रियस्यापि पथ्यस्य वक्तृणि मित्रेऽलं क्रोधेन ।
नप्तुर्लाभेऽतीवोत्कण्ठा भारतवर्षीयाणाम् ।
परमं कारुण्यं साधूनां भूतेषु ।
कन्यां जामातुर्गृहं नयति ।

Rāma was (the) chief of the Raghus.

(I) got a book from (the) author.

Lakṣmī* was (the) wife of Viṣṇu.

[hearers.

(He) begs pardon of (his)

Janaka saw (the) chariot of (his) grandsons.

Nārāyaṇa saw (the) horses of Hari's son-in-law.

(The) Āryas lived in (the) Kurus.

(A) parrot sat on (the) tree.

(A) servant of Hari's grandson went to a village.

Karṇa was (the) first among donors.

---

* This noun takes स् in the nom. sing.

(The) lion is (the) lord of beasts.

Hari is (the) friend of Ramā's husband.

The disc of (the) moon increases and decreases.*

By order of (his) brother, Rāma, Lakṣmaṇa abandoned Sītā in a forest.

From (the) Creator was born the universe.

(She) obtained news of (her) husband.

By (the) strength of (his) arm (he) conquered (his) enemies.

(There) is no fear for (the) mountains even from (a) strong wind.

Wise men get knowledge even from children.

Sins afflict (my) heart, O Śambhu!

In sages is seen great love for God.

Birds sit on (the) branches of trees.

Servants do not transgress (the) orders of (their) lords.

From (her) husband (she) obtained permission for going to (her) mother's house.

(A) residence in *Vaikuṇṭha* is obtained by the devotees of Viṣṇu.

EXAMINATION.

1. Decline द्रष्टृ *m.* and *n.*, मधु, मनु, जामातृ, अश्रु, धातृ *m.*, नृ, देवृ, शत्रु, विभु *m.* and *n.*, ज्ञातृ, स्रष्टृ *m.*, वस्तु, वायु, &c. &c.

2. Compare the declensions of masculine nouns ending in उ and neuter nouns ending in उ and ऋ with those of nouns ending in इ.

---

*Use क्षि *Pass.*

3. What change or changes does the ending ऋ of masc. nouns undergo in the first five inflexions ?

4. When is छ changed to च्छ ? When is the change optional and when necessary ?

LESSON XXI

FEMININE NOUNS ENDING IN इ, उ, ऊ, and ऋ

Feminine nouns ending in ऊ are declined like those in ई, उ, ऊ, or व् being substituted for the इ, ई, or य् occurring in the latter. The termination of the nominative singular is स्.

The termination of the instrumental singular of feminine nouns ending in इ or उ is आ, and that of the accusative plural is स्, before which latter the final vowel is lengthened. In other respects these nouns are declined like the corresponding masculine. The forms of the dative, ablative, genitive, and locative singulars are optionally made up like those of nouns ending in ई or ऊ respectively.

Feminine nouns ending in ऋ are such as express relationship. They are स्वसृ, मातृ, दुहितृ, ननान्दृ and यातृ. The accusative plural termination is स्, before which the ऋ of all these nouns is lengthened. In other respects स्वसृ is declined like नप्तृ or गन्तृ *m.*, and the rest like पितृ.

Adjectives ending in ऋ such as श्रोतृ, गन्तृ, &c. form their feminine by adding ई, as श्रोत्री, गन्त्री, &c.

श्वश्रू

	Singular	*Dual*	*Plural*
Nom.	श्वश्रूः	श्वश्र्वौ	श्वश्र्वः
Acc.	श्वश्रूम्	श्वश्र्वौ	श्वश्रूः
Instr.	श्वश्र्वा	श्वश्रूभ्याम्	श्वश्रूभिः
Dat.	श्वश्र्वै	श्वश्रूभ्याम्	श्वश्रूभ्यः
Abl.	श्वश्र्वाः	श्वश्रूभ्याम्	श्वश्रूभ्यः
Gen.	श्वश्र्वाः	श्वश्र्वोः	श्वश्रूणाम्
Loc.	श्वश्र्वाम्	श्वश्र्वोः	श्वश्रूषु
Voc.	श्वश्रु	श्वश्र्वौ	श्वश्र्वः

मति.

	Singular	*Dual*	*Plural*
Nom.	मतिः	मती	मतयः
Acc.	मतिम्	मती	मतीः
Instr.	मत्या	मतिभ्याम्	मतिभिः
Dat.	मतये–मत्यै	मतिभ्याम्	मतिभ्यः
Abl.	मतेः-मत्याः	मतिभ्याम्	मतिभ्यः
Gen.	मतेः-मत्याः	मत्योः	मतीनाम्
Loc.	मतौ–मत्याम्	मत्योः	मतिषु
Voc.	मते	मती	मतयः

धेनु.

	Singular	*Dual*	*Plural*
Nom.	धेनुः	धेनू	धेनवः
Acc.	धेनुम्	धेनू	धेनूः
Instr.	धेन्वा	धेनुभ्याम्	धेनुभिः
Dat.	धेनवे–धेन्वै	धेनुभ्याम्	धेनुभ्यः
Abl.	धेनोः–धेन्वाः	धेनुभ्याम्	धेनुभ्यः
Gen.	धेनोः–धेन्वाः	धेन्वोः	धेनूनाम्
Loc.	धेनौ–धेन्वाम्	धेन्वोः	धेनुषु
Voc.	धेनो	धेनू	धेनवः

मातृ

	Singular	*Dual*	*Plural*
Nom.	माता	मातरौ	मातरः
Acc.	मातरम्	मातरौ	मातॄः
Inst	मात्रा	मातृभ्याम्	मातृभिः
Dat.	मात्रे	मातृभ्याम्	मातृभ्यः
Abl.	मातुः	मातृभ्याम्	मातृभ्यः
Gen.	मातुः	मात्रोः	मातॄणाम्
Loc.	मातरि	मात्रोः	मातृषु
Voc.	मातर्	मातरौ	मातरः

SUBSTANTIVES

(*Feminine*).

आङ्ग्लभूमि England
अनुरक्ति love
कान्ति splendour, light
कीर्ति fame
कृति action
गति mode of walking, going, gait
जाति caste, kind
दुष्कृति a wicked action
दुहितृ a daughter
धृति courage
धेनु a cow
ननान्दृ husband's sister
नीति politics
प्रकृति ministry; disposition, nature
प्रतिकृति image or copy
प्रीति affection satisfaction
बुद्धि talent
भक्ति devotion
भूति prosperity
भूमि ground, land; the earth
मातृ mother
मुक्ति absolution
मूर्ति an image or idol
यातृ husband's brother's wife
रति pleasure; the wife of the god of love
रात्रि night
वधू a young woman, a daughter-in-law
वसति a place of residence
वृत्ति profession avocation

श्रुति hearing; Hindu religious books, the *Vedas*

श्वश्रू mother-in-law

सुकृति a virtuous or good action

सृष्टि creation

स्तुति praise

स्मृति remembrance; Hindu law-book

स्वसृ sister

आङ्ग्ल *m.* an Englishman

आध्यान *n.* meditation.

आश्रम *m.* hermitage

ऋष्यशृङ्ग *m.* son-in-law of दशरथ and brother-in-law of राम

एलापुर *n.* a name of a city, Verul

कृ *with* अधि to authorize; (*Pass.*) to be authorized.

चल् *1st Conj. Parasm.* to go astray, to go wrong

चिह्न *n.* a token

धा (धी *Pass.*) *with* अभि, to call, to name

धीर *m.* a bold man

निन्दा *f.* censure

निपुण *adj.* proficient.

पद् *with* उद् *4th Conj. Ātm.* to be produced, to result.

पर *adj.* great, greatest

परिणाम *m.* result

पश्चात् *ind.* afterwards

पिण्ड *m.* a ball of rice given to the dead

प्रकर्ष *m.* intensity greatness

प्रच्छ् [पृच्छ्] *with* आ, *Ātm.* to take leave of as at the time of departure

बहु *adj.* many

मदन *m.* god of love

मन्द *adj.* slow

लोभ *m.* avarice

विकास *m.* development

विवर *n.* a cave

शम्बूक *m.* name of a person

शान्ता *f.* sister of Rāma

शूद्र *m.* a person of the lowest Hindu caste

शौर्य *n.* valour

श्लिष् *with* आ *4th Conj. Parasm.* to embrace

सद् [सीद्] *1st Conj. Parasm, with* नि [निषीद्] to sit

संनिधि *m.* proximity, vicinity.

सुजन *m.* a good person, a good man

सृ *with* प्र to spread

स्निह् *4th Conj. Parasm.* to feel affection for

SENTENCES.

सुजनस्य कीर्तिर्लोके प्रसरति ।

संकटे धीरो धृतिं न मुञ्चति ।

रामःप्रीत्या पुत्रामाश्लिष्यति ।

मुक्तये देवं भजति ।

यक्षाणां वसत्या आगच्छत् ।

दुःखं दुष्कृतेरुत्पद्यते ।

मदनो रतेर्वल्लभः ।

सृष्ट्याः पालक ईश्वरः ।

बुद्धेः प्रकर्षः कीर्तये भवति ।

भूमौ निषीदति ।

जामातुर्ऋष्यशृङ्गस्याश्रमं रामस्य मातरोऽगच्छन् ।

यातॄर्ननान्दरं चापृच्छत सीता पश्चादगच्छत्पितुर्गृहम् ।

रघोः पिता वसिष्ठस्य धेनुमरक्षत् ।

नारायणस्य कृतयो हरेः प्रीत्यै न भवन्ति ।

श्रुत्यां शूद्रो नाधिक्रियते ।

मूर्खाणां स्तुतीर्निन्दा वा न गणयन्ति बुधाः ।

प्रकृतिभिर्नृपः सेव्यते ।

गोपो धेनू रक्षति ।

वध्वो नद्या जलमानयन्ति ।

श्वश्रूर्जामातरि स्निह्यति ।

चन्द्रस्य कान्तिं पश्यति ।

सुकृतीनां फलमनुभवति ।

लोभेन बुद्धिश्चलति ।

हरिः प्रकृत्या साधुर्वर्तते

रामः पित्रे मात्रे च पिण्डानयच्छत् ।

स्मृत्यां धर्मः कथ्यते ।

Sītā bowed to Ṛṣyaśṛṅga, (the) husband of (her) husband's sister.

Viśvāmitra was (a) Kṣatriya by caste; afterwards (he) became (a) Brāhmaṇa.

Śambūka is (a) husbandman by profession.

Sītā always pleased (her) mother-in-law.

(The) king's counsellor is proficient in politics.

Among *Smṛtis*, Manu's is (the) best.

(The) modesty of young women in Mahārāṣtra is praiseworthy.

Rāma saw (his) sister Śāntā and bowed to (his) mother.

Rāma asked (the) man (his) [caste.

Men desire prosperity.

Englishmen come here from England.

In (the) caves in (the) vicinity of Verul (there) are many images of gods.

Hari passed* (his) nights in meditation.

Kṛṣṇa† had many daugh-[ters.

Valour contributes to (is for) fame.

(A) man's disposition is known from (the) actions.

Nārāyaṇa's ruin is (the) result of (his) wicked actions.

Courage is the greatest ornament of men.

Great love for God is called devotion.

(The) development of (a) man's talent is (the) result of teaching.

Sītā's face is like (the) moon in (by) splendour.

(An) elephant's gait is [slow.

(The) father gave much wealth to (his) daughters.

(The) sister's present was (a) taken of affection.

---

* Use the root नी here.

† Use the gen. of 'Kṛṣṇa' and nom. of 'daughters' and the Sanskrt verb corresponding to 'were'.

The feminine of adjectives ending in उ is optionally the same as the masculine. The other form is made up by adding ई.

EXAMINATION

1. Compare :—(*a.*) The declension of feminine nouns ending in ऊ with that of those in ई.

(*b.*) The declension of feminine nouns in इ and उ with that of the corresponding masculine. What do the optional forms of the former resemble ?

(*c.*) The declension of स्वसृ, मातृ, पितृ, नप्तृ, and गन्तृ *m.* with one another.

2. How is the feminine of adjectives ending in उ and ऋ formed ?

3. Decline ननान्दृ, स्वसृ, रुचि, कीर्ति, वधू ,रज्जु *f.*, नीति, पृथु *m.* and *f*, &c., &c.

LESSON XXII.

ON THE IMPERATIVE MOOD.

Parasmaipada Terminations.

	Singular	*Dual*	*Plural*
*1st pers.	आनि	आव	आम
2nd pers.	(none)	तम्	त
3rd pers.	तु	ताम्	अन्तु
	वदानि	वदाव	वदाम
	वद	वदतम्	वदत
	वदतु	वदताम्	वदन्तु

The conjugational signs are added on to the roots before the termination of the Imperative.

---

* The Imperative forms of अस् and अद् are given in the Second Book.

WORDS.

अनृत *n.* a falsehood, an untruth
अभिधान *n.* name
डिम्भ *m.* a child
दुर्ग *n.* difficulty
दृढम् *adv.* firmly, closely
पाठ *m.* a lesson
पितृ *du.* parents
पूज्य *adj.* worthy of honour
प्रतिक्रिया *f.* retaliation, revenge, the way to revenge.
भद्र *n.* well-being, [benefit
भू *with* अनु, to experience, to feel
मद् *with* प्र, to err, to fall off
मा *ind.* not (prohibitive)
रस *m.* juice
रेरे *interj.* O! Oh!
वंश *m.* race
वत्स *m.* a child
वयस्य *m.* a companion, friend
शङ्का *f.* doubt
श्रम् *with* वि to rest
सत्त्व *n.* truth, goodness; an animal, a creature
सद् [सीद्] *1st Conj. Parasm with* प्र, to favour, to be pleased
सर्वदा *ind.* always
सुवर्णकार *m.* a goldsmith
सोम *m.* a plant used in sacrifices, or its juice
स्था *with* अनु to carry out, to act according to

SENTENCES.

सत्त्वं जयतु ।
वत्स पितरं प्रणम ।
अयोध्यां दूता गच्छन्तु ।
पुत्रावश्वमारोहताम् ।
रेरे मा विनयं त्यजत ।
सख्यौ पुष्पाण्यानयतम् ।
वयस्योपवनं प्रविशाव ।
जलं त्यज घृतं पिब ।
कथं व्याघ्राणां संनिधौ निवसानि ।
लोको दुर्गाणि तरतु भद्राणि पश्यतु ।
नराणां व्याधयो नश्यन्तु ।
मयूरौ प्रासादस्य शिखरे नृत्यताम् ।
बालका अनृतं मा वदत ।

आसनयोर्निषीदतम् ।

डिम्भ जननीमाह्वय ।

भूपतयः सर्वदा प्रजा धर्मेण रक्षन्तु ।

जनः सदानन्दमनुभवतु ।

शत्रोः प्रतिक्रियामुपदिशत ।

पितरौ प्रसीदतम् ।

सत्यान्मा प्रमाद्याम ।

सुवर्णकारस्सुवर्णं तोलयतु ।

पित्रोर्गुर्वोश्च वचनमनुतिष्ठ ।

पूज्यान्पूजय ।

विश्राम्यन्तु पान्थास्तरोश्छायायाम् ।

क्षालयतां हस्तौ बालौ ।

Tell (your) brother's name.

Children, go to school and learn (your) lessons.

God save (the) King!

* Let (us) follow (the) counsels of wise men.

(The) gods be satisfied!

Hari and Mādhava, do not prattle.

Leave off doubt as to† Rāma's success.

May (the) enemies of men thus perish!

Give money to (the) poor.

Caṇḍāla, do not touch (a) Brāhmaṇa.

Let (him) drink (the) juice of *Soma*.

May (he) remember (the) good deeds of (his) race!

Let (us) deserve (the) praises of men.

Let (us) forgive (the) faults of (our) friends.

Embrace closely (thy) father, boy.

Children, do not give pain to dumb creatures.

May not Hari's mind be agitated by anger!

May we not wallow in sin.

Let (the) herdsman take (the) kine home.

---

*Use the Imperative of the infinitive depending on "Let," and put the object of 'Let' into the nominative case.

†Use the locative here.

May (the) greed of (the) people for gold decrease!

May (the two) sons please (their) mother!

Let (the) beggars glean (the) (grains of) rice.

Let (the) fools prattle.

LESSON XXIII.

Imperative Mood—(*Continued*).

Ātmanepada Terminations.

	Singular	*Dual*	*Plural*
1st pers.	ऐ	आवहै	आमहै
2nd pers.	स्व	इथाम्	ध्वम्
3rd pers.	ताम्	इताम्	अन्ताम्
	मोदै	मोदावहै	मोदामहै
	मोदस्व	मोदेथाम्	मोदध्वम्
	मोदताम्	मोदेताम्	मोदन्ताम्

Roots.

जि *with* वि *Ātm.* to conquer

पद् *with* प्रति, to step towards, to do.

मन् *4th Conj. Ātm.* to think, to maintain, to regard.

लम्ब् *1st Conj. Ātm. with* अव, to resort to, to adopt

वृत् *with* प्र, to set about.

Substantives.

अभिलाष *m.* desire.

आचार *m.* proper conduct, conduct.

ऋजुता *f.* straight-forwardness.

खल *m.* a villain.

देवदत्त *m.* name of a person.

पात्र *n.* a deserving person or object.

पार्थिव *m.* a king.

प्रश्रय *m.* courtesy, civility

विद्या *f.* learning.

श्रम m. labour.

समृद्धि *f.* plenty, abundance.

सूनु *m.* a son.

SENTENCES.

शत्रुभिः सह युध्यस्व ।

चित्तं स्वास्थ्यं लभताम् ।

शिष्या गुरून् वन्दध्वम् ।

प्रजाया हिताय पार्थिवाः प्रवर्तन्ताम् ।

कन्ये गीतं शिक्षेताम् ।

भर्तारं सेवेथाम् ।

कथं दुःखं सहे ।

कीर्तये यतामहे ।

भूपते विजयस्व ।

भ्रातुर्गुणान् मा श्लाघध्वम् ।

नरा धान्यस्य समृद्ध्या मोदन्ताम् ।

आचारं प्रतिपद्येथाम् ।

जनानां धर्मेऽभिलाषो वर्धताम् ।

शृगालौ म्रियेताम् ।

वार्ताः श्रूयन्ताम् ।

प्रश्रयमवलम्बस्व ।

प्रकाशन्तां पराक्रमेण नृपस्य सूनवः ।

रमतां चित्तं छात्राणां विद्यायाम् ।

संगीतमारभामहे ।

प्रजानां कल्याणाय क्लेशा सह्यन्तां नृपैः ।

प्रेक्षस्व वनस्य शोभाम् ।

संकटेऽप्यनृतं मा भाषावहै ।

मा निष्टमाशङ्केथाम् ।

शोभन्तां तरवः फलानामुद्गमेन ।

दुराचारेभ्यः कल्याणं माशंसध्वम् ।

Tremble, (the) enemies of the King!

Taste (thou a) mango.

Begin (you the) study of Sanskṛt.

May (we) obey (the) commands of God!

Let (the) moon shine.

Let (the two) books be brought here.

Do not (you both) regard Devadatta (an) enemy.

Rejoice at men's prosperity.

Die, villain!

May men blush at (their) misdeeds!

Let (the) virtues of (the) medicine be examined.

Let riches be given to deserving persons.

May men always seek (the) truth!

Flatter not sinners.

Let (the) birds fly from (the) branches of the tree.

Let rogues smile at (the) straight-forwardness of (the) good.

Let heaps of corn be given to Brāhmanas.

May (a) son be born to (the) king!

Obtain (thou thy) desires.

May (I) not disregard (the) orders of (my) father!

Let (us two) destroy (our) enemies.

Let (the two) faults of (the) servant be forgiven by (the) master.

Earn wealth by labour, do not beg.

Let (the two) children taste (the) sweetmeats.

May (we two) not be killed in (the) battle!

LESSON XXIV.

SOME OF THE MORE IMPORTANT VERBAL DERIVATIVES.

The past passive participle* is formed by adding त to the root; as श्रु *to hear*, श्रुत *heard.*

The infinitive of purpose is formed by adding तुम्† to the root; as श्रु *to hear*, श्रोतुम् *for hearing.*

---

* The feminine of this is formed by adding आ.

† The final vowel or the penultimate short takes its *guṇa* substitute before this termination.

The indeclinable past participle or absolutive is formed by adding त्वा to the root; श्रु *to hear*, श्रुत्वा *having heard*. य takes the place of त्वा, when a preposition is prefixed to the root; अनुभूय *having experienced*. त् is prefixed to this य, when the roots ends in a short vowel; अनुकृत्य *having imitated*.

Before all these terminations except य some roots take the augment इ. As a general rule, however, roots ending in short vowels do not take it. There are some other modifications which the roots undergo, which are too various to be noticed here.

To form the present participle, the conjugational sign* is first affixed to the root, and then the termination अत् (see note*, p. 6) is added on to it when the root takes Parasmaipada terminations, and मान when it takes Atmanepada terminations. आन, however, takes the place of मान when the base† does not end in अ. Passive presents participles are formed by adding मान to the passive base.

List of Passive Participles of several roots.

अस् to throw	अस्त	क्षुभ् to be agitated	क्षुब्ध
आप् to obtain	आप्त	खन् to dig	खात
कम् to desire, to love	कान्त	गम् to go	गत
कृष् to draw lines,		गुह् to hide	गूढ
to plough	कृष्ट	जन् to be produced	जात
क्रम् to go	क्रान्त	तुष् to be satisfied	तुष्ट
क्रुध् to be angry	क्रुद्ध	त्यज् to abandon	त्यक्त
क्लम् to be weary	क्लान्त	दह् to burn	दग्ध
क्षम् to forgive	क्षान्त	दिश् to show	दिष्ट

* Or, more generally, take that form which the root assumes before the 3rd pers. plural termination of the present tense, and then add on the participial suffix instead of that termination.

† That form of a noun or root to which the termination is appended is called the *base*.

दुष्	to be made bad	दुष्ट
दृश्	to see	दृष्ट
धा	to put, to bear	हित
धृष्	to be proud, to dare	धृष्ट
नम्	to bow	नत
नश्	to perish	नष्ट
पच्	to cook	पक्व
पद्	to go	पन्न
पुष्	to nourish	पुष्ट
प्रच्छ्	to ask	पृष्ट
बन्ध्	to bind	बद्ध
भज्	to worship	भक्त
भुज्	to eat, to enjoy	भुक्त
मन्	to mind, to think	मत
मस्ज्	to plunge	मग्न
मुच्	to liberate	मुक्त
मुह्	to be foolish	मूढ or मुग्ध
मृ	to die	मृत
यज्	to worship	इष्ट
युज्	to join	युक्त
रभ्	to be engaged in	रब्ध
रम्	to sport	रत
रुह्	to grow	रूढ
लभ्	to obtain	लब्ध
लुभ्	to covet	लुब्ध
वच्	to speak	उक्त
वद्	to speak	उदित
वप्	to sow	उप्त
वह्	to bear	ऊढ
विश्	to enter	विष्ट
वृत्	to be	वृत्त
शंस्	to praise	शस्त
शम्	to be quiet	शान्त
श्लिष्	to embrace	श्लिष्ट
सह्	to endure	सोढ
सृज्	to create, to abandon	सृष्ट
स्पृश्	to touch	स्पृष्ट
हन्	to kill	हत

WORDS.

अखिल *adj.* all, whole

अभिषेक *m.* coronation

अस् (to throw) *with* **निर्**, to scatter

उटज *m.* a hut

उद्यत (*past part.* of **यम्** *with* **उद्**) ready, prepared

उपाय *m.* a remedy

कारागृह *n.* prison

कुम्भकार *m.* potter

कूप *m.* a well

क्षेत्र *n.* a field

खन् *1st Conj. Parasm. & Ātm. with* **उद्**, to dig to excavate

घट *m.* a jar

तूष्णीम् *ind.* silent, silently

दिश् *with* **निर्** to indicate

धा (to put, to bear) *with* नि, to place.

ह *1st Conj. Parasm* and *Ātm.* to seize; *with* उद्, to save, to release, to lift up.

नी *with* वि, to educate

पङ्क *m.* mud.

पीडा *f.* pain.

प्रातर् *ind.* in the morning

भज् *1st Conj. Parasm.* and *Ātm.* to resort to, to have recourse to

भाष् *with* प्रति, to reply

मति *f.* intellect.

मद *m.* pride, arrogance

मूल *n.* root, foot

मूर्छ् *1st Conj. Parasm.* to faint away, to swoon

यज्ञिय *adj.* belonging to a sacrifice.

राजपुरुष *m.* a king's officer

रुह् *with* आ, to ascend

वृत् *with* प्रति and नि, to come back, to return

समर्थ *adj* able, powerful

सर्प *m.* a serpent

सम्यक् *adv.* well

सारमेय *m.* a dog

हृ *1st Conj. Parasm.* and *Ātm.* *with* परि, to dispel, to remove

SENTENCES.

जलं पातुं नदीमगच्छत् ।
कुम्भकारेण घटः कृतः* ।
हरिणा सर्पो दृष्टः ।
ग्रामं गन्तुमिच्छामि ।
जनानां पीडाः परिहर्तुमीश्वरः समर्थोऽस्ति ।
भार्यां त्यक्त्वा वनं गतः ।

रामस्य पीडा नष्टा ।
उपायश्चिन्तितः ।
गृहं प्रविष्टः किंकरः ।
शम्बूकेन कथितां वार्तां श्रुत्वा रामोऽमुह्यत् ।
नद्यास्तीरे चिरं विहृत्योटजं निवृत्ता सीता ।

---

* In sentences in which the past participle is thus used, the copula अस्ति 'is' may be supposed to be understood.

गृहं प्रविश्य क मातेत्यपृच्छत् ।

लक्ष्म्या मदेन स्पृष्टोऽसि ।

रामेण बहवः कूपास्तडागाश्चोत्खाताः ।

एवमुक्तो हरिर्ब्राह्मणाय धनमयच्छत् ।

अश्वमारोढुं* मतिर्जाता ।

शत्रून् जित्वा नगरीं प्राविशत् ।

सखीभिः पृष्टा ललनाऽलज्जत ।

क्लेशः सोढः सीतया ।

पृथिव्यां चरितुं यज्ञियोऽश्वो मुक्तः ।

वनात्प्रतिनिवृत्य रामो राज्यं कर्तुमारभत ।

पङ्के पतितां धेनुमुद्धरति ।

रक्षितोऽस्मि देवेन ।

बहूनि काव्यानि पठितानि हरिणा ।

आतपेन क्लान्तास्तरोर्मूलं भजामः ।

(The) clouds †have been scattered by (the) wind.

(The) fields have been ploughed by (the) husbandmen, and corn has been sown.

Having well educated (the) pupil, (the) preceptor gave (him) permission to marry.

(The) sea is agitated by the wind.

Having followed (the) dog's steps, (he) came to (the) place indicated.

Śiva became satisfied with Rāvaṇa's devotion.

(The) seed of virtues is placed by God in (the) heart of men.

Be ready to conquer (your) enemy.

Many soldiers were killed in (the) battle.

---

* From रुह्.

† In translating these sentences, use the verbal derivatives taught in this lesson, wherever they can be used.

Having remembered (her) dead husband, (she) again swooned.

At (the) time of (the) coronation, all men were released from prison.

(The) child wishes to seize (the) moon.

(The) fruit of (his) exertion has been obtained by Nārāyaṇa.

Having saluted (the) goddess, (he) returned from (the) temple.

Hari's faults have been forgiven by (his) father.

Having ascended (the) mountain, (he) saw (a) lake.

(The) cause of fear is gone

(He) attempts to lead villains to (the) path of (the) good.

(The) child was abandoned on (the) shore of (the) sea.

Having experienced (the) sorrows of (the) world, (he) became (an) ascetic.

Many villages were burnt by the soldiers on (the) way.

Having replied to (his) friend, (he) stood silent.

(A) son is born to Hari's wife.

Having got up* in (the) morning, men wash (their) faces.

(The) thieves were bound by (the) king's officers.

EXAMINATION.

1. Give the Imperative (all numbers and persons) of जीव्, ईक्ष्, जन्, स्पृश्, कृ, हृ, स्था act. and pass., पा 'to drink,' स्फुर्, अद्, निन्द्, क्षुभ्, भू *with* अनु act. and pass., सह्, &c., &c.

2. How do you form :—

a. The Past Passive Participle,

b. The Present Participle Active,

---

* The स् of स्था is dropped after the preposition उद्.

c. The Present Participle Passive,

d. The Infinitive of purpose,

e. The Indeclinable Past Participle or Absolutive with and without a preposition ?

3. *Give the infinitive of purpose and all participles of मन्, यज्, मुच्, खन्, दह्, सृज्, वह्, लभ्, रभ्, क्षिप्, &c., &c.

4. When is the initial स् of स्था dropped ?

LESSON XXV

NOUNS ENDING IN CONSONANTS

The general scheme of case-endings given in Sanskṛt Grammars is as follows :—

	Singular	*Dual*	*Plural*
Nom. & Voc.	स्	औ	अस्
Acc.	अम्	औ	अस्
Instr.	आ	भ्याम्	भिस्
Dat.	ए	भ्याम्	भ्यस्
Abl.	अस्	भ्याम्	भ्यस्
Gen.	अस्	ओस्	आम्
Loc.	इ	ओस्	सु

These terminations are applied without any change to masculine and feminine nouns ending in consonants, but the crude form itself undergoes certain modifications, which we will shortly notice.

---

* The pupil will require the teacher's assistance in answering this question, which is rather too advanced for him.

1. There are a number of nouns which undergo no change, and are declined alike, whether masculine or feminine ; as भूभृत् *m.*, मरुत् *m.*, दृषद् *f.*, &c.

मरुत् *m.*

	Singular	*Dual*	*Plural*
Nom. & Voc.	मरुत्*	मरुतौ	मरुतः
Acc.	मरुतम्	मरुतौ	मरुतः
Instr.	मरुता	मरुद्भ्याम्	मरुद्भिः
Dat.	मरुते	मरुद्भ्याम्	मरुद्भ्यः
Abl.	मरुतः	मरुद्भ्याम्	मरुद्भ्यः
Gen.	मरुतः	मरुतोः	मरुताम्
Loc.	मरुति	मरुतोः	मरुत्सु

वाच् *f.*

	Singular	*Dual*	*Plural*
Nom. & Voc.	वाक्†	वाचौ	वाचः
Acc.	वाचम्	वाचौ	वाचः
Instr.	वाचा	वाग्भ्याम्	वाग्भिः
Dat.	वाचे	वाग्भ्याम्	वाग्भ्यः
Abl.	वाचः	वाग्भ्याम्	वाग्भ्यः
Gen.	वाचः	वाचोः	वाचाम्
Loc.	वाचि	वाचोः	वाक्षु‡

*When there are more consonants than one at the end of a word, the first is retained and the others dropped; as मरुत् with स् becomes मरुत्स्, but स् is dropped and the form is मरुत्.

†च् or ज् is changed to क् before hard consonants, and to ग् before any soft consonant except a nasal or a semi-vowel. This change takes place also when these consonants end a word, even before a nasal or a semi-vowel; वाच्+यत=वाग्यत. A consonant (except a nasal) at the end of a word is changed to the first or third of its class.

‡स् following a vowel except अ and आ, or a letter of the guttural class, or र्, generally becomes ष्.

2. Nouns ending in वत् and मत्, when masculine, prefix a न् to the final त् in the first five inflections.

भगवत् *m.*

	Singular	*Dual*	*Plural*
Nom.	भगवान्	भगवन्तौ	भगवन्तः
Acc.	भगवन्तम्	भगवन्तौ	भगवतः
Instr.	भगवता	भगवद्भ्याम्	भगवद्भिः
Dat.	भगवते	भगवद्भ्याम्	भगवद्भ्यः
Abl.	भगवतः	भगवद्भ्याम्	भगवद्भ्यः
Gen.	भगवतः	भगवतोः	भगवताम्
Loc.	भगवति	भगवतोः	भगवत्सु
Voc.	भगवन्	भगवन्तौ	भगवन्तः

3. Present participles differ from this only in the nominative singular, the अ of the last syllable being short, as गच्छत् *pr. part.*, गच्छन् *nom. sing.*

4. The terminations of the nominative, vocative and accusative forms of neuter nouns ending in consonants are as follows :—

Singular	*Dual*	*Plural*
(none)	ई	इ

Before the इ of the plural न् is prefixed to the final consonant, if it be not a nasal or a semi-vowel. The other cases are, as in the case of nouns ending in अ, formed exactly like those of the corresponding masculine.

Nom., Voc. and Acc. जगत् जगती जगन्ति

5. Before the ई of the nom., voc. and acc. dual of the neuter, न् is prefixed the final त् of the present participles of roots of the 1st, 4th and 10th conjugations, and optionally to the त् of those of roots of the 6th conjugation.

Nom., Voc. and Acc. गच्छत् गच्छन्ती गच्छन्ति

Nom., Voc., and Acc. विशत् विशन्ती or विशती विशन्ति

WORDS.

आपद् *f.* adversity
आयुष्मत् *adj.** long-lived
गुणवत् *adj.* meritorious
जगत् *n.* the world
दृषद् *f.* stone
धीमत् *adj.* sensible, talented
परवत् *adj.* dependent
प्रतिपद् *f.* the first day of a lunar fortnight
भगवत् *adj.* divine, majestic
भवत् *pron.* your Honour
भूभृत् *m.* a king
मरुत् *m.* wind ; a god
मूर्तिमत् *adj.* having form
मृद् *f.* earth
यशस्वत् *adj.* famous
वाच् *f.* speech
विद्युत् *n.* lightning
विपद् *f.* adversity
वियत् *n.* the sky
शरद् *f.* autumn
श्रीमत् *adj.* prosperous
संपद् *f.* wealth, prosperity
सुखभाज् *adj.* happy, those who enjoy happiness
सुहृद् *m.* a friend
हुतभुज् *m.* fire

अकाल *m.* (अ + काल *m.* time) not the time, improper time
अत्यय *m.* passing away, destruction
अधमर्ण *m.* a debtor
अन्तःकरण *n.* the heart
अर्थ् *10th Conj. Ātm.* with अभि, to request, to beg of, to solicit
इह *ind.* here
ईक्ष् *with* उप, to neglect

---

* The feminine forms of adjectives ending in मत् or वत् are formed by adding ई; as आयुष्मती long-lived (she). Of present participles the fem. form is the same as that of the neuter nom., voc. and acc. dual : as भवत् *pr. part.* भवन्ती *f.* ; विशत् *pr. part.*, विशन्ती or विशती *f.*

उच्चैस् *ind.* aloft, nobly

उद्भव *m.* birth

उद्धत (*past part. pass.* of हन् *with* उद्) proud

कार्त्तिक *m.* name of a month

चञ्चल *adj.* transitory

जीवित *n.* life

नल *m.* name of a king

निषण्ण (*past. part. pass.* of सद् *with* नि) seated, sitting

प्रवृत्ति *f.* predilection

प्राण *m. pl.* life

बहुशस् *ind.* often, in many cases

महोत्सव *m.* a festival

मृदु *adj.* soft

वासुदेव *m.* name of the god Kṛṣṇa

विकार *m.* change of form, transformation

विद् *4th Conj. Ātm.* to be

विहित (*past. pass. part.* of धा *with* वि) laid down

वृन्त *n.* a stalk

श्लथ *adj.* loosened

संदेह *m.* doubt

सर्वथा *ind.* wholly

होतृ *m.* a sacrificial priest

Present Participles.

कुर्वत् doing

गच्छत् going

चोदयत् going

जयत् conquering

पश्यत् seeing

वसत् dwelling

शासत्* ruling

सत् (*pr. part.* of अस् to be) being good; *m.* a good or virtuous man

SENTENCES.

नृशंसेभ्यो गुणवतामपि भयं विद्यते ।

चन्द्रस्य प्रकाशः शरद्याह्लादको भवति ।

---

* न् is not prefixed to त् in the first five inflections in this case. Only before the इ of the nom., voc., and acc. plur. it is prefixed optionally.

विद्युता सह मेघो वियति वर्तते ।

वत्स आयुष्मान् भव ।

धीमन्तो लोके यशस्वन्तो भवन्ति ।

रामो मूर्तिमान् धर्म इव ।

जयतः शत्रून् मोपेक्षस्व ।

भवद्भिरादिष्टः किंकरो नगरमगच्छत् ।

नमो भगवते वासुदेवाय ।

पश्यतो गुरोः* शिष्येणाविनयः कृतः ।

हुतभुजा दग्धमरण्यमपश्यज्ज्वलः ।

दिनेषु गच्छत्सु† नारायणः पण्डितोऽभवत् ।

महीं शासति दशरथे भूभृति जनाः सुखभाजोऽभवन् ।

मरुतां भर्तार्जुनं द्रष्टुमिच्छति ।

कवीनां वाक्षु माधुर्यमस्ति ।

सुहृदोर्वचनमलङ्घनीयम् ।

भवन्तः पुत्रैः सहागच्छन्त्विति श्रीमतो देवस्याज्ञा ।

घटा मृदो विकारा अलंकाराश्च सुवर्णस्य ।

प्राणानामत्ययेऽप्यसन्तः सद्भिर्नाभ्यर्थ्यन्ते ।

इह जगति पुत्रस्योद्भव उत्सवस्य हेतुः ।

संदेहे सतामन्तःकरणस्य प्रवृत्तयः प्रमाणम् ।

विपद्युच्चैः स्थीयते सद्भिः ।

दृशदि निषण्णो गुरुः शिष्यान्धर्ममुपादिशत् ।

---

*This is an instance of the genitive absolute; it has the sense of 'notwithstanding.'

†This is an instance of the locative absolute; the meaning is like that of the English nominative absolute—*days having elapsed.*

अधमर्णाः सर्वथा परवन्तो भवन्ति ।

अकालो नास्ति धर्मस्य जीविते चञ्चले सति ।

Nārāyana is not dependent.

Deer sit on stones in (a) [forest.

Indra is (the) lord of (the) gods.

On (the) first of *Kārttika* there is (a) festival.

(I) saw (a) boy going to school.

In prosperity many persons follow (a) man.

(A) man is abandoned by (his) friends in adversity.

Kṛṣṇa saw men driving horses.

Ascetics regard (the) world as (a) wilderness.

(A) work is written by (the) talented Nārāyaṇa.

Even (the) meritorious are censured by (the) wicked.

Men always desire to be long-lived.

(It) has been so laid down by (the) divine Manu.

Anger cools down by soft speech.

Nārada descended from (the) sky.

(The) good do not become proud on account of (by) wealth.

(It) was advised by (our) preceptor (when he was) going to heaven.

(While) living in (a) forest Rāma and Lakṣmaṇa destroyed many demons.

(I) am very pleased by seeing (a sight of) your Honour.

(The) talented are honoured at (the) courts of kings.

(The) wind takes away (the) loosened flower from (the) stalk.

Lightning is considered by poets (as the) wife of (the) cloud.

Fire, (if) touched, burns even (the) *Hotr.*

(The) desire for happiness of those who enjoy happiness often increased by (their) enjoyment of happiness.

Rāma lived in (the) prosperous city of Ayodhyā.

EXAMINATION.

1. Repeat the case-terminations occurring in Śanskṛt Grammars.

2. Compare the *declension* of nouns in वत् or मत् with that of present participles, and of these with that of any ordinary noun ending in a consonant, such as भूभृत्.

3. How do you form the neuter dual (nom., voc., acc.) or feminine of present participles, and of adjectives in वत् or मत् ?

4. How is म् or न् treated when followed by hard or soft consonants, or when it is at the end of a word ?

5. In what circumstances is स् generally changed to ष् ?

6. Decline प्रतिपद्, हुतभुज्, यशस्वत् *m., f. & n.*, कुर्वत् *m., f. & n.*, सुखभाज् *m. & n.*, आयुष्मत् *m. & n.*, द्विषत् *m., f. & n.*, परवत् *m.*, आपद्, चोदयत् *m., f. & n.* &c., &c.

7. Explain, with instances, the use of the Loc. and Gen. absolute.

LESSON XXVI.

NOUNS ENDING IN अन् AND इन्.

1. स्, the nominative and vocative singular termi nation, is dropped (see note*, page 97).

2. न् is dropped in the nominative singular, and before all terminations begining with consonants.

3. The अ is lengthened in the first five inflections, and इ in the nominative singular only. The rule does not hold good fn the case of neuter nouns. But in the plural of the nom., voc. and acc, of these, the अ and इ are lengthened.

4. अ is dropped before the vowel terminations, beginning with the अस् of the accusative plural, but not in cases when the अ is preceded by a conjunct consonant of which म् or व् is final member. This rule is applied optionally in the locative singular of masculine and neuter nouns, and in the nom , voc. and acc. dual of the latter.

5. The vocative singular does not differ from the crude. In the neuter न् is optionally dropped.

राजन् *m.*

	Singular	*Dual*	*Plural*
Nom.	राजा	राजानौ	राजानः
Acc.	राजानम्	राजानौ	राज्ञः*
Instr.	राज्ञा	राजभ्याम्	राजभिः

*The अ of the final syllable अन् being dropped, we have राजन्. By rule of *saṁdhi* (see page 21, note*) न् becomes ञ्, which, with the preceding ज्, becomes ज्ञ्.

	Singular	*Dual*	*Plural*
Dat.	राज्ञे	राजभ्याम्	राजभ्यः
Abl.	राज्ञः	राजभ्याम्	राजभ्यः
Gen.	राज्ञः	राज्ञोः	राज्ञाम्
Loc.	राज्ञि—राजनि	राज्ञोः	राजसु
Voc.	राजन्	राजानौ	राजानः

आत्मन् *m.*

Nom.	आत्मा	आत्मानौ	आत्मानः
Acc.	आत्मानम्	आत्मानौ	आत्मनः
Instr.	आत्मना	आत्मभ्याम्	आत्मभिः
Dat.	आत्मने	आत्मभ्याम्	आत्मभ्यः
Abl.	आत्मनः	आत्मभ्याम्	आत्मभ्यः
Gen.	आत्मनः	आत्मनोः	आत्मनाम्
Loc.	आत्मनि	आत्मनोः	आत्मसु
Voc.	आत्मन्	आत्मानौ	आत्मानः

नामन् *n.*

Nom. and Acc.	नाम	नामनी or नाम्नी	नामानि
Instr.	नाम्ना	नामभ्याम्	नामभिः
Dat.	नाम्ने	नामभ्याम्	नामभ्यः
Abl.	नाम्नः	नामभ्याम्	नामभ्यः
Gen.	नाम्नः	नाम्नोः	नाम्नाम्
Loc.	नामनि-नाम्नि	नाम्नोः	नामसु
Voc.	नामन् or नाम	नामनी or नाम्नी	नामानि

शशिन् *m.*

Nom.	शशी	शशिनौ	शशिनः
Acc.	शशिनम्	शशिनौ	शशिनः

	Singular	*Dual*	*Plural*
Instr.	शशिना	शशिभ्याम्	शशिभिः
Dat.	शशिने	शशिभ्याम्	शशिभ्यः
Abl.	शशिनः	शशिभ्याम्	शशिभ्यः
Gen.	शशिनः	शशिनोः	शशिनाम्
Loc.	शशिनि	शशिनोः	शशिषु
Voc.	शशिन्	शशिनौ	शशिनः

भाविन् *n.*

Nom. and acc.	भावि	भाविनी	भावीनि
Voc.	भाविन् or भावि	भाविनी	भावीनि

The rest like शशिन्.

WORDS.

अनुजीविन् *m.* a servant

अन्तरात्मन् *m.* the internal soul, the heart

अपराधिन् *adj.* guity, offending

अश्मन् *m.* a stone.

आत्मन् *m.* the soul, self

उत्सङ्गवर्तिन् *adj.* (उत्सङ्ग *m.* lap resting in the lap

कञ्चुकिन् *m.* an attendant on the women's apartments, a chamberlain

कर्मन् *n.* action

कुशलिन् *adj* happy, well

क्षयिन् *adj.* lessening, decreasing

क्षेत्रगामिन् *adj.* going to a holy place

चर्मन् *n.* leather

नामन् *n.* a name

पक्षिन् *m.* a bird

प्राणिन् *m.* an animal

प्रियवादिन् *adj.* speaking sweetly

प्रेमन् *m. n.* affection

फलाशिन् *adj. m. n.* a fruit-eater. or

ब्रह्मन् *m.* the Creator

भाविन् *adj.* what is to be, future

महिमन् *m.* greatness

मूर्धन् *m.* the head
मेधाविन्* *adj.* talented, intelligent
योगिन् *m.* an ascetic
राजन् *m.* a king
लघिमन् *m.* littleness
वर्त्मन् *n.* a way, path
विश्वकर्मन् *m.* the architect of the gods
शिखरिन् *m,* a mountain
शूलिन् *m.* name of the god Śiva
सद्मन् *n.* a house
सीमन् *f.* boundary bounds
स्वामिन् *m.* a lord
हेमन् *n.* gold

अनर्थ *m.* disadvantage, evil
अन्तःपुर *n.* the apartment occupied by women in a house
अमात्य *m.* counsellor
अम्बर *n.* the sky
अर्थ *m.* a thing, occurrence, event
अवतरत् (*pr. part.* of तॄ *with* अव) descending [ter
आत्मजा *f.* daughter
आरम्भ *m.* beginning, performance
उपकार *m.* doing good to another, obligation, benefiting another
उपानह् † *f.* a shoe
कुण्ठित (*past pass. part.* of कुण्ठ्) hampered, impeded
कृ *with* आविस् [आविष्कृ‡] to manifest, to show, to expose
केवलम् *adv.* solely
कैकेयी *f.* name of a wife of Daśaratha
कौशल *n.* skill proficiency
क्रमेण (*instr. sing.* of क्रम) gradually
गण् *10th Conj.* to count, to reckon, to consider
गुरु *adj.* long
जगत्कर्तृ *m.* Creator of the world
जीविका *f.* livelihood
दिन *n.* a day
दुष्ट (*past pass. part.* of दुष्) wicked
दूर *adj.* distant
दैन्य *n.* meanness

---

* The feminine form of an adjective ending in इन् is made up by adding ई; as मेधाविनी 'talented' (woman).

†The ह् of this word becomes त् and द् in the circumstances mentioned in note †, page 97.

‡ See note ‡, p. 97.

द्रु 1st Conj. Parasm to melt with pity

न कदापि never

निर्मित (*past pass. part* of मा *with* निर्) created constructed, formed, made

निर्वृतिमत् *adj*. happy

निवेशित *past pass. part.* of the *causal* of विश् *with* नि placed

परार्ध *m.* the second or latter half

पश्चात् *ind.* afterwards

पुण्यवत् *adj.* virtuous

पूर्वार्ध *m.* the first half

प्रसन्न (*past pass. part*, or सद् with प्र) pleased

प्रियवादित्व *n.* kindliness of speech

बुद्धि *f.* intellect

मधुरम् *adv.* sweetly

यात्रिक *m.* a pilgrim

लक्ष् 10th Conj. with सम्, to observe to test, to prove

लघु *adj.* short

वसुदेव *m.* name of Kṛṣṇa's father

विनाश *m.* destruction

विशुद्धि *f.* purity

विश्वास *m.* confidence

वृद्धिमत् *adj.* lengthening

व्याली *f.* a tigress

शुभ *adj.* good, virtuous [purity

श्यामिका *f.* impurity

श्रवण *n.* hearing

श्रीषेण *m.* name of a person

साशङ्क *adj.* suspicious

सुख *n.* ease

सोत्कण्ठ *adj.* anxious

स्वप्न *m.* a dream

SENTENCES.

योगिनः फलाशिनो भवन्ति।

अपराधिनं मा क्षमस्व।

अनुजीविने कुप्यति भर्ता।

दशरथस्य पुत्रो नाम्ना रामः।

ब्रह्मणः प्रजाः प्रजायन्ते।

राजन् कुशली भव।

कञ्चुकी राज्ञामन्तःपुरेऽधिकृतः पुरुषः।

भाविनोऽनर्थाञ् ज्ञातुं न समर्थोऽस्ति जनः।

अश्मभिरश्वस्य गतिः कुण्ठिता।

जगत्कर्तुर्महिम्नां फलं सर्वत्र दृश्यते ।

क्षेत्रगामिना वर्त्मना गच्छ- न्तं यात्रिकमपश्यम् ।

जनस्य कल्याणाय यतमा- नेन रामेणात्मा क्लेशमु- पानीयत ।

आत्मनः पुत्राणां कर्मसु कौशलं प्रशंसति ।

कृष्णो वसुदेवस्य सद्मनि वसन्न*म्बरादवतरन्तं नारदमपश्यत् ।

श्रीषेणस्य राज्ञो महिषी सूर्यं चन्द्रं चात्मन उत्सङ्गव- र्तिनौ स्वप्नेऽपश्यत् ।

अपराधिनः पुरुषान्दण्डय- न्तु राजानः ।

अस्मन्नेव निर्मितं दुष्टानां हृदयं परकीयस्य दुःख- स्य श्रवणेन न कदापि द्रवति ।

शुभानां कर्मणामारम्भः कल्याणाय ।

जगता कुटुम्बिनं मन्यत † आत्मानं साधुः ।

प्राणिनामुपकारायैव साधू- नां जगति जीवितम् ।

प्रियवादिनां प्रियवादित्वं दैन्यं गण्यते शठैः ।

अज्ञानादात्मनो विनाशायैव केवलं राज्ञा दशरथेन व्यालीव कैकेय्यात्मनः सद्मनि निवेशिता ।

प्रसन्नो भवतोऽन्तरात्मा ।

---

* When ङ्, ण् and न् at the end of a word or grammatical form are preceded by a short vowel and followed by any vowel, they are doubled.

† If a nominal or verbal form ending in ए, ऐ, ओ, or औ is followed by a vowel, the य् and व् of the substitute for the former are optionally dropped. The two vowels thus brought together by the dropping of य् or व् do not coalesce.

दिनस्य पूर्वार्धे वृक्षाणां छाया आरम्भे गुर्व्यः क्रमेण च क्षयिण्यः परार्धे तु पुरा लघवः पश्चाच्च वृद्धिमत्यः ।

हेम्नः संलक्ष्यते ह्यग्नौ विशुद्धिः श्यामिकापि वा ।

Devadatta is intelligent.

(The) father embraced (his) son with affection.

Nala was (the) son of Viśvakarman.

Birds fly in (the) sky.

Servants follow (their) lord.

Trees grow on mountains.

(I) do not remember (the) names of (the) boys.

Shoes are made of leather.

Hari's ruin is (the) result of (his) actions.

(The) mind of (a) guilty person is always suspicious.

(The) message of (the) queen was taken to (the) king by (the) chamberlain.

Though speaking sweetly, (I) speak (the) truth.

(The) whole creation was born of Brahman.

Men are often anxious to know future events.

Śiva is sought in (the) heart by ascetics.

(His) foot was placed by (the) king on (the) heads of (his) enemies.

(An) educated man does not transgress (the) bounds of good conduct.

On hearing intelligence of (his) happy sons in (a) distant country (he) rejoiced.

Affection for (their) young is shown by even (the) beasts.

In (a) forest livelihood is made by fruit-eaters with ease.

(He) worshipped guests in (his) house as gods.

(A) man becomes famous by greatness of intellect.

(The) confidence of subjects grows in (a) good king.

(The) littleness of men is exposed by (their) own actions.

Brahmā created animals, and stones, and (the) sky.

EXAMINATION.

1. In what cases is the न् of nouns ending in अन् dropped, and in what cases the अ? Give examples of nouns which do not drop the latter.

2 Compare the declension of nouns ending in अन् with that of those in इन्.

3. Decline मूर्धन्, महिमन्, वर्त्मन्, यज्वन्, कधिमन्, कुशलिन्, सद्मन्, पक्षिन्, कर्मन्, सीमन्, &c. &c.

4. How do you form the feminine of adjectives ending in इन्?

5. When are ङ्, ण् and न् doubled?

6. What changes taken place when the ending ए, ऐ, ओ or औ of a nominal or verbal form is followed by a vowel? Give the rules and illustrate them.

LESSON XXVII.

NOUNS ENDING IN स्, वस् AND ईयस् OR इयस्.

1. The nom. sing, of nouns ending in स् is formed by dropping the termination स् and lengthening अ if it precedes. The स् of the noun is then changed to a *visarga* (*vide* note ‡, p. 9).

2. Before the terminations beginning with consonants the स् is changed to a *visarga*, which, in being compounded with the terminations, follows the *Saṁdhi* rules that have been given (see note* page 15, and † and ‖ page 17).

3. Nouns in वस् and ईयस् or एयस् prefix in the masculine a न् to the final स्, and their penultimate अ is lengthened, in the first five inflections. The nominative singular ends in वान् and यान्.

4. The व of वस् is changed to उ* before the vowel terminations, beginning with that of the accusative plural, and before the ई of the nom., voc. and acc. dual of the neuter; and the स् to द् before the consonantal, and in the nom., voc. and acc. sing. of the neuter.

5. The rule mentioned in 2 holds also in the case of ईयस् or एयस्.

6. The preceding अ, if any, is not lengthened in the case of the nom., voc, and acc. sing, of neuter nouns. Before the इ of the plural, the penultimate vowel is lengthened and a nasal inserted after it.

7. In the vocative singulars of all these, the penultimate is not lengthened; as चन्द्रमस्, विद्वस्; &c.

चन्द्रमस् *m.*

	Singular	*Dual*	*Plural*
Nom.	चन्द्रमाः	चन्द्रमसौ	चन्द्रमसः
Acc.	चन्द्रमसम्	चन्द्रमसौ	चन्द्रमसः
Instr.	चन्द्रमसा	चन्द्रमोभ्याम्	चन्द्रमोभिः

---

* Before this the preceding इ, if any, is dropped; सेदिवस्, सेदुषः acc. pl.

	Singular	*Dual*	*Plural*
Dat.	चन्द्रमसे	चन्द्रमोभ्याम्	चन्द्रमोभ्यः
Abl.	चन्द्रमसः	चन्द्रमोभ्याम्	चन्द्रमोभ्यः
Gen.	चन्द्रमसः	चन्द्रमसोः	चन्द्रमसाम्
Loc.	चन्द्रमसि	चन्द्रमसोः	चन्द्रमःसु-स्सु
Voc.	चन्द्रमः	चन्द्रमसौ	चन्द्रमसः

विद्वस् *m.*

Nom.	विद्वान्	विद्वांसौ*	विद्वांसः
Acc.	विद्वांसम्	विद्वांसौ	विदुषः†
Instr.	विदुषा	विद्वद्भ्याम्	विद्वद्भिः
Dat.	विदुषे	विद्वद्भ्याम्	विद्वद्भ्यः
Abl.	विदुषः	विद्वद्भ्याम्	विद्वद्भ्यः
Gen.	विदुषः	विदुषोः	विदुषाम्
Loc.	विदुषि	विदुषोः	विद्वत्सु
Voc.	विद्वन्	विद्वांसौ	विद्वांसः

श्रेयस् *m.*

Nom.	श्रेयान्	श्रेयांसौ	श्रेयांसः
Acc.	श्रेयांसम्	श्रेयांसौ	श्रेयसः
Instr.	श्रेयसा	श्रेयोभ्याम्	श्रेयोभिः
Dat.	श्रेयसे	श्रेयोभ्याम्	श्रेयोभ्यः
Abl.	श्रेयसः	श्रेयोभ्याम्	श्रेयोभ्यः
Gen.	श्रेयसः	श्रेयसोः	श्रेयसाम्
Loc.	श्रेयसि	श्रेयसोः	श्रेयःसु-स्सु
Voc.	श्रेयन्	श्रेयांसौ	श्रेयांसः

*In the body of a word or grammatical form न् is changed to an *anusvāra* when followed by श, ष, स, or ह

†See note‡, p. 97.

मनस् *n.*

	Singular	*Dual*	*Plural*
Nom., Voc. and Acc.	मनः	मनसी	मनांसि
The rest like	चन्द्रमस्.		

तस्थिवस् *n.*

Nom., Voc. And Acc.	तस्थिवत्	तस्थुषी*	तस्थिवांसि
The rest like	विद्वस्.		

अर्चिस् *f.*

Nom.	अर्चिः	अर्चिषौ	अर्चिषः
Acc.	अर्चिषम्	अर्चिषौ	अर्चिषः
Instr.	अर्चिषा	अर्चिर्भ्याम्	अर्चिर्भिः
Dat.	अर्चिषे	अर्चिर्भ्याम्	अर्चिर्भ्यः
Abl.	अर्चिषः	अर्चिर्भ्याम्	अर्चिर्भ्यः
Gen.	अर्चिषः	अर्चिषोः	अर्चिषाम्
Loc.	अर्चिषि	अर्चिषोः	अर्चिःषु-ष्षु
Voc.	अर्चिः	अर्चिषौ	अर्चिषः

WORDS.

अध्युषिवस् *adj.* dwelt
कनीयस् *adj.* younger
चक्षुस् *n.* the eye
चन्द्रमस् *m.* the moon
छन्दस् *n.* *Veda*
†ज्यायस् *adj.* elder
तपस् *n.* religious austerity
तमस् *n.* darkness
तस्थिवस् *adj.* sat
तेजस् *n.* light. heat
दिवौकस् *m.* an inhabitant of heaven
दुर्वासस् *m.* name of a sage
धनुस् *n.* a bow
नभस् *n.* the sky
पयस् *n.* water

*The feminine of adjectives ending in वस् is the same as the Nom., Voc. and Acc. dual. of the neuter while that of adjectives in ईयस् and एयस् is formed by the simple addition of ई.

†This and भूयस् are declined like श्रेयस्.

प्रेयस् *adj.* very dear, dearer

भूयस् *adj.* very great, greater

मनस् *n.* mind

यशस् *n.* fame, glory

रक्षस् *n.* an evil spirit, a *Rākṣasa*

रजस् *n.* dust, pollen

वक्षस् *n.* the breast

वचस् *n.* speech

वनौकस् *adj.* one dwelling in a forest

वयस् *n.* age

वासस् *n.* a cloth

विद्वस् *adj.* learned

वेधस् *m.* Brahmā

शिरस् *n.* the head

श्रेयस् *adj.* superior, prosperous

सरस् *n.* lake

हविस् *n.* an offering

अधर्म *m.* sin

अनन्तरम् *adv.* after

अभूमि *f.* not ground

अविचालित (अ+विचलित *past pass. part.* of चल् *with* वि) steady

कण्टक *m. n.* a thorn

कीचक *m.* name of the commander-in-chief of king Virāṭa

कुश *m.* name of a son of Rāma

कृत (*past pass. part.* of कृ) done, made

कृते *ind.* for, for the sake (of)

गुणिन् *adj.* meritorious

जीर्ण (*past pass. part.* of जृ) worn out, old

दरिद्र *adj.* poor

दारुण *adj.* dreadful

द्वारका *f.* name of a town

नव *adj.* new

निश्चेष्ट *adj.* motionless

परिहित (*past pass. part.* of धा *with* परि) worn

पूजास्थान *n.* an object of worship of reverence

प्रियंवदा *f.* name of a female companion of Śakuntalā

भगीरथ *m.* name of a king of the solar race

महाराज *m.* a great king

लिङ्ग *n.* sex

वर *m.* a boon

शाखा *f.* a branch

श्वेत *adj.* white

संतप्त (*past pass. part.* of तप् *with* सम्) heated, oppressed by heat

सहसा *adv.* at once, suddenly

हरण *n.* taking away

अस् *4th Conj. Parasm. with* प्र, to throw; आप् *with* वि, to cover; यत् *pr. part. with* उद्, उद्यत् rising; व्रज् *1st Conj. Parasm.* to go; श्रि *1st Conj Parasm.* and *Ātm. with* आ, to resort to, to depend upon; हृ *with* आ, to eat, to perform (a sacrifice).

SENTENCES.

मुनयो वनौकसोऽभवन्।

देवान् दिवौकसो वदन्ति।

कनीयांसं भ्रातरमाह्वय।

कुशो लवस्य ज्यायान् भ्राता। [कृष्णः।

प्रेयसो जनान् स्मरति

उद्यन्तं चन्द्रमसं प्रेक्षस्व।

तमोभिर्नभो व्याप्यते।

वाससी परिहिते कन्यया।

श्रेयसे यतते।

शत्रूञ् शिरस्सु प्रहरति।

मनसा हरिं व्रजति।

तपसां फलमनुभवतु।

दुर्वासाः पाण्डवानां वसतिमगच्छत्।

भूयांसोऽत्र धान्यस्य राशयो वर्तन्ते।

रामो रक्षांसि हत्वा यशोऽविन्दत। [श्रूयते।

गङ्गायाः पयांसि श्वेतानीति

विद्वद्भिरुपदिष्टो दशरथो यज्ञमाहरत्।

भीमेन वक्षसि ताडितः कीचकोऽमुह्यत्।

बहूनि हवींष्यग्नौ प्रास्यति ।

नगरस्य समीपे तस्थिवद्राजसैन्यमपश्यम् ।

सूर्यस्य तेजसा संततः पांथश्छायामाश्रयते ।

*द्वारकामध्यूषुषो जनस्य संपदो मनसोऽप्यभूमिरभवन् ।

वसिष्ठस्य वचांसि श्रुत्वा विश्वामित्रेण सह रामस्य गमनं दशरथोऽन्वमन्यत ।

गुणाः पूजास्थानं गुणिषु न च लिङ्गं न च वयः ।

कैकेय्याः दारुणं वचः श्रुत्वा महाराजो दशरथः सहसा भूमावपतन्निश्चेष्टश्चाभवत् ।

Hari appeased (his) mother by (his) speech.

Nārāyaṇa's younger brother is at Kāśī.

Pāṇini speaks of (the) *Vedas* as *Chandases.*

(The) wind brings pollen from flowers.

May (the) glory of (the) King spread over (the) earth !

Priyaṁvadā went to Durvāsas and begged pardon.

Hari saw with (his) eyes (the) charioteer driving horses.

Rāma was waited upon (served) by (his) younger brothers.

(The) hermitages of (the)

*That is, their wealth and general prosperity exceeded their desire.

forest-dwelling *Ṛṣis* were made of leaves and branches of trees.

Bhagīratha pleased Vedhas by (his) austerities.

(There) are lotus-flowers in the waters of (the) lakes.

(The) king reveres learned men.

As (a) man leaves worn-out clothes and wears new ones, so (the) soul leaves old bodies and enters new ones.

Raghu conquered (the) earth by (his) bow and arrows.

(The) offerings thrown into (the) fire are carried by (the) fire to (the) gods.

(The) people, who dwelt in Ayodhyā, were happy.

After light comes darkness and after darkness comes (the) light.

Leaving (the) net on (the) thorns, (the) birds flew into (the) sky.

(There) is very great sin in taking away (the) wealth of (the) poor.

Warriors do not mind even death for the sake of fame.

(The) younger brother followed (the) elder brother.

(He) obtained many boons from (the) gods.

Truth is dearer than life to (the) virtuous.

God is sought by (His) devotees with steady minds.

(A) learned person is honoured everywhere.

EXAMINATION.

1. Compare the declensions of nouns ending in **अस्**, **इस्**, **ईयस्**, or **प्यस्**, and **वस्**.

2. When is the **व** of **वस्** changed to **उ**, and how is the preceding **इ**, if any, treated in this ease ?

3. How is the feminine of nouns ending in वस् and ईयस् or एयस् formed ?

4. Decline नभस्, धनुस्, जग्मिवस् *m. f. & n.*, लघीयस् *m, f. & n.*, पयस्, चकृवस्, *m., f. & n.*, ज्यायस् *m., f. & n.*, चक्षुस्, वनौकस् *m. & f.*, सेदिवस् *m., f. & n. &c, &c.*

LESSON XXVIII.

ON THE POTENTIAL MOOD.

Terminations.

Parasmaipada.

	Singular	*Dual*	*Plural*
1st pers.	ईयम्	ईव	ईम
2nd pers.	ईस्	ईतम्	ईत
3nd pers.	ईत्	ईताम्	ईयुस्

Ātmanepada.

1st pers.	ईय	ईवहि	ईमहि
2nd pers.	ईथाः	ईयाथाम्	ईध्वम्
3nd pers.	ईत	ईयाताम्	ईरन्*

---

* These terminations are the same as those of the Imperfect with the following exceptions and modifications. —The *Parasm.* 3rd pers. plur. termination is उस् instead of अन् and those of the *Ātm.* 3rd pers. plu., 1st pers. sing., 3rd and 2nd pers. duals are रन्, अ, आताम् and आथाम् respectively, instead of अन्त, इ, इताम् and इथाम्. To these terminations ई is to be prefixed when they begin with a consonant and ईय् when they begin with a vowel.

The conjugational signs must be added on to the roots before the terminations of the Potential.

Parasmaipada.

	Singular	*Dual*	*Plural*
1st pers.	वसेयम्	वसेव	वसेम
2nd pers.	वसेः	वसेतम्	वसेत
3rd pers.	वसेत्	वसेताम्	वसेयुः

Ātmanepada.

1st pers.	युध्येय	युध्येवहि	युध्येमहि
2nd pers.	युध्येथाः	युध्येयाथाम्	युध्येध्वम्
3rd pers.	युध्येत	युध्येयाताम्	युध्येरन्

The potential expresses (1) probability, commands, prayers, wishes, hopes, &c., and (2) is used in dependent clauses implying these. (3) It is also used in conditional† sentences in which one statement depends on another as its reason or condition. In these two latter respects it resembles the English subjunctive.

WORDS.

अध्वखेद *m.* (अध्वन् *m.* a road, खेद *m.* fatigue) the fatigue of a journey
अनुरञ्जन *n.* pleasing, giving delight to [person
अपण्डित *m.* an illiterate
अपाय *m.* harm
अभिभूत (*past pass. part.* of भू *with* अभि) overcome, overpowered
अहित *n.* injury, harm, damage.

* The potential forms of अस् and अद् are given in the Second Book.

† Except pluperfect conditionals.

आवरण *n.* covering, obstruction

उत *ind.* or

क्लृप् *1st Conj. Ātm.* to be able

क्षुद्र *adj.* insignificant, mean

गाह् *1st Conj. Ātm. with* अव, to bathe in

जायापती *m. du.* wife and husband

तप् *1st Conj. Parasm.* to shine, to be hot

तमिस्रा *f.* night

तृषित *adj.* thirsty

दारिद्र्य *n.* poverty

दीन *adj.* poor

दुर्दशा *f.* bad state, misfortune

द्रुह् *4th conj. Parasm.* to act the traitor

धीर *adj.* wise, of fortitude or patience

नीचैराख्य *adj.* (नीचैस्, आख्या *f.* name) named नीचैस्

न्यायसभा *f.* (न्याय *m.* justice, सभा *f.* court) court of justice

पद् *with* निस् [निष्पद्*] to result

परकीय *adj.* another's

प्रतिहत (*past pass. part.* of हन् *with* प्रति) obstructed

प्रथमसुकृत *n.* (प्रथम *adj.* first, previous; सुकृत *n.* a good action) a previous good action

प्राप्त (*past pass. part.* of आप् *with* प्र) arrived at, come to

बहिस् *ind.* out of (used with the Abl.)

भागीरथी *f.* the Ganges

भूरि *adj.* much

†भोस् *ind.* a vocative particle

रक्षण *n.* defence

रज्जु *f.* a rope

वस् *with* अधि, to sit upon, to rest upon

विघ्न *m.* a obstacle

विपत्ति *f.* adversity

विमार्ग *m.* a wrong path, evil conduct

विमुख *adj.* with the face turned away from

विश्रामहेतोः (*abl.* or *gen sing.* of विश्रामहेतु *m.* विश्राम *m.* rest हेतु *m.* purpose) for the purpose of rest

---

* See Note ‡ p. 97.

† भोस् drops its स् when followed by a vowel or a soft consonant.

शोभन *adj.* good

संश्रय *m.* resting-place

समाज *m.* an assembly

सुकृत *n.*, सुचरित *n.* } a good action

सुरभि *adj.* fragrant

सुवृत्त *adj.* virtuous, good

स्मृ *with* वि. to forget

SENTENCES.

विपदाभिभूतोऽपि न धर्मं त्यजेयम् ।

इच्छामि सोमं पिबेद्भवान् ।

किं भो नृत्यं शिक्षेयोत गानम् ।

भूरिणा प्रयत्नेन तत्त्वमवगच्छेः ।

पुत्राः सुचरितैः पितरौ प्रीणयेयुः ।

ईश्वरस्य पूजया शान्तिं विन्देवहि ।

रज्जुं सर्पं न मन्येध्वम् ।

दुर्दशां गते नरि क्षुद्रोऽप्यहितमाचरेत् ।

वर्धमानं व्याधिं जयन्तं शत्रुं च नोपेक्षेत ।

पण्डितानां समाजेऽपण्डिता मौनं भजेयुः ।

कुसुमैः सुरभिणि हर्म्येऽध्वखेदं नयेथाः ।

प्रजानामनुरञ्जनाय राजानो यतेरन् ।

सुवृत्ताय नृपतये प्रजा न द्रुह्येयुः ।

यदि हरिर्धर्ममार्गान्निवर्तेत शोभनं भवेत् ।

धर्मे रताः प्रज्ञा हरिं पश्येयुः ।

वत्सौ मातुराज्ञामनुरुध्येयाथाम् ।

धैर्यमवलम्ब्य शत्रुभिः सह युध्येथाः ।

नारायणस्यालस्याद्दारिद्र्यं निष्पद्येत ।

शिष्यस्याविनयं गुरुर्न सहेत ।

विपत्तौ धीरो न मुह्येद्धर्मं वा न परित्यजेत् ।

इच्छामि पुनरपि पुण्यां भागीरथीमवगाहेवहीत्यवदद्रामं सीता ।

संश्रयाय प्राप्ते मित्रे प्रथमसुकृतानि स्मृत्वा क्षुद्रोऽपि न विमुखो भवेत् ।

तृषिताय जलं यच्छेद्दरिद्दीनस्य चापदम् ।

नीचैराख्यं गिरिमधिवसेस्तत्र विश्रामहेतोः ।

सूर्ये तपत्यावरणाय दृष्टेः कल्पेत लोकस्य कथं तमिस्रा ।

(You two) should wash (your) hands and feet when (you) return home.

Men should not forget (their) friends.

If (thou) wert to taste poison, (thou) wouldst die.

(The two) books may be carried in (the two) hands.

(You two) should learn *Nyāya* from (your) teacher.

Let (us) sit here in the shade of (a) tree.

Kings should protect (their) subjects from harm.

Let (us) worship God with (a) pure heart.

(Thou) shouldst give money to poor persons.

(You) should not err in [from] (your) duties.

Men should not become agitated without cause.

No man shall covet another's wealth.

(The) king ordered that (the two) rogues should be beaten.

(We) should obtain fame, if (we) died in defence of (our) country.

Witnesses shall always tell (the) truth in courts of justice.

If (I) go to Kāśī, (I) will bring many Sanskṛt books.

If (you) were to tell (a) lie, (you) would be beaten by (your) masters.

(The) king led (his) soldiers out of (the) city that (he) might fight with (his) enemy.

(I) should be punished by (my) masters, if (I) were seen doing evil (sin).

Would (the) poor Brāhmanas get (any) money if (they) should beg through (the) town?

(I) gave much money to (my) sisters that (my) parents might be pleased.

(A) wife and husband should worship *Agni* every day in (the) house.

(A) man should not mind trouble in (the) performance of duty.

Pupils should salute (their) teacher.

Though obstructed by obstacles, (you) should not abandon (a) work begun.

EXAMINATION.

1. Compare the terminations of the Imperfect and the Potential.
2. In what senses is the Potential used?
3. When does भोस् drop its स्?

4. Give the Potential (all numbers and persons) of मृ, ईक्ष्, मन्त्र् *with* नि, सृज, हृ, डी, मृग्, स्था, जन्, पा act. and pass, कृ pass., भू *with* अनु act. and pass., श्रु pass, मुच act. and pass. &c., &c.

LESSON XXIX.

PRONOUNS.

The chief pronouns in Sanskṛt are—सर्व 'all,' तद् 'that', एतद् 'this', यद् 'who' or 'which' (relative), किम् 'who,' or 'which' (interrogative), अस्मद् 'I' or 'we,' युष्मद् 'thou' or 'you' इदम्, 'this' अदस् 'this' or 'that.'

1. The following five terminations are peculiar to pronouns of the masculine gender ending in अ; in other respect the pronouns are declined like the corresponding nouns—

Nom.	Pl.	ई
Dat.	Sing.	स्मै
Abl.	Sing.	स्मात्
Gen.	Pl.	इषाम्
Loc.	Sing.	स्मिन्

	Singular	*Dual*	*Plural*
Nom.	सर्वः	सर्वौ	सर्वे
Acc.	सर्वम्	सर्वौ	सर्वान्
Instr.	सर्वेण	सर्वाभ्याम्	सर्वैः
Dat.	सर्वस्मै	सर्वाभ्याम्	सर्वेभ्यः
Abl.	सर्वस्मात्	सर्वाभ्याम्	सर्वेभ्यः
Gen.	सर्वस्य	सर्वयोः	सर्वेषाम्
Loc.	सर्वस्मिन्	सर्वयोः	सर्वेषु

2. Pronouns of the feminine gender ending in आ take the following peculiar terminations before all of which, except साम्, the आ is shortened; in other respects they are declined like nouns in आ—

Dat.	Sing.	स्यै
Abl.	Sing.	स्यास्
Gen.	Sing.	स्यास्
Gen.	Pl.	साम्
Loc.	Sing.	स्याम्

	Singular	*Dual*	*Plural*
Nom.	सर्वा	सर्वे	सर्वाः
Acc.	सर्वाम्	सर्वे	सर्वाः
Instr.	सर्वया	सर्वाभ्याम्	सर्वाभिः
Dat.	सर्वस्यै	सर्वाभ्याम्	सर्वाभ्यः
Abl.	सर्वस्याः	सर्वाभ्याम्	सर्वाभ्यः
Gen.	सर्वस्याः	सर्वयोः	सर्वासाम्
Loc.	सर्वस्याम्	सर्वयोः	सर्वासु
Neut. Nom. Acc.	सर्वम्	सर्वे	सर्वाणि

The rest like the Masculine.

3. तद्, एतद्, यद्, and किम् in the masculine gender are declined as if they were त, एत, य and क respectively, *i. e.*, pronouns ending in अ. The nom. sing. forms of तद् and एतद्, however, are सः* and एषः respectively.

4. In the feminine gender these pronouns are declined as if they were ता, एता, या and का, *i. e.*, ending in आ. The Nominative singulars of the first two are सा and एषा respectively.

---

* सः and एषः drop the final स् or *visarga* when followed by a consonant in a sentence ; स पुरुषः, &c.

	Singular	Dual	Plural
Neuter Nom. and Acc.	तद्	ते	तानि
	एतद्	एते	एतानि
	यद्	ये	यानि
	किम्	के	कानि

5. एन is used optionally for एत in the accusative, the instrumental singular, and the genitive and locative dual in the three genders.

MASCULINE.

Acc. एतम् or एनम्, एतौ or एनौ, एतान् or एनान्
Instr Sing. एतेन or एनेन
Gen. & Loc. Du. एतयोः or एनयोः

FEMININE.

Acc. एताम् or एनाम्, एते or एने, एताः or एनाः
Instr Sing. एतया or एनया
Gen. & Lod. Du. एतयोः or एनयोः
Neut. Acc. एतद् or एनद्, एते or एने, एतानि or एनानि

WORDS.

अक्षर *adj.* immutable

अखिल *adj.* all, whole

अटवी *f.* a forest

अर्थ् *10th Conj. Ātm. with* प्र, to seek, to desire

अल्प *adj.* small, little

अवदात *adj.* pure, noble

आत्मज *m.* a son

आयास *m.* effort, trouble

इष्ट (*past pass. part.* of इष्) wished, desired.

कपिल *m.* name of a great sage

काञ्चन *n.* gold

कुलीन *adj.* born of a good family

गुणज्ञ *adj.* (गुण merit, add ज्ञा to know) one who appreciates merit

चारु *adj.* beautiful

चौर्य *n.* theft

जाल्म *m.* a wretch, a rascal

दक्षिणा *f.* money given to Brāhmaṇas

दर्शनीय *adj.* handsome.

दिश्* *f.* direction, quarter

दुराप *adj.* difficult to obtain

दुर्गा *f.* name of a goddess

देवायतन *n.* a temple

द्यावापृथिवी *f. du.* the sky and the earth

नाट् *10th Conj. Parsm. & Ātm.* to act as in a dramatic play.

निष्णात *adj.* well-versed

पुराण *n.* name of the sacred poetical works comprising the whole body of Hindu mythology

पूत (*past pass. part* of **पू**) purified, holy

प्रपन्न (*past pass. part* of **पद्** *with* **प्र**) joined with

प्रयाग *n.* Allahabad

ब्रह्मविद् *adj.* a metaphysical philosopher; one knowing the *Brahman*

महत् † *adj.* great

महिषासुर *m.* an evil spirit in the form of a buffalo

मेदिनी *f.* the earth

राजपुत्र *m.* a prince

राज्ञी *f.* a queen

रोदन *n.* weeping

वित्त *n.* wealth

विधृत (*past pass. part. of* **धृ** *with* **वि**) upheld, supported

श्रद्धेय *adj.* credible

श्रुतिमत् *adj.* one who knows the *Vedas*

सगर *m.* name of a king of the solar race

साध्य *adj.* obtainable, possible to make

सामर्थ्य *n.* power

---

*The श् of this is changed to क् in the nom. sing., and before the consonantal terminations. The क् is changed to ग् before soft consonants. (See note †, p. 28).

† As in the case of nouns in वस् and ईयस् or एयस् (see rules 3, 6 and 7, p. 112), the penultimate अ of this is lengthened and न् prefixed to the final त् in the first five inflections of the masculine, and nom., voc. and acc. plural of the neuter. When compounded as an adjective with a following substantive, it becomes महा.

SENTENCES.

कोऽत्रागतः ।

कस्यैतानि पुस्तकानि ।

कस्याः पुत्रा एते ।

यं पुरुषं ह्योऽपश्यं तमेवाह्वयामि ।

सा बाला न* किंचिदवदत् ।

तेभ्यो ब्राह्मणेभ्यो दक्षिणामयच्छम् ।

कस्मान्नगराद्भवानागतः ।

एतेषां यद्यदिष्टं तत्तत्क्रियताम् ।

याः कथाः पुराणेषु श्रूयन्ते ता एवैते नाटयन्ति ।

स एवैष प्रदेशो यस्मिन् प्रियया सह चिरमवसम् ।

येनैतदखिलं जगन्निरमीयत तस्मै नम ईश्वराय ।

तेषु तेषु शास्त्रेषु निष्णातैः पण्डितैः सह राजाऽभाषत ।

कयोस्ते वाससी ।

ययात्मानं पूतं मन्यते वसिष्ठस्तामरुन्धतीं वन्दस्व ।

सर्वासु कलासु प्रावीण्यमुपगतो राजपुत्रः ।

यया महिषासुरो हतस्तस्यै दुर्गायै नमः ।

ते नद्यौ प्रयागे संगच्छेते ।

याभ्यां चौर्यं कृतं तौ पुरुषौ राजाऽदण्डयत् ।

एतस्यामटव्यां पुरा ब्रह्मविदो मुनयो न्यवसन् ।

यैर्मेदिन्युत्खाता ये च कपिलस्य कोपेन दग्धास्तान्

* The addition of चित् or अपि to किम् in all its genders gives it an indefinite sense; किंचित् 'something' or 'anything,' कश्चित् 'somebody,' &c.

† See rule, page 61, footnote*.

सगरस्यात्मजान् भगीरथो गङ्गाया जलेनोद्धरत् ।

यासां विवाहाः स्वपुत्रैः सह समजायन्त ताभिर्जनकस्य कन्याभिः प्रपन्नो राजा दशरथोऽयोध्याम गच्छत् । [इ श्रूयते ।

न दृश्यतेऽत्र कोऽपि रोदनं

पुरा यानि वस्तूनि महता श्रमेण साध्यान्यासंस्तान्यधुना यन्त्राणां सामर्थ्यादल्पेनैवायासेन साध्यानि ।

किं तया धेन्वा क्रियते यस्या दुग्धं नोपलभ्यते ।

यस्यास्ति वित्तं स नरः कुलीनः
स पण्डितः स श्रुतिमान् गुणज्ञः ।
स एव वक्ता स च दर्शनीयः
सर्वे गुणाः काञ्चनमाश्रयन्ते ॥

Who are these ?

What is their avocation ?

She is Hari's daughter.

What is her name ?

To whom did Rāma say so ?

He is Govinda's brother.

I went to school with him

He saw Nārāyaṇa playing with those boys.

Which of his friends does he remember ?

(There) are fishes in that river.

He is followed by her.

Where are the men that have come from those villages ?

They come from that country of which Śūdraka is (the) king.

(The) queen directed those of her maids who were near (in proximity with) her to bring flowers for her.

In this house did (the) king of (the) Mahārāṣṭrīyas live.

Which of those girls sing?

By whom was this book placed here?

(The) sky and (the) earth stand upheld by (the) power of this immutable soul.

No noble deed has been done by them (two).

In that forest (I) lived for (a) long time.

In (by) what direction did the wretch go?

In that temple (there) is (a) beautiful idol of Lakṣmī.

Hari told him (an) incredible story.

How would he, whom Lakṣmī seeks, be difficult for her to obtain?

EXAMINATION.

1. In what respects does the Pronominal declension differ from the nominal?

2. Do the crude forms of Pronouns (Demonstrative, Relative, and Interrogative) end in vowels or consonants? Does their declension resemble that of nouns ending in a vowel or in a consonant?

4. How is the *visarga* of सः and एषः treated in combination in a sentence?

4. Decline यद् *m.,f.* & *n*, तद् *m.,f.* & *n.*, किम् *m. f,* & *n.*, एतद् *m.,f,* & *n.*, दिश्, महत् *m. n.*

LESSON XXX.

PRONOUNS OF THE 1ST AND 2ND PERSONS.

अस्मद् (*I or we*)

	Singular	*Dual*	*Plural*
Nom.	अहम्	आवाम्	वयम्
Acc.	माम् or मा	आवाम् or नौ	अस्मान् or नः
Instr.	मया	आवाभ्याम्	अस्माभिः
Dat.	मह्यम् or मे	आवाभ्याम् or नौ	अस्मभ्यम् or नः
Abl.	मत्	आवाभ्याम्	अस्मत्
Gen.	मम or मे	आवयोः or नौ	अस्माकम् or नः
Loc.	मयि	आवयोः	अस्मासु

युष्मद् (*Thou or you*)

Nom.	त्वम्	युवाम्	यूयम्
Acc.	त्वाम् or त्वा	युवाम् or वाम्	युष्मान् or वः
Instr.	त्वया	युवाभ्याम्	युष्माभिः
Dat.	तुभ्यम् or ते	युवाभ्याम् or वाम्	युष्मभ्यम् or वः
Abl.	त्वत्	युवाभ्याम्	युष्मत्
Gen.	तव or ते	युवयोः or वाम्	युष्माकम् or वः
Loc.	त्वयि	युवयोः	युष्मासु

WORDS.

अपराधलव *m.* a small fault

अव् *1st Conj. Parasm.* to protect

अविश्वास्य *adj.* faithless

आर्या *f.* a venerable woman

उचित *adj.* proper

ऋत्विज् *m.* a sacrificial priest

एतादृश *adj.* of this sort

कारुणिक *adj.* merciful

गम् (with *acc. sing.* of **शरण** or **वश** prefixed to it) to submit oneself to

जेतृ *m.* a conqueror

ताडन *n.* beating

त्वर् *1st Conj. Ātm.* to hasten, to be impatient.

दासजन *m.* a person who is a slave

दूरम् *adv.* far

दैव *n.* fortune

नन्दिनी *f.* a girl

निमित्त *n.* a cause, reason

निष्फल *adj.* fruitless

पत् *with* आ, to happen

पर्याकुल *adj.* agitated, bewildered

पार् *10th Conj. Parasm. & Ātm.* to surmount

प्रतनु *adj.* little, small

भूतार्थ *m.* reality

मति *f.* thought, view, feeling

मानिनी *f.* a proud woman

मेघजाल *n.* an assemblage of clouds

रघुनाथ *m.* the lord of the Raghus

लव *m.* a particle

वियोग *m.* separation

शिव *n.* welfare, happiness

सवितृ *m.* the sun

साक्षिन् *m.* a witness

सोमवासर *m.* Monday

SENTENCES.

नाहमपराधी ।

रघुनाथः खिद्यत्यावयोः ।

कुत्रास्ति मे पुत्रकः ।

भगवति त्वामहं वन्दे ।

मास्मानवधीरय ।

विष्णुर्वोऽवतु

त्वया सहोपवनं गन्तुमिच्छामि ।

आर्ये कथयामि ते भूतार्थम् ।

मह्यं धनं न यच्छसि ।

शिवो वः शिवाय भवतु ।

बालकौ युवयोः पिता क्वास्ति ।

पृथिवीं रक्षत्सु युष्मासु कुतो नो भयम् ।

युष्मदधिगतां वार्तां सर्वेभ्यः शंसामि ।

तस्य पीडां हर्तुमस्माभिश्चिन्तित उपायो निष्फलोऽभवत् ।

तव सुचरितं ममेव प्रतनु यतो न दीर्घं कालमावां सुखमन्वभवाव ।

त्वरते मम मनोऽध्ययनाय ।

अस्माकमश्व एषः ।

क्व गता ते माता ।

एतस्य वृत्तान्तस्य श्रवणेन पर्याकुलमावयोर्मनः ।

दीनेष्वस्मास्वप्येतादृशो भवतः स्नेहः ।

मरुता मेघजालमिव दैवेनास्माकं सर्वे मनोरथा निरस्ताः ।

किं तव पापं रामेण मया वा पापं कृतमित्यपृच्छत्क्रुद्धो दशरथः कैकेयीम् । केन निमित्तेन तस्यैवं त्वमनर्थायोद्यता ।

*कमपराधलवं मयि पश्यसि त्यजसि मानिनि दासजनं यतः ।

†तेषां वधूस्त्वमसि नन्दिनि पार्थिवानाम्
येषां कुलेषु सविता च गुरुर्वयं च ।
यूय वयं वयं यूयमित्यासीन्मतिरावयोः ।
किं जातमधुना येन यूयं यूयं वयं वयम् ॥

Thou art (a) wise man.

Dost thou suspect me to be (a) faithless person ?

Who was your guide when you ascended the mountain ?

Who told thee this story ?

My father went to Kāśī, and, when he returned, he brought many books, and gave them to me.

---

* Said by a husband to his wife.

† Said to Sītā by Vasiṣṭha, who was the preceptor or chaplain to the solar race of kings, to which Rāma belonged.

Tell us what happened there.

I asked you where my book was.

Do not be sorry at (a) separation from us.

By thy favour, we surmounted all perils.

I remember what was done by you at the time.

The witnesses were ordered by me to come on Monday.

I gave you heaps of corn when you came to my house.

Thou being defeated, thy soldiers submitted to the conqueror.

We (two) saw (the) hermitages of many *Ṛṣis*.

These flowers have been brought by us (two).

He got that intelligence from me.

You (two) censure all men.

I give thee this reward.

From thee was (the) path of (the) wise known by me.

Without (any) fault, (the) sacrificial priests beat me.

Do not be angry with us, thy children, (O) merciful father.

He wandered far from us, his friends.

(An) improper action has been done by thee in beating that dog.

Thou being protector, how would thy subjects experience adversity ?

Amongst us, Hari is (the) best.

LESSON XXXI.

अदस् *That* or *This* and इदम् *This.*

अदस् *That* or *This*

MASCULINE.

	Singular	*Dual*	*Plural*
Nom.	असौ	*अमू	अमी
Acc.	अमुम्	अमू	अमून्
Instr.	अमुना	अमूभ्याम्	अमीभिः
Dat.	अमुष्मै	अमूभ्याम्	अमीभ्यः
Abl.	अमुष्मात्	अमूभ्याम्	अमीभ्यः
Gen.	अमुष्य	अमुयोः	अमीषाम्
Loc.	अमुष्मिन्	अमुयोः	अमीषु

FEMININE.

	Singular	*Dual*	*Plural*
Nom.	असौ	अमू	अमूः
Acc.	अमूम्	अमू	अमूः
Instr.	अमुया	अमूभ्याम्	अमूभिः
Dat.	अमुष्यै	अमूभ्याम्	अमूभ्यः
Abl.	अमुष्याः	अमूभ्याम्	अमूभ्यः
Gen.	अमुष्याः	अमुयोः	अमूषाम्
Loc.	अमुष्याम्	अमुयोः	अमूषु

---

*A short way of learning the masc. forms of अदस्, except that of the Nom. sing.:—Suppose the word अदस् to be अद masculine, and decline it like सर्व, and for द in each form put म् and for the vowel following, if it be short, put उ, if long, ऊ: for ए in the plural put ई, and you will get the forms given in the text. The forms of the Instr. sing. and pl. are to be taken as अमुना and अमीभिः, and not अदेन and अदैः The rule about the change of स् to ष् given in a former note should be applied. The same may be done with regard to the feminine forms, अदा being declined like सर्वा.

NEUTER:

	Singular	*Dual*	*Plural*
Nom. and Acc.	अदः	अमू	अमूनि

The rest like tha Masculine.

इदम *This*

MASCULINE.

	Singular	*Dual*	*Plural*
Nom.	अयम्	इमौ	इमे
Acc.	इमम्	इमौ	इमान्
Instr.	अनेन	आभ्याम्	एभिः
Dat.	अस्मै	आभ्याम्	एभ्यः
Abl.	अस्मात्	आभ्याम्	एभ्यः
Gen.	अस्य	अनयोः	एषाम्
Loc.	अस्मिन्	अनयोः	एषु

FEMININE.

Nom.	इयम्	इमे	इमाः
Acc.	इमाम्	इमे	इमाः
Instr.	अनया	आभ्याम्	आभिः
Dat.	अस्यै	आभ्याम्	आभ्यः
Abl.	अस्याः	आभ्याम्	आभ्यः
Gen.	अस्याः	अनयोः	आसाम्
Loc.	अस्याम्	अनयोः	आसु

NEUTER.

Nom. and Acc.	इदम्	इमे	इमानि

The rest like the Masculine.

WORDS.

अक्षमा *f.* jealousy

अथवा *ind.* or

उर्वशी *f.* name of a celestial woman

कदर्य *m.* a miser

कवीश *m.* (कवि poet, ईश *m.* a lord) the lord of poets, the chief of poets.

किल *ind.* verily

कृ *with* अलम् to beautify, to adorn

गर्ता *f.* a pit

गृध्रराज *m.* Jaṭāyu, the lord of vultures

छन्न (*past pass. part.* of छद्) concealed, covered

जव *m.* speed

दुःखित *adj.* sorry, sad, afflicted

दृश्य *adj.* visible

देवदारु *m.* a species of pine

द्रुतम् *adv.* soon, quickly

पुत्रीकृत *adj.* (पुत्र son, and कृत made) made a son, adopted

पुरः *ind.* before (*space*)

पुष्पधारिन् *adj.* having flowers

पूर् *10th Conj.* to fill

प्रदेय *adj.* to be given, to be given in marriage

प्रभव *m.* source

प्रियतमा *adj. f.* beloved, dearest

प्रियाप्रवृत्ति *f.* (प्रिया *f.* beloved and प्रवृत्ति *f.* intelligence) intelligence about one's beloved

भिक्षा *f.* alms

भीरू *adj. f.* timid (woman)

मदिराक्षी *f.* a woman with fascinating eyes

मधुकर *m.* a bee

रथ्य *m.* a horse

रम् *with* वि *Parasm.* to stop, to desist

रीति *f.* manner, way

लतागृह *n.* a bower of creepers

वरतनु *adj.* one whose form is elegant; handsome, beautiful

भार्या *f.* a wife, a mate

वास *m.* habitation [fence
विप्रिय *adj.* disliked; *n.* of-
वीथि *f.* a road
वृषभध्वज *m.* Śiva
व्याख्येय *adj.* to ba expounded
शिवालय *n.* a temple of Śiva
संगत *n.* companionship, friendship
संगम *m.* a confluence
संगमोत्सुक *adj.* eager for union
सारङ्ग *m.* a kind of bird
साहस *n.* an adventure
स्त्रीरत्न *n.* a jewel amongst women
स्वादु *adj.* delicious

SENTENCES.

इदमासनमलंक्रियतां भवता ।
मृगस्य जवस्याक्षमयेवामी रथ्या धावन्ति ।
अनया रीत्या व्याख्येयोऽयं ग्रन्थः ।
वत्स विरमास्मात्साहसात् ।
अमू तौ तरू यौ ह्योऽपश्यम् ।
अस्मै विदुषे ब्राह्मणाय दक्षिणां प्रयच्छ ।
अनयोः कन्ययोः संगतं मे रोचते ।
*इमं सारङ्गं प्रियाप्रवृत्तयेऽभ्यर्थये ।
†अयं स ते तिष्ठति संगमोत्सुको

---

*The sentences marked with an asterisk on this and the next page are spoken by a king who, while enjoying the company of his beloved wife in a grove, suddenly loses her by some miraculous occurrence, and wanders about asking birds and beasts whether they can give him any intelligence about her.

The second speech bearing this mark is addressed to an elephant.

†Said by a lover to a maid who was afraid of meeting with a repulse at his hands.

विशङ्कसे भीरु यतोऽवधीरणाम् ।

†अमुं पुरः पश्यसि देवदारुं

पुत्रीकृतोऽसौ वृषभध्वजेन ।

*स्त्रीरत्नेषु ममोर्वशी प्रियतमा यूथे तवेयं वशा ।

*मधुकर मदिराक्ष्याः शंस तस्याः प्रवृत्तिं

वरतनुरथवासौ नैव दृष्टा त्वया मे ।

*हंस प्रयच्छ मे कान्तां गतिरस्यास्त्वया हृता ।

अस्मिन्नेव लतागृहे त्वमभवः ।

अस्यैवासीन् महति शिखरे गृध्रराजस्य वासः ।

मनोहरा अमी वृक्षा दृश्यन्ते पुष्पधारिणः ।

अगच्छदमुया वीथ्या वास्यमूं द्रुतमानय ।

कृतं किमेभिस्तव विप्रियं य-

दनिष्टमेषामसि कर्तुमुद्यतः ।

पादानमीषां प्रणतो यतोऽसौ

भद्रं ततोऽमीभिरमुष्य कार्यम् ।

पुर्यां पुराऽस्यां किल कालिदासो

नाम्नाभवद्यो न्यवसत्कवीशः ।

यदि प्रसन्ना भगवतीमं वरं याचे ।

---

† Said by one to another about a tree which was a great favourite with Siva.

अस्मिँल्लोके* यत्क्रियते तस्य फलममुष्मिँल्लोकेऽनुभूयते ।
एभिर्वचोभिः सान्त्वय मे दुःखितां भार्याम् ।
हे सीते पुत्राविमौ ते ।

This is my book.

These men rejoice at their king's victory.

These girls learn to dance (dancing).

(There) are many learned men in these villages.

I do not see with these eyes.

There is (a) monkey on [this tree.

There is much water in these rivers.

From these mountains many stones have fallen.

I beat (a) thief with these sticks.

I saw these women in (the) temple of Śiva.

(The) sources of these rivers are in the Himālaya.

Give some sweetmeat to these boys, and to those girls.

I saw (a) tiger coming down from (the) top of that mountain.

I guarded my gold from these (two) thieves.

I saw that soldier running away from (the) battle-field.

The traveller went by that [path.

Fill these (two) pits with earth.

I do not expect alms from [the miser.

The king's palace is (two) coss from this river.

Give me that delicious mango.

What fault has been committed by this deer?

(The) confluence of these (two) rivers is holy.

Covered by this cloth, I become invisible.

These (two) girls too are to be given in marriage.

---

* A dental consonant followed by ल् is changed to ल्, and न् to a nasal ल्, which is written as in the text.

EXAMINATION.

1. Which of the pronouns is or are the most irregular ?

2. Decline अदस् *m. f. & n.*, इदम् *m. f. & n.*, अस्मद् and युष्मद्.

3. Explain the shortest way of arriving at the forms of अदस्.

4. What change do dentals undergo when compounded with the follwing ल् ?

LESSON XXXII

SELECTIONS FOR EXERCISE.

विद्वत्त्वं च नृपत्वं च नैव तुल्यं कदाचन ।
स्वदेशे पूज्यते राजा विद्वान् सर्वत्र पूज्यते ॥
वरमेको गुणी पुत्रो न च मूर्खशतान्यपि ।
एकश्चन्द्रस्तमो *हन्ति न च तारागणोऽपि च ।
†एकेनापि सुवृक्षेण पुष्पितेन सुगन्धिना ।
वासितं तद्वनं सर्वं सुपुत्रेण कुलं यथा ॥
उत्सवे व्यसने चैव दुर्भिक्षे शत्रुविग्रहे ।
राजद्वारे श्मशाने च यस्तिष्ठति स बान्धवः ॥
दुर्जनः प्रियवादी च नैतद्विश्वासकारणम् ।
मधु तिष्ठति जिह्वाग्रे हृदये तु हलाहलम् ॥

---

* Pres. 3rd pers. sing. of हन् 2nd conj. Parasm. to kill.
† एक is a pronoun, and should be declined like सर्व.

दुर्जनः परिहर्तव्यो विद्ययालंकृतोऽपि सन् ।
मणिना भूषितः सर्पः किमसौ न भयंकरः ॥
कुलीनैः सह संपर्कं पण्डितैः सह मित्रताम् ।
ज्ञातिभिश्च समं मेलं कुर्वाणो *न विनश्यति ॥
यो ध्रुवाणि परित्यज्य अध्रुवं परिषेवते ।
ध्रुवाणि तस्य नश्यन्ति अध्रुवं नष्टमेव च ॥
पादपानां भयं वातः पद्मानां शिशिरो भयम् ।
पर्वतानां भयं वज्रः साधूनां दुर्जनो भयम् ॥

तस्मात्स्वविषये रक्षा कर्तव्या भूतिमिच्छता ।
यज्ञैर्नावाप्यते स्वर्गो रक्षणात्प्राप्यते यथा ॥
यथा फलानां पक्वानां नान्यत्र पतनाद्भयम् ।
एवं नरस्य जातस्य नान्यत्र मरणाद्भयम् ॥

न भीतो मरणादस्मि केवलं दूषितं यशः ।
विशुद्धस्य हि मे मृत्युः पुत्रजन्मसमः किल ॥
अपापानां कुले जाते मयि पापं न विद्यते ।
यदि संभाव्यते पापमपापेन च किं मया ॥

अर्थमनर्थं भावय नित्यं नास्ति ततः सुखलेशः सत्यम् ।
पुत्रादपि धनभाजां भीतिः सर्वत्रैषा विहिता रीतिः ॥

---

* Masc. Nom. sing. of the Ātm. pres. part. of कृ 8th conj. to do.

का तव कान्ता कस्ते पुत्रः संसारोऽयमतीव विचित्रः ।
कस्य त्वं वा कुत आयातस्तत्त्वं चिन्तय तदिदं भ्रातः ॥

शत्रौ मित्रे पुत्रे बन्धौ मा कुरु यत्नं विग्रहसन्धौ ।
भव समचित्तः सर्वत्र त्वं वाञ्छस्यचिराद्यदि सत्तत्त्वम् ॥
महता पुण्यपण्येन क्रीतेयं कायनौ *स्त्वया ।
पारं दुःखोदधेर्गन्तुं तर यावन्न भिद्यते ॥

धैर्यं यस्य पिता क्षमा च जननी शान्तिश्चिरं गेहिनी
सत्यं सूनुरयं दया च भगिनी भ्राता मनःसंयमः ।
शय्या भूमितलं दिशोऽपि वसनं ज्ञानामृतं भोजन-
मेते यस्य कुटुम्बिनो वद सखे कस्माद्भयं योगिनः ॥

विपदि धैर्यमथाभ्युदये क्षमा
सदसि वाक्पटुता युधि विक्रमः ।
यशसि चाभिरुचिर्व्यसनं श्रुतौ
प्रकृतिसिद्धमिदं हि महात्मनाम् ॥

आलस्यं मनुष्याणां शरीरस्थो महारिपुः ।
नास्त्युद्यमसमो बन्धुः कृत्वा यं नावसीदति ॥

अस्ति ब्रह्मारण्ये कर्पूरतिलको नाम हस्ती । तमवलोक्य सर्वे शृगालाश्चिन्तयन्ति स्म यद्ययं केनाप्युपायेन म्रियते

---

* The word is declined by simply appending the terminations given at the head of lesson XXV, and observing the Saṁdhi rules.

† The declension of this word is irregular.

तदास्माकमेतद्देहेन मासचतुष्टयस्य भोजनं भविष्यति। तत्रैकेन वृद्धशृगालेन प्रतिज्ञातं मया बुद्धिप्रभावादस्य मरणं साधयितव्यम्। अनन्तरं स वञ्चकः कर्पूरतिलक-समीपं गत्वा साष्टाङ्गपातं प्रणम्यावदद्देव दृष्टिप्रसादं कुरु। हस्ती ब्रूते कस्त्वं कुतः समायातः। सोऽवदज्जम्बूकोऽहं सर्वैर्वनवासिभिः पशुभिर्मिलित्वा भवत्सकाशं प्रस्थापितो यद्विना राज्ञाऽवस्थातुं न युक्तं तदत्राटवीराज्येऽभिषेक्तुं भवान्सर्वस्वामिगुणोपेतो निरूपितस्तद्यथा लग्नवेला न विचलति तथा कृत्वा सत्वरमागम्यतां देवेन। इत्युक्त्वो-त्थाय चलितः। ततोऽसौ राज्यलोभाकृष्टः कर्पूरतिलकः शृगालवर्त्मना धावन् महापङ्के निमग्नः। ततस्तेन हस्तिनोक्तं सखे शृंगाल किमधुना विधेयं पङ्के निपतितोऽहं म्रिये परावृत्य पश्य। शृगालेन विहस्योक्तं देव मम पुच्छकावलम्बनं कृत्वोत्तिष्ठ। यन्मद्वचसि त्वया प्रत्ययः कृतस्तदनुभूयतामशरणं दुःखम्।

APPENDIX.

SAMDHI RULES.

Guṇa and Vṛddhi.

1. The *Guṇa* of इ or ई is ए, of उ or ऊ is ओ, of ऋ or ॠ is अर्, and of ऌ is अल्.

2. The *Vṛddhi* of अ is आ, of इ, ई or ए is ऐ, of उ, ऊ or ओ is औ, of ऋ or ॠ is आर्, and of ऌ is आल्.

Vowels.

3. In Sanskṛt, two vowels cannot come together without coalescing.

4. There are a few cases, in which two vowels, though coming together, do no coalesce.

5. When the dual of a noun or a verb ends in ई, ऊ, or ए, these vowels do not combine with another following them ; गिरी + आरोहन्ति = गिरी आरोहन्ति. See also 13,37 and 42.

6. ऋ (short), after any vowel except the last four is optionally not combined, and the preceding vowel, if long, is made short ; अर्घेण + ऋषिम् = अर्घेण ऋषिम् or (by 7) अर्घेणर्षिम्.

7. If अ or आ is followed by इ, ऊ, ऋ, or ऌ, short or long, the corresponding *Guṇa* letter is substituted for both; फल + ई = फले.

8. If ए, ऐ, ओ or औ follow अ or आ, the vowel which takes the place of both is ऐ in the first two, cases and औ in the last two; नृप + औ = नृपौ.

9. When any vowel, short or long, except the last four, is followed by the same vowel, short or long, the

substitute for both is the same vowel lengthened; दैत्य+अरि=दैत्यारि, कवि+ईश=कवीश; &c.

10. When इ, उ, ऋ, and ऌ, short or long, are followed by a dissimilar vowel, य्, व्, र, and ल् are respectively substituted for them; तृणानि+अत्ति=तृणान्यत्ति.

11. When ए or ओ at the end of the word or grammatical form is followed by अ, the latter merges into the former, *i. e.*, it is neither pronounced nor written. In its place the mark ऽ is generally put; रामो (by 36) + अश्वम्=रामोऽश्वम्.

12. ए, ओ, ऐ, and औ, when followed by a vowel become अय्, अव्, आय्, and आव् respectively. ने+अ=नय.

13. If a nominal or verbal form ending in ए, ऐ, ओ or औ is followed by a vowel, the य् and व् of the substitute for the former are optionally dropped. The two vowels thus brought together by the dropping of य् or व् do not coalesce; मन्यते+आत्मानम्=मन्यतयात्मानम् or मन्यतआत्मानम्.

Consonants.

14. When there are more consonants than one at the end of a word, the first is retained and the others dropped; as मरुत् with स् becomes मरुत्स् but स् is dropped and the form is मरुत्.

15. A consonant (except a nasal) at the end of a word is changed to the first or third of its class; मरुत् or मरुद्.

16. Before hard consonants, the preceding consonants except nasals, substitute the first (*i. e.* hard unaspirate) letter of their class; as ककुभ्+प्रान्त=ककुप्प्रान्त, and दृषद्+पतति=दृषत्पतति.

17. The preceding consonant (except a nasal) takes the third consonant of its class as its substitute when

compounded with a soft consonant or the initial vowel of a word; प्रासादात् + जनम् = प्रासादाद् + जनम् (=प्रासाद्राज्जनम् by 19)

18. A consonant at the end of a word or grammatical form followed by a nasal is changed to the nasal of its class optionally; as एतद् + मुरारि=एतन्मुरारि or एतमुरारि. This change is necessary, when the nasal belongs to a nominal termination; as चित्+मय=चिन्मय.

19. When स् or a consonant of the dental class is compounded with श् or a consonant of the palatal class, a letter of the latter class is substituted for the former, and in this order, *viz.*, श् for स्, च for त्, ज् for द् &c.; अरीन् + जयति=अरीञ्जयति. The same happens when dentals are combined with linguals, ष् being substituted for स्, ट for त्, ड for थ् &c.; तत्+ टीका=तट्टीका.

20. A consonant of the dental class followed by ल् is changed to ल् (भगवत्+लीला=भगवल्लीला), and न् to a nasal ल्, which is written as in line 1, page 141.

21. When ङ्, ण् and न् at the end of a word or grammatical form are preceded by a short vowel and followed by any vowel, they are doubled; वसन् + अम्बरात्=वसन्नम्बरात्.

22. च् or ज् is changed to क् before hard consonants, and ग् before any soft consonant except a nasal or a semi-vowel; मुच्+त=मुक्त. This change takes place also when the consonants end a word, even before a nasal or a semi-vowel: वाच्+यत=वाग्यत.

23. छ following a vowel is changed to च्छ; अ+ छिद्यन्त=अच्छिद्यन्त. This change takes place optionally when the vowel is long and at the end of a word or

grammatical form; लक्ष्मी+छाया=लक्ष्मिछाया or, लक्ष्मीच्छाया: but after मा (negative particle) and आ (preposition) it is necessary.

24. In the body of a word or grammatical form न् is changed to an *anusvāra* when followed by श्, ष्, स् or ह्; विद्वांसौ.

25. A final न् when followed by च, छ्, त्, थ्, and ट्, ठ्, is changed to an *anusvāra* and *visarga*: बिडालान् + ताडयति=बिडालां:ताडयति(=बिडालांस्ताडयति by 39).

26. न् coming after ऋ, र्, ष्, in the same word is changed to ण्. This change takes place even if a vowel, a semi-vowel (ल् excepted), the aspirate ह्, or a letter of the guttural or labial class comes between ऋ, र्, or ष् and न्; गृहाणि. This change does not take place when न् ends a word; as नरान्.

27. म् at the end of a word or particle, followed by a consonant in general, is changed to an *anusvāra* optionally; and necessarily when it is followed by श्, ष्, स्, or ह्. When it is not changed to an *anusvāra*, it is changed to the nasal of the class to which the following letter belongs and to a nasal य्, व्, ल्, when followed by य्, व्, ल्, respectively; सम्+गच्छते=संगच्छते or सङ्गच्छते.

28. At the end of the word, र्, followed by a hard consonant or by nothing, is changed to a *visarga*;मातर् +पश्य=मातः पश्य.

26, र् followed by र् is dropped, and the preceding vowel (except ऋ) if short, is made long : धूर्जटिर् (by 38) +रक्षति=धूर्जटी रक्षति.

30. When a word or form ending in any of the first four consonants of a class is followed by श्, the श् is

optionally changed to छ्, when it is itself followed by a vowel, a semi-vowel or a nasal; अवदत् + शठः = अवदच् (by 19) शठः or अवदच्छठः

31. The स् of स्था is dropped after the preposition उद्; उद्+स्था + य = उद्+थाय (=उत्थाय by 16).

32. ह् preceded by any the first four letters of a class is changed to the fourth letter of that class optionally; उद्यमाद् (by 17)+हरेः=उद्यमाद् हरेः or उद्यमाद्धरेः

33. The ह् of उपानह् becomes त् and द् in the circumstances mentioned in 22.

34. स् following a vowel except अ and आ, or a letter of the guttural class, or र्, generally becomes ष्; वाक् (by 22)+सु=वाक्षु.

35. At the end of words, स्, whether followed by any letter or not, is changed to a *visarga*; वद्यामस्=वद्यामः.

स् or *Visarga*.

36. When a *visarga* is preceded by अ and followed by अ or a soft consonant, it is changed to उ, which, with the preceding अ, becomes ओ (see 7); नृपः जयति= नृपो जयति.

37. *Visarga* preceded by आ and followed by a vowel or a soft consonant is dropped. It is also dropped when preceded by अ and followed by any vowel except अ. The two vowels, thus brought together by the dropping of *visarga*, do not coalesce, *e. g.*, नरा इमे for नराः इमे; बुध इच्छति for बुधः इच्छति.

38. स् or *visarga* preceded by any vowel except अ or आ, and followed by a vowel or a soft consonant, is changed to र्; नृपतिस्+यजति=नृपतिर्यजति.

39. *Visarga* followed by च् or छ् is changed to श्; by त् or थ् to स्; and by ट् or ठ् to ष्; as हरिश्चरति for हरिः चरति; रामस्तरति, रामष्टीकते.

40. *Visarga* followed by श्, ष् or स् is either retained or changed to श्, ष् or स् respectively; ऋषयः + शाम्यन्ति = ऋषयः शाम्यन्ति or ऋषयश्शाम्यन्ति.

41. सः and एषः drop the final स् or *visarga* when followed by a consonant in a sentence; स पुरुषः, &c.

42. भोस् drops its स् when followed by a vowel or a soft consonant; भोस् + नृत्यम् = भो नृत्यम्.

SYNTAX.

There are some roots that govern two accusatives; नी, प्रच्छ् and याच् are instances. The synonyms of these also govern two: सैनिकान् नगरं नयति.

कथ् sometimes governs two accusatives, or the indirect object may be in the dative or genitive case; नृपं नृपाय नृपस्य कथयति वार्ताम्.

Verbs implying motion govern the accusative, and sometimes the dative, of the place to which the motion is directed; नगरं or नगराय गच्छामि.

विना governs an accusative, instrumental or ablative; वधं, वधेन or वधाद् विनारिर्न शाम्यति.

सह governs the instrumental ; पुत्रैः सह.

रुच् and other verbs having the same sense govern the dative of the person or thing pleased or satisfied; मोदकौ बालकाय रोचते.

Verbs implying anger, malice, rivalry and jealousy (*i. e.*, having the sense of क्रुध्, द्रुह्, ईर्ष्या, and असूया)

govern the dative of the person or thing against whom or which the feeling is directed; हरये कुप्यति. स्पृह् also governs the dative of the object of the wish; मोदकेभ्यः स्पृहयति.

धृ in the sense of 'to owe' governs the dative of the person to whom something is owing; निष्कान् धारयति रामाय.

नमः and स्वस्ति govern a dative; नमो देवेभ्यः.

च or वा is used after each of the parts of speech joined together, or once only, that is, after them all; हरिश्च गोविन्दश्च or हरिर्गोविन्दश्च जल्पतः.

GENERAL GLOSSARY

I

अ.

अकाल (अ and काल) *m.* improper time
असूया *f.* jealousy, rivalry
अक्षर *adj. m. n.* immutable
अखिल *adj. m.n.* all, whole
अगद *m.* medicine
अग्नि *m.* fire
अग्र *n.* the tip
अङ्गल *m.* an Englishman
अङ्गलभूमि *f.* England
अचिराद् *ind.* soon
अज *m.* a goat
अज्ञान *n.* ignorance
अट् *1 st Conj. Parasm.* to wander, to ramble
अटवी *f.* a forest
अतः *ind.* hence
अतिथि *m.* a guest
अतीव *ind.* greatly. very
अत्यय *m.* passing away, destruction
अत्र *ind.* here
अथवा *ind.* or
अद् *2nd Conj. Parasm.* to eat
अद्य *ind.* to-day
अधमर्ण *m.* a debtor
अधर्म *m.* a sin
अधिपति *m.* a master
अधुना *ind.* now
अध्ययन *n.* study
अध्युषितवत् *adj. m. n.* dwelt
अध्रुव *adj. m. n.* uncertain
अध्वखेद *m.* (अध्वन् *m.* a road, खेद *m.* fatigue) the fatigue of a journey
अनन्तरम् *adv.* after
अनर्थ *m.* a disadvantage, an evil
अनल *m.* fire
अनिष्ट *n.* evil, calamity
अनुजीविन् *adj. m. n.* a servant, dependent
अनुज्ञा *f.* permission
अनुरञ्जन *n.* pleasing, giving delight to
अनुराग *m.* love.
अनुष्ठान *n.* performance, execution
अनृत *n.* a falsehood. an untruth; *adj. m.n.* false, untrue
अनेकशस् *ind.* frequently
अन्तःकरण *n.* the heart
अन्तःपुर *n.* the apartment

occupied by women in a house

अन्तरात्मन् *m.* the internal soul, the heart

अन्न *n.* food

अन्यत्र *ind* in another place

अपण्डित *m.* an illiterate [person

अपराध *m.* a fault

अपराधलव *m.* (अपराध, and लव *m.* a particle) a small fault

अपराधिन् *adj. m. n.* guilty, offending

अपाय *m.* harm

अपि *ind.* even

अप्रिय *adj. m. n.* disliked, unpalatable

अभिधान *n.* a name

अभिभूत (*pastpass part.* of भू *with* अभि) overcome, overpowered

अभिरुचि *f.* liking

अभिलाष *m.* a desire

अभिषेक *m.* coronation

अभिषेक्तुम् (*inf.* of सिच् *with* अभि) to crown

अभूमि *f.* not the ground: not the subject or proper place

अभ्युदय *m.* rise, prosperity

अमरावती *f.* Indra's capital

अमात्य *m.* a counsellor

अम्बर *n.* the sky

अयोध्या *f.* name of a city

अरण्य *n* a forest

अरि *m.* an enemy

अरुन्धती *f.* name of the wife of Vasiṣṭha (a great sage)

अर्घ्य *n.* materials of worship

अर्चन *n.* worship

अर्जुन *m.* one of the sons of Pāṇḍu

अर्थ् *10 th Conj. Ātm. with* अभि, to request, to beg of, to solicit; *with* प्र, to request, to seek, to desire

अर्थ *m.* a thing; on occurrence, an event; wealth

अर्ह् *1 st Conj. Parasm.* to deserve

अलंकार *m.* an ornament

अलङ्घनीय *adj. m. n.* that cannot be transgressed

अलम् *ind.* enough, away [with

अलि *m.* a bee

अल्प *adj m.n.* small, little,

अव् *1 st Conj. Parasm.* to protect

अवकाश *m.* room, space

अवचय *m.* gathering, collecting

अवतरत् (*pr. part.* of तृ *1st Conj. Parasm. with* अव) descending

अवदात *adj. m. n.* pure, noble

अवधीरणा *f.* repulsion, repulse

अवन्ती *f.* name of a town, Ujjain

अवलोक्य (*ind. past part.* of लोक् *with* अव) having seen

अवस्तु *n.* not a thing an unreal thing

अवस्त्वारोप *m.* ascribing something that is not real

अविचलित (अ + विचलित *past pass. part,* of चल् *with* वि) steady

अविश्वास्य *adj. m n.* faithless

अशरण *adj. m. n.* helpless

अश्मन् *m.* a stone

अश्रु *n.* a tear

अश्व *m.* a horse

अश्वपति *m.* name of a man

अस् *2nd Conj Parasm.* to be

अस् *4th Conj. Parasm.* to throw; *with* निर्, to scatter; *with* प्र, to throw

असंख्येय *adj. m. n.* innumerable

असत्य *n.* a lie, falsehood

असारता *f.* worthlessness

असि *m.* a sword

असुर *m.* demons, the enemies of the gods (*plur.*)

अस्त्र *n.* a miraculous weapon

अहित *n.* injury, harm, damage

आ.

आकाश *m. n.* the sky

आङ्ग्ल *m.* an Englishman

आचार *m.* conduct, proper conduct

आचार्य *m.* a perceptor, a tutor

आज्ञा *f.* command

आतप *m.* sun (sunshine)

आत्मज *m.* a son

आत्मजा *f.* a daughter

आत्मन् *m.* soul, self

आत्मीय *adj. m. n.* one's own

आदर *m.* respect

आदेश *m.* a command

आध्यात्मिक *adj. m. n.* spiritual

आध्यान *n.* meditation

आप् to obtain; *with* अव or *with* प्र, to obtain, to reach; *with* वि, to cover

आपद् *f.* adversity

आम्र *n* a mango (fruit)

आयास *m.* effort, trouble

आयुष्मत् *adj. m. n.* long-lived

आरम्भ *m.* beginning: performance

आराधन *n.* propitiation, pleasing

आरोप *m.* ascribing

आरोपण *n.* planting sowing

आर्य *m.* a respectable person; name of the remote ancestors of the Hindus

आर्या *f.* a venerable woman

आवरण *n.* covering, obstruction

आशा *f.* hope

आशीर्वाद *m.* a blessing

आश्रम *m.* a hermitage

आसन *n.* a seat

आह्लादक *adj. m. n.* delighting

इ, ई

इच्छा *f.* wish

इति *ind.* so, thus

इत्थम् *ind.* in this manner

इन्दु *m.* the moon

इन्द्र *m.* god of thunder

इन्द्राणी *f.* the wife of Indra

इन्धन *n.* fuel

इव *ind.* like, as,

इष् [इच्छ्] *6th Conj. Parasm* to wish

इष् *4th Conj. Parasm. with* **अनु**, to search for

इषु *m.* an arrow

इष्ट (*past pass. part.* of **इष्**) wished, desired

इह *ind.* here

ईक्ष् *1st Conj. Ātm.* to see, to take into account, to care for; *with* **अप**, to expect; *with* **उप**, to neglect; *with* **परि**, to examine; *with* **प्र**, to see

ईश्वर *m.* God

उ

उक्त (*past pass. part.* of **वच्**) spoken, spoken to

उचित *adj. m. n.* proper

उच्चैस् *ind.* aloft, nobly

उज्जयिनी *f.* name of a town Ujjain

उज्ज्वलम् *adv.* brightly

उञ्छ् *6th Conj. Parasm.* to glean

उटज *m.* a hut

उत *ind.* or

उत्कण्ठा *f.* anxiety, longing

उत्खात (*past. pass. part.* of **खन्** *with* **उद्**) dug

उत्थाय (*ind. past part.* of **स्था** *with* **उद्**) having stood up

उत्सङ्गवर्तिन् *adj. m. n.* (**उत्सङ्ग** *m.* lap) resting on the lap

उत्सव *m.* a festive occasion

उत्साह *m.* happiness, cheerfulness, energy

उदक *n.* water

उदधि *m.* the ocean

उद्गम *m.* coming to birth, appearance

उद्धत (*past pass. part.* of **हन्** *with* **उद्**) proud

उद्भव *m.* birth

उद्यत(*past pass. part.* of **यम्** with **उद्**) ready, prepared

उद्यम *m.* exertion, industry

उद्यमसम *adj. m, n.* (**सम** like) like exertion

उद्यान *n.* garden

उद्योग *m.* application, exertion

उपकार *m.* doing good to another, obligation, benefiting another

उपदेश *m.* advice, counsel

उपवन *n.* a garden

उपहार *m.* a present

उपानह् *f* a shoe

उपाय *m.* a remedy

उपालम्भ *m.* a taunt

उर्वशी *f.* name of a celestial woman

ऋ.

ऋजुता *f.* straightforwardness

ऋतुपर्ण *m.* name of a king

ऋत्विज् *m.* a sacrificial priest

ऋध् *4th Conj. Parasm with* **सम्**, to prosper

ऋषि *m.* a sage

ऋष्यशृङ्ग *m.* name of the son-in-law of **दशरथ** and brother-in-law of **राम**

ए.

एक *pron.* one

एतादृश *adj. m. n.* of this sort

एलापुर *n.* name of a city, Verul

एव *ind.* only

एवम् *ind.* thus

ओ.

ओदन *m.* cooked rice

औ.

औषध *n.* medicine

क.

कञ्चुकिन् *m.* an attendant on the women's apartment, chamberlain

कट *m.* a mat
कण्टक *m. n.* a thorn
कण्ठ *m.* the neck
कत्थ् *1stConj.Ātm.* to praise, to flatter
कथ् *10th Conj.* to tell
कथम् *ind.* in what manner?
कथा *f.* a story
कदर्य *m.* a miser
कदा *ind.* when ?
कनीयस् *adj. m. n.* younger
कन्या *f.* daughter, a girl
कपट *n.* a fraud, a deceit
कपि *m.* a monkey
कपिल *m.* name of a great sage
कपोल *m.* the cheek
कबरी *f.* a braid of hair
कम्प् *1st Conj. Ātm.* to shake (*intr.*)
कमल *n.* lotus
कर *m.* the hand
करभक *m.* the young (of an elephant)
कर्ण *m.* name of a hero: the ear
कर्तव्य *adj. m. n.* what should be done
कर्तृ *adj. m. n.* doer, author
कर्पूरतिलक *m.* name of an elephant; कर्पू...समीपं near Karp.
कर्मन् *n.* an action
कलङ्क *m.* a stain, a spot
कलह *m.* a strife, a quarrel
कला *f.* an art
कलि *m.* a strife, a quarrel
कल्याण *n.* welfare, good
कवि *m.* a poet
कवीश *m.* (कवि, ईश *m*, a lord) the lord of poets
काञ्चन *n.* gold
कान्ता *f.* a female beloved a wife.
कान्ति *f.* splendour, light
काम *m.* desire
कारण *n.* a cause
कारागृह *n* a prison
कारुणिक *adj. m. n.* merciful
कारुण्य *n.* compassion, kindness
कार्त्तिक *m.* name of a month
कार्य *n.* an action, a work
काल *m.* time, proper time
काश् *1st Conj. Ātm. with* प्र to shine
काष्ठ *n.* wood
कासार *m.* a lake
किंकर *m.* a servant
किंतु *ind.* but

किरि *m.* a boar

किल *ind.* verily

कीचक *m.* name of the commander-in-chief of king Virāṭa

कीर्ति *f.* fame

कुटुम्बिन् *adj. m.n.* one possessed of a family; *m.* a member of a family

कुण्ठित (*past pass. part.* of कुण्ठ्) hampered, impeded

कुतः *ind.* whence ?

कुत्र *ind.* where ? [angry

कुप् 4*th Conj. Parasm.* to be

कुमारी *f.* a virgin

कुम्भकार *m.* a potter

कुरु *m.* name of a country (*in the plural*)

कुर्वत् (*pr. part. Parasm.* of कृ to do) doing

कुर्वाण (*pr. part. Ātm.* of कृ) doing

कुलीन *adj. m. n.* born of a good family

कुश *m.* name of a son of Rāma [well

कुशलिन् *adj. m.* happy,

कुष् 4*th Conj. Parasm*, to embrace

कुसुम *n*, a flower

कूप *m.* a well

कूर्म *m.* a tortoise

कृ to do; *with* अधि, to authorise; *with* अलम्, to beautify, to adorn; *with* आविस्, to manifest, to show, to expose

कृत *past pass. part.* of कृ) made, done

कृतज्ञता *f.* gratitude

कृति *f.* an action

कृते *ind.* for, for the sake (of)

कृपा *f.* favour

कृष् 1*st Conj. Parasm.* or 6*th Conj. Parasm.* & *Ātm.* to plough

कृषीवल *m.* a husbandman

कृष्ण *m.* name of a person

क्लृप् 1*st Conj. Ātm* to be able

केवल *adj. m. n.* only

केवलम् *adv.* solely

कैकेयी *f.* name of one of the wives of Daśaratha

कोश *m.* a treasure

कौमुदी *f.* moonlight

कौशल *n.* skill, proficiency

कौशाम्बी *f.* name of a town

कौशिक *m.* a descendant of कुशिक

क्रमेण (*instr. sing.* of क्रम) gradually

क्रीड् *1st Conj. Parasm.* to play

क्रीडा *f.* sport, play

क्रीत (*past pass. part.* of **क्री**) bought

क्रुध् *4th Conj. Parasm.* to be angry

क्रोध *m.* anger

क्रोश *m.* two miles

क्लेश *m.* pain, distress

क्व *ind.* where ?

क्षम् *1st Conj. Ātm.* to forgive

क्षम् [**क्षाम्**] *4th Conj. Parasm.* to forgive, to pardon

क्षमा *f.* forgiveness

क्षयिन् *adj. m. n.* lessening, decreasing

क्षल् *10th Conj.* to wash off; *with* **प्र**

क्षि *1st Conj. Parasm.* to waste away

क्षिप् *6th Conj. Parasm., & Ātm.* to throw

क्षुद्र *adj. m. n.* insignificant, mean

क्षुभ् *4th Conj. Parasm.* to be agitated

क्षुधित *adj. m. n.* hunrgy

क्षेत्र *n.* a field

क्षेत्रगामिन् *adj. m. n.* going to a holy place

ख.

खञ्ज *m. n.* a lame man

खड्ग *m.* a sword

खन् *1st Conj. Parasm & Ātm.* to dig; with **उद्**, to dig, to excavate

खनित्र *n.* a spade.

खल *m.* a villain

ग.

गङ्गा *f.* the Ganges

गच्छत् (*pr. part.* of **गम्** *1st Conj. Parasm.* to go) going

गज *m.* an elephant

गण् *10 Conj.* to count, to reckon, to consider, to care for, to mind

गत (*past pass. part.* of **गम्**) gone [going

गति *f.* mode of walking,

गन्तृ *adj. m.* goer

गन्धर्व *m.* an individual of a class of celestial beings

गम् [**गच्छ्**] *1st Conj. Parasm.* to go; *with* **अधि**, to obtain; *with* **अनु**, to go after, follow ; *with*

अव, to know; *with* निर्, to depart; *with* प्रति and आ, to return; *with acc. sing.* of शरण or वश prefixed to it, to submit; *with* सम् *Atm.* to join, to go or flow together

गमन *n.* departure

गर्ता *f.* a pit

गर्ह्य *adj. m. n.* censurable

गल् *1st Conj. Parasm.* to drop

गल्भ् *1st Conj. Ātm. with* प्र to swagger

गात्र *n.* a limb

गान *n.* singing

गाहू *1st Conj. Ātm. with* अव, to bathe in

गायक *m.* a songster

गिरि *m.* a mountain

गीत *n.* a song

गुण *m.* a merit, quality, virtue

गुणज्ञ *adj. m. n.* (गुण, and ज्ञा to know) one who appreciates merit

गुणवत् } गुणिन् } *adj. m. n.* meritorious

गुरु *adj. m. n. f.* long

गुरु *m.* a preceptor, a venerable person

गृध्रराज *m.* Jaṭāyu, the king of vultures, who was friend to Rāma's father; the lord of vulturs

गृह *n.* a house

गेहिनी *f.* wife

गै *1st Conj. Parasm.* to sing

गोत्र *n.* a family, race

गोदावरी *f.* name of a river

गोप *m.* a herdsman

गोष्ठ *m. n.* a cowpen

ग्रथन *n.* wreathing

ग्रन्थ *m.* a work, book

ग्रहण *n.* capture

ग्राम *m.* a village

ग्रीष्म *m.* summer

घ

घट *m.* a jar

घुष् *10th Conj.* to proclaim

घृत *n.* ghee

च

च *ind.* and

चकोर *m.* a species of bird

चक्र *n.* a wheel

चक्षुस् *n.* the eye

चञ्चल *adj. m. n.* transitory

चण्ड *adj. m. n.* hot, fierce

चन्द्र *m.* the moon

चन्द्रमस् *m.* the moon

चन्द्रापीड *m.* name of a prince

चर् *1st Conj. Parasm.* to go, to walk, to stalk abroad; *with* **आ** to practise, to do

चरित *n.* the manner of leading life

चर्मन् *n.* leather

चल् *1st Conj. Parasm.* to go, to move, to go astray, to go wrong

चातुर्य *n.* skill

चाप *m.* a bow

चारु *adj. m. n. f.* beautiful

चित्त *n.* mind

चित्रकूट *m.* name of a mount

चिन्त् *10th Conj.* to contemplate

चिन्ता *f.* anxiety

चिन्तित (*past pass. part.* of **चिन्त्**) thought

चिर *adj. m. n.* long (*time*)

चिरम् *adv.* long (*time*)

चिह्न *n.* a token

चुर् *10th Conj.* to steal

चोदयत् (*pr. part* of **चुद्** *10th Conj.* to drive) driving

चोर *m.* a thief

चौर्य *n.* theft

छ

छन्दस् *n.* Veda; a metre

छन्न (*past pass. patr.* of **छद्**) concealed, covered

छात्र *m.* a scholar, a pupil

छाया *f.* shade

छिद् *pass.* to be cut off

ज

जगत् *n.* the world

जगत्कर्तृ *m.* Creator of the world

जन् [**जा**] *4th Conj. Ātm.* to be produced, to result

जन *m.* people; a person

जनक *m.* a father; father of Sītā, the wife of Rāma

जननी *f.* a mother

जम्बूक *m.* a jackal

जयत् (*pr. part.* of **जि**) conquering

जयन्त *m.* name of India's son

जरठ *m.* an old man

जरा *f.* old age

जल *n.* water

जल्प् *1st Conj. Parasm.* to prattle

जव *m.* speed

जाड्य *n.* sluggishness

जात (*past pass. part.* of जन्) produced, resulted

जाति *f.* a caste; a kind

जामातृ *m.* a son-in-low

जायापती *m. du.* wife and husband

जाल *n.* net

जाल्म *m.* a wretch, a rascal

जि *1st Conj. Parasm.* to conquer; *with* वि *Ātm.* to conquer

जिह्वा *f.* the tongue

जिह्वाग्र *n.* (जिह्वा, अग्र *n.* the tip) the tip of the tongue

जीर्ण (*past pass. part.* of जृ) worn out, old

जीव् *1st Conj. Parasm.* to live

जीव *m.* life; an animal

जीविका *f.* livelihood

जीवित *n.* life

जेतृ *adj. m. n.* a conqueror

ज्ञा know

ज्ञाति *m.* a relation

ज्ञान *n.* knowledge

ज्ञानामृत *n.* (ज्ञान, अमृत *n.* nectar) nectar in the shape of knowledge

ज्यायस् *adj. m. n.* elder

ज्योत्स्ना *f.* moonlight

ड

डिम्भ *m.* a child

डी *1st Conj. Āmt.* to fly

त

तड् *10th Conj.* to beat

तडाग *m.* a tank

तण्डुल *m.* rice

ततः *ind.* thence

तत्त्व *n.* reality, truth

तत्र *ind.* there

तथा *ind.* in that manner

तदा *ind.* then

तनय *m.* a son

तनु *adj. m. n. f.* small, little

तन्त्र् *10th Conj. Ātm.* to tend, to take care of

तप् *1st Conj. Parasm.* to shine, of be hot

तपस् *n.* religious austerity

तमस् *n.* darkness

तमिस्रा *f.* night

तरु *m.* a tree

तस्थिवस् *adj. m. n.* sat

ताडन *n.* beating
तारक *n.* a star
तारागण *m.* (तारा *f.* a star, गण *m.* a crowd or cluster) cluster of stars
तालु *n.* the palate
तिल *m.* sesamum
तीर *n.* a bank, shore
तु *ind.* but, however
तुद् *6th Conj. Parasm. & Ātm.* to inflict pain on
तुल् *10th Conj.* to weigh
तुल्य *adj. m. n.* equal
तुष् *4th Conj. Parasm* to be pleased or satisfied
तूल *m.* cotton
तूष्णीम् *ind.* silent, silently
तृण *n.* grass
तृषित *adj. m. n.* thirsty
तृष्णा *f.* thirst, greed
तृ *1st Conj. Parasm.* to cross, to surmount; *with* अव, to descend
तेजस् *n.* light, heat
त्यज् *1st Conj Parasm.* to abandon
त्याग *m.* leaving
त्वर् *1st Conj. Ātm.* to hasten, to be impatient
त्वष्टृ *m.* the architect of the gods

द

दक्ष *adj. m. n.* diligent
दक्षिणा *f.* money given to Brāhamaṇas
दण्ड् *10th Conj.* to punish
दण्ड *m.* a stick; punishment
दण्डका *f.* name of a forest
दरिद्र *adj. m. n.* poor
दर्शन *n.* a sight, seeing
दर्शनीय *adj. m. n.* handsome
दशरथ *m.* the name of a king, the father of the hero Rāma
दह् *1st Conj. Parasm.* to [burn
दा [यच्छ्] *1st Conj. Parasm.* to give, offer; *with* प्र, to give: *with* प्रति, to exchange
दा [दी *pass.*] to give
दातृ *adj. m. n.* giver, donor
दारिद्र्य *n.* poverty
दारुण *adj. m. n.* dreadful
दासजन *m.* (दास *m.* a slave, जन *m.* a person) a person who is a slave
दासी *f.* a maid, a maid- [servant
दिन *n.* a day
दिवा *ind.* by day [heaven
दिवौकस् *m.* an inhabitant of
दिश् *6th Conj. Parasm. & Ātm.* to show: with आ,

to command: *with* उप, to teach, advise; *with* निर्, to indicate

दिश् *f.* a direction, quarter

दीन *adj. m. n.* poor

दीप *m.* a lamp

दीर्घ *adj. m. n.* long

दुःख *n.* misery

दुःखित *adj. m. n.* sorry, sad, afflicted

दुःखोदधि *m.* (दुःख *n.* sorrow, उदधि *m.* an ocean) the ocean of sorrow or pain

दुराचार *m.* bad conduct

दुराप *adj. m. n.* difficult to obtain

दुर्ग *n.* a difficulty

दुर्गा *f.* name of a goddess

दुर्जन *m.* a wicked person

दुर्दशा *f.* bad state

दुर्भिक्ष *n.* scarcity, dearth, famine

दुर्वासस् *m.* name of a sage

दुष्कृत *n.* } a wicked action
दुष्कृति *f.* }

दुष्ट (*past pass. part.* of दुष् 4*th Conj. Parasm*). wicked

दुहितृ *f.* a daughter

दूत *m.* a messenger

दूर *adj. m. n.* distant

दूरम् *adv.* far

दूषित (*past pass. part.* of दूष्) polluted

दृढम् *adv.* firmly, closely

दृश् [पश्य्] 1*st Conj. Parasm.* to see.

दृषद् *f.* a stone

दृश्य *adj. m. n.* visible

दृष्ट (*past pass. part.* of दृश्) seen

दृष्टिप्रसाद *m.* (दृष्टि *f.* seeing, प्रसाद *m.* a favour) favour of seeing

दॄ 10*th Conj.* to tear

देव *m.* God, a god

देवता *f.* a deity

देवदत्त *m.* name of person

देवदारु *m.* a species of pine

देवायतन *n.* a temple

देवी *f.* a woman of distinction; a goddess

देवृ *m.* husband's brother

देश *m.* country

देह *m.* a body

दैन्य *n.* meanness

दैव *n.* fortune

द्यावापृथिवी *f. dual* the sky and the earth

द्युत् 1*st Conj. Ātm.* to shine

द्रव्य *n.* money

द्रष्टृ *m.* seer; *adj. m. n.*

द्रु 1*st Conj. Parasm.* to

water, to be wet, to melt with pity

द्रुतम् *adv.* soon, quickly

द्रुह् *4th Conj. Parasm.* to act the traitor

द्वारका *f.* name of town

द्विज *m* one of the first three Hindu castes

द्वीप *m. n.* an island, a continent

द्वेष्टृ *m* hater; *adj. m. n.*

ध.

धन *n.* wealth

धनपति *m.* god of wealth, Kubera

धनभाज् *adj. m. n. f.* possessor of wealth

धनिक *m.* a rich man; *adj. m. n.*

धनुस् *n.* bow

धर्म *m.* a duty, virtue

धा [धी *pass.*] *with* अभि, to call, to name; *with* नि, to place

धातृ *m.* the Creator

धान्य *n.* corn

धार्तराष्ट्र *m.* son of धृतराष्ट्र

धाव् *1st Conj. Parasm.* to run

धीमत् *adj. m. n.* sensible, talented

धीर् *with* अव *10th Conj.* to disregard, to despise

धीर *adj. m. n.* wise, of fortitude or patience; *m.* a bold or wise man

धूर्जटि *m.* the god Śiva

धृ *10th Conj.* to hold, to wear: to owe

धृ *1st Conj. Parasm. & Ātm* to seize; *with* उद्, to save, to release, to lift up

धृति *f.* courage

धेनु *f.* a cow

ध्यान *n.* contemplation

ध्रुव *adj. m n.* certain

ध्वंस् *1st Conj. Ātm,* to perish

ध्वनि *m.* a sound

न.

न *ind.* not

न कदापि never

नख *n.* a nail

नगर *n.* } a town
नगरी *f.* }

नटी *f.* an actress

नद *m.* } a river
नदी *f.* }

ननान्दृ *f.* husband's sister

नन्द् *1st Conj. Parasm. with* अभि, to rejoice in, to like

नन्दिनी *f.* a girl

नप्तृ *m.* a grandson

नभस् *n.* the sky

नम् *1st conj. Parasm.* to bow to, to salute; *with* अव, to become bent, to bend down

नमस् *ind.* bow

नयन *n.* the eye

नर *m.* a man

नल *m.* name of a king

नव *adj. m. n.* new

नश् *4th conj. Parasm* to perish

नष्ट (*past pass. part.* of नश्) perished

नाग *m.* an elephant

नाट् *10th conj.* to act as in a dramatic play

नाटक *n.* a play, a drama

नाम *ind.* by name, namely

नामन् *n.* a name

नायक *m.* a leader

नारद *m.* name of a heavenly *Ṛṣi*

नारायण *m.* name of a man

नारी *f.* a woman

नाविक *m.* a sailor

नाश *m.* ruin

नित्यम् *adv.* always

निधि *m.* a store

निन्द् *1st conj. Parasm.* to censure

निन्दा *f.* censure

निपुण *adj. m. n.* proficient

निमग्न (*past pass. part.* of मस्ज् *with* नि) plunged in, immersed

निमित्त *n.* a cause, reason

निरतिशय *adj. m. n.* unsurpassed, full, perfect

निरस्त (*past pass. part.* of अस् *4th conj.* to throw *with* निर्) scattered

निरूपित (*past pass. part.* of रूप् *with* नि) found out, marked out

निर्देश *m.* a direction

निर्बन्ध *m.* importunity

निर्मित (*past pass. part.* of मा *with* निर् to create) created, constructed, formed, made

निर्वृतिमत् *adj m. n.* happy

निवृत्त (*past pass. part.* of वृत् *with* नि) returned

निवेशित (*past. pass part.* of *the causal of* विश् *with* नि) placed

निशा *f.* night

निशाचर *m.* an evil spirit, wicked person

निशित *adj. m. n.* sharp

निश्चेष्ट *adj m. n.* motionless

निषण्ण (*past pass. part.* of सद् *with* नि) seated, sitting

निष्क *m.* a golden coin

निष्णात (*past pass. part.* of स्ना *2nd conj. with* नि) well-versed

निष्फल *adj. m. n.* fruitless

नी *1st conj. Parasm. & Ātm.* to lead or carry; *with* अप, to take away, to remove; *with* आ, to bring; *with* परि, to marry; *with* प्र, to compose, write; *with* वि, to educate

नीचैराख्य *adj.* नीचैस् ; आख्या *f.* name) named नीचैस्

नीति *f.* politics

नृ *m.* a man

नृत् *4th conj. Parasm.* to dance

नृत्य *n.* dancing, a dance

नृप *m.* }
नृपति *m.* } a king

नृपत्व *n.* royalty

नृशंस *adj. m. n.* wicked

नेत्र *n.* the eye

नैयायिक *m.* a follower of *Nyāya*

नौ *f.* a ship, a boat; कायनौ *f.* a boat in the shape of the body

न्याय *m.* a school of philosophy

न्यायसभा *f.* (न्याय *m.* justice, सभा *f.* a court) a court of justice

प

पक्षिन् *m.* a bird

पङ्क *m.* mud

पच् *1st conj. Parasm & Ātm.* to cook

पञ्चवटी *f.* name of a place

पञ्जर *m.* a cage

पठ् *1st conj. Parasm.* to learn

पण्डित *m.* a learned man

पण्य *n.* price; पुण्यपण्य *n.* religious merit as the price

पत् *1st conj. Parasm.* to fall; *with* आ, to happen; *with* उद्, to rise up, to fly up

पतन *n.* falling

पतित (*past pass. part.* of **पत्**) fallen

पत्ति *m.* a foot-soldier

पत्नी *f.* a wife

पथ्य *n.* a wholesome thing, what is wholesome

पद् *4th conj. Ātm. with* **उद्**, to be produced, to result: *with* **निस्**, to result; *with* **प्रति**, to step towards, to do.

पद *n.* a step

पद्म *n.* a lotus

पयस् *n.* water

पर *adj. m. n.* great, greatest

परकीय *adj. m. n.* another's

परम् *ind.* however, but

परम *adj. m. n.* very great

परवत् *adj. m. n.* dependent

परशु *m.* an axe

परशुराम *m.* a Brāhmaṇa hero who exterminated the warrior caste

पराक्रम *m.* an exploit

परार्ध *m.* the second or latter half

परिणाम *m.* a result

परिहर्तव्य *adj. m. n.* what should be shunned

परिहित (*past pass. part.* of **धा** *with* **परि**) worn

पर्ण *n.* a leaf

पर्याकुल *adj. m. n.* agitated

पर्वत *m.* a mountain

पल्वल *m. n.* a small pond, a puddle

पवन *m.* wind

पवि *m.* Indra's thunderbolt

पशु *m.* a beast

पश्चात् *ind.* afterwards

पश्यत् (*pr. part.* of **दृश्** *1st conj. Parasm.*) seeing

पा [**पिब्**] *1st conj. Parasm.* to drink; **पी** *passive*

पांसु *m.* dust

पाठ *m.* lesson

पाठशाला *f.* a school

पाणि *m.* the hand

पाण्डव *m.* son of **पाण्डु**, a king

पात *m.* a fall

पात्र *n.* a deserving person or thing

पाद *m.* the foot

पादप *m.* a tree

पान्थ a traveller

पाप *m.* a sinner; *adj. m. n.* sinful; *n.* a sin

पार् *10th conj.* to surmount

पार *m.* the other bank or side

पारितोषिक *n.* a reward

पार्थिव *m.* a king

पालक *m.* a protector; *adj. m. n.*

पिण्ड *m.* a ball of rice given to the dead

पितृ *m.* father; *du.* parents

पितृव्य *m.* a paternal uncle

पीड् *10th conj.* to give pain

पीडा *f.* pain

पुच्छकावलम्बन *n.* (**पुच्छक** *n.* a tail, **अवलम्बन** *n.* holding) holding the tail

पुण्य *n.* merit; *adj. m. n.* holy

पुण्यवत् *adj. m. n.* virtuous, meritorious

पुत्र *m.* a son

पुत्रजन्मसम *adj. m. n.* like the birth of a son

पुत्रीकृत *adj.* (**पुत्र**, and **कृत** made) made a son, adopted

पुनर् *ind.* again

पुरः *ind.* before (*space*)

पुरतस् *ind.* in front, in the presence (of)

पुरा *ind.* formerly, at first

पुराण *n.* name of the sacred poetical works comprising the whole body of Hindu mythology

पुरी *f.* a town

पुरुष *m.* a man

पुष् *4th conj. Parasm.* to nourish

पुष्पधारिन् *adj. m. n.* having flowers

पुष्पित *adj. m. n.* flowered

पुस्तक *n.* a book

पूज् *10 th conj.* to adore

पूजा *f.* worship

पूजास्थान *n.* an object of worship or reverence

पूज्य *adj. m. n.* worthy of honour

पूत (*past pass. part.* of **पू**) purified, holy

पूर् *10th conj.* to fill

पूर्वार्ध *m.* the first half

पृथ्वी *f.* the earth

पृष्ट (*past pass. part.* of **प्रच्छ्**) asked

पौर *m.* an inhabitant of a city, a citizen

प्रकर्ष *m.* intensity, greatness

प्रकाश *m.* light

प्रकृति *f.* ministry; disposition, nature

प्रकृतिसिद्ध *sdj. m. n.* (**प्रकृति**

सिद्ध *past pass. part.* of **सिध्** *1st & 4th conj.*) ready, natural

प्रच्छ [**पृच्छ**] *6th conj. Parasm.* to ask ; *with* **आ** *Ātm.* to take leave of (as at the time of departure)

प्रजा *f.* subjects ; progeny

प्रज्ञ *m.* a wise man

प्रतनु *adj. m. n. f.* little, small

प्रतिकृति *f.* an image or copy

प्रतिक्रिया *f.* retaliation, revenge, the way to revenge

प्रतिज्ञात (*past pass. part* of **ज्ञा** *with* **प्रति**) promised, vowed

प्रतिपद् *f.* the first day of a lunar fortnight

प्रतिष्ठापन *n.* establishing, establishment

प्रतिहत (*past pass. part.* of **हन्** *with* **प्रति**) obstructed

प्रत्यय *m.* conviction, belief

प्रथ् *10th conj.* to publish

प्रथम *adj. m. n.* first

प्रथमसुकृत *n.* (**प्रथम** first, previous, **सुकृत** *n.* a good action) a previous good action.

प्रदेय *adj. m. n.* to be given, to be given in marriage

प्रधानतम *adj. m. n.* chief

प्रपन्न (*past pass. part.* of **पद्** *4th conj. with* **प्र**) joined with

प्रबल *adj. m. n.* strong

प्रभव *m.* a source

प्रभा *f.* light

प्रभु *m.* a lord

प्रभूत *adj. m. n.* plentiful, much

प्रमदा *f.* a young woman

प्रमाण *n.* evidence, authority

प्रयाग *n.* Sanskṛt name of Allahabad

प्रवर्तन *n.* inciting, establishing

प्रवाह *m.* a current, flow

प्रविष्ट (*past pass. part.* of **विश्** *with* **प्र**) entered

प्रवृत्ति *f.* predilection; intelligence

प्रशस्य *adj. m. n.* praiseworthy

प्रश्रय *m.* courtesy, civility

प्रसन्न (*past pass. part.* of **सद्** *1st conj. with* **प्र**) pleased.

प्रसाद *m.* favour, grace

प्रस्थापित (*past pass part. of the causal form of* **स्था** *with* **प्र**) sent

प्राची *f.* the east

प्राज्ञ *m.* an intelligent man

प्राण *m. plur.* life

प्राणिन् *m.* an animal

प्रातर् *ind.* in the morning

प्राप्त (*past pass. part.* of **आप्** *with* **प्र**) arrived at, come to

प्रायस् *ind.* generally

प्रावीण्य *n.* proficiency

प्राश्निक *m.* an examiner

प्रासाद *m.* a palace, and **तल** *n* a surface; **प्रासादतल** *n.* the upper surface or terrace of a palace

प्रिय *adj. m. n.* beloved

प्रियंवदा *f.* name of a female companion of Śakuntalā

प्रियतमा *f.* beloved, dearest

प्रियवादिन् *adj. m. n.* speaking sweetly

प्रियवादित्व *n.* kindliness of speech

प्रियाप्रवृत्ति *f.* (**प्रिया** beloved, and **प्रवृत्ति**) intelligence about one's beloved

प्री [**प्रीण्**] *10th conj.* to please

प्रीति *f.* affection; satisfaction

प्रेमन् *m. n.* affection

प्रेयस् *adj. m. n.* very dear

फ

फल् *1st conj. Parasm.* to fructify, to be fulfilled

फल *n.* a fruit

फलाशिन् *adj. m. n.* a fruit-eater

ब

बन्धु *m.* a relation

बल *n.* strength; an army

बलि *m.* name of a king; an oblation (food)

बहिस् *ind.* out of (used with the Abl.)

बहु *adj. m. n. f.* many

बहुशस् *ind.* often, in many cases

बाण *m.* an arrow

बान्धव *m.* a brother, a relation

बाल *m.* a child

बाहु *m.* an arm

बाहुल्य *n.* multiplicity

बिडाल *m.* a cat

बिन्दु *m.* a drop

बिम्ब *n.* a disc

बीज *n.* seed

बुद्धि *f.* talent, intellect

बुद्धिप्रभाव *m.* (प्रभाव *m.* power) the power of talent

बुध् *1st conj. Parasm.& Ātm.* to know or understand

बुध *m.* a wise man

ब्रह्मन् *m.* the Creator ; *n.* the soul of the universe

ब्रह्मविद् *adj. m. n. f.* a metaphysical philosopher, one knowing the *Brahman*

ब्रह्मारण्यं *n.* name of a forest

ब्राह्मण *m.* a person of the highest Hindu caste

ब्रूते (*present tense 3rd pers sing. Atm.* of ब्रू *2nd conj.*) says

भ.

भक्त (*past pass part.* of भज्) devoted ; *m.* a devotee

भक्ति *f.* devotion

भक्ष् *10th conj.* to eat

भगवत् *adj. m. n* divine, prosperous

भगिनी *f.* a sister

भगीरथ *m.* name of a king of the solar race

भङ्ग *m.* violation, breaking

भज् *1st conj. Parasm. & Ātm.* to worship, to resort to, to have recourse to

भद्र *n.* well-being, benefit

भय *n.* fear

भयंकर *adj. m. n.* causing fear, frightful

भर *m.* weight

भर्तृ *m.* husband ; master

भवत् *pron.* your honour

भवत्सकाश *m.* (भवत् and सकाश *m.* vicinity) to your honour

भविष्यति *3rd pers. sing. future tense* of भू

भागीरथी *f.* the Ganges

भार *m.* a burden

भारतवर्षीय *m.* a native of Bhāratavarṣa or India

भार्या *f.* wife

भावय (*2nd pers. sing. imp. of the causal form* of भू) feel, make; संभाव्यते *pass. of the causal*, appears credible

भाविन् *adj. m. n.* what is to be, future

भाष् *1st conj. Atm.* to speak, *with* प्रति, to reply

भास्वरशुक्ल *adj. m. n.* brilliant white

भिक्ष् *1st conj. Ātm* to beg

भिक्षा *f.* alms
भिक्षुक *m.* a beggar
भिद् to break
भीति *f.* fear, danger
भीम *m.* name of the second of the sons of Pāṇḍu
भीरु *adj. f.* timid (woman)
भू *1st conj. Parasm.* to be, to become, *with* अनु, to experience, *with* उद्, to be produced, to result
भूत *n.* a creature, an animal
भूतार्थ *m.* reality
भूति *f.* prosperity
भूप, भूभृत *m.* a king
भूमि *f.* ground, land; the earth
भूयस् *adj. m. n.* very great, greater
भूरि *adj. m. n.* much
भूष् *10th conj.* to adorn
भूषण *n.* an ornament
भृ *1st conj. Parasm.* & *Ātm.* to fill; भ्रियते *pass.*
भृत्य *m.* a servant
भोग *m.* enjoyment
भोजन *n.* a dinner
भोस् *ind.* a vocative particle
भ्रमर *m.* a bee
भ्रातृ *m.* a brother
भ्रान्त (*past pass. part.* of भ्रम्) bewildered

म.

मणि *m.* a jewel
मणिकार *m.* a jeweller
मण्डप *m.* a bower
मति *f.* intellect, thought, view, feeling
मत्स्य *m.* a fish
मद् [माद्] *4th conj. Parasm.* to be mad, to err; *with* प्र, to err, to fall off
मद *m.* pride, arrogance, insolence, intoxication
मदन *m.* the god of love
मदिरा *f.* wine
मदिराक्षी *f.* a woman having fascinating or lovely eyes
मधु *n.* honey
मधुकर *m.* a bee
मधुरम् *adv.* sweetly
मन् *4th conj. Atm.* to think, to maintain, to regard, *with* अनु, to consent to, to agree to, *with* अव, to disregard
मनःसंयम *m.* (संयम *m.* restraint) the restraining of the mind

मनस् *n.* the mind
मनु *m.* the Hindu legislat
मन्त्र् *with* नि *10th conj. Ātm.* to invite
मन्त्र *m.* a Vedic verse
मन्द *adj. m. n.* slow
मयूर *m.* a peacock
मरण *n.* death
मरुत् *m.* wind, or the deity that presides over it; a god
महत् *adj. m. n.* great
महात्मन् *m.* a great soul, a magnanimous person
महाराज *m.* the great king
महारिपु *m.*(रिपु *m.*an enemy) a great enemy
महिमन् *m.* greatness
महिष *m.* a buffalo
महिषासुर *m.* an evil spirit in the form of a buffalo
महिषी *f.* a crowned queen
मही *f.* the earth
महोत्सव *m.* a festival
मा *ind.* not (prohibitive)
मा *with* निर्, to produce, to create; निर्मीयते *pass.*
मांस *n.* flesh
माणवक *m.* name of an individual
मातृ *f.* mother
माधुर्य *n.* sweetness
मानव *m.* a man, a human being
मानिनी *f.* a proud woman
मारुत *m.* wind, or the deity that presides over it
मार्ग् *10th conj.* to seek
मार्ग *m.* a road
माला *f.* a garland, a wreath
माष *m.* a kind of pulse
मास *m.* month
मासचतुष्टय *n.* (चतुष्टय *n.* a collection of four) four months, a fourfold month
मित्र *n.* a friend
मित्रता *f.* friendship
मिलित्वा (*ind. past part.* of मिल्) having joined
मुक्त (*past pass. part.* of मुच्) released, left
मुक्ता *f.* a pearl
मुक्ति *f.* absolution
मुख *n.* the mouth
मुख्य *adj.* chief
मुच् [मुञ्च्] *6th conj. Parasm. & Ātm.* to leave or release
मुद् *1st conj. Ātm.* to rejoice

मुष्टि *m.* a handful

मुह् *4th conj. Parasm.* to be silly; to lose sense, to faint

मूक *adj. m. n.* silent, dumb

मूर्ख *m.* a fool

मूर्खशत *n.* (शत *n.* a hundred) a hundred fools

मूर्च्छ् *1st conj. Parasm.* to faint away, to swoon

मूर्ति *f.* an image or idol

मूर्तिमत् *adj. m. n.* having [form

मूर्धन् *m.* the head

मूल *n.* root, foot

मृ [म्रिय्] *6th conj. Ātm.* to die

मृग् *10th conj. Ātm.* to seek

मृग *m.* a deer

मृत्यु *m.* death

मृद् *f.* earth

मृदु *adj. m, n, f:* soft

मृश् *6th conj. Parasm. with* वि, to test, to examine

मेघ *m.* a cloud

मेघजाल *n.* an assemblage of clouds

मेदिनी *f.* the earth

मेधाविन् *adj. m. n.* talented, intelligent

मेल *m.* union, company

मैत्रावरुण *m.* a priest at the Soma sacrifice

मोक्ष *m.* absolution

मोदक *m.* sweetmeat

मौक्तिक *n.* a pearl

मौन *n.* silence

य.

यक्ष *m.* servant of Kubera

यज् *1st conj. Parasm. & Ātm.* to worship

यजमान *m.* a sacrificer

यज्ञिय *adj. m. n.* belonging to a sacrifice

यत् *1st conj. Ātm.* to strive

यत् *pr. part. with* उद्, उद्यत् rising

यतः *ind.* whence (*relative*)

यति *m.* an ascetic

यत्न *m.* effort

यत्र *ind.* where (*relative*)

यथा *ind.* in which manner (*relative*)

यदा *ind.* when (*relative*)

यदि *ind.* if

यन्त्र *n.* a machine

यशस् *n.* fame, glory

यशस्वत् *adj. m. n.* famous

या *with* आ, to come

या *with* सम् and आ, to come *past pass. part.* समायात

याच् *1st conj. Parasm. & Ātm* to beg

याचक *m.* a mendicant
यात (*past pass. part.* of या to go) gone
यातृ *f.* husband's brother's wife
यात्रिक *m* a pilgrim
यावत् *ind.* as long as
युक्त (*past pass. part.* of युज्) joined
युद्ध *n.* a battle
युध् *4th conj. Ātm.* to fight
युध् *f.* a war, a battle
यूथ *n.* a herd
योगिन् *m.* an ascetic
योजन *n.* eight miles
योध *m.* a warrior

र

रक्ष् *1st conj. Parasm.* to protect
रक्षण *n.* defence
रक्षस् *n.* an evil spirit, a *Rākṣasa*
रक्षा *f.* protection
रक्षित (*past pass. part.* of रक्ष्) protected
रक्षितृ *m.* a defender, protector; *adj. m. n.*
रक्त *adj. m. n.* red
रघु *m.* (*in the plural*) the descendants of a king named रघु
रघुनाथ *m.* the lord of the Raghus
रच् *10th conj.* to arrange
रजनी *f.* a night
रज्जु *f.* a rope
रजस् *n.* dust, pollen
रति *f.* pleasure ; the wife of the god of love
रत्न *n.* jewel
रथ *m.* a chariot
रथ्य *m.* a horse
रथ्या *f.* a street
रभ् *1st conj. Ātm.* to be engaged; *with* आ, to begin
रम् *1st conj. Ātm.* to sport, to be diverted, to feel happy; *with* वि, *Parasm* to stop, to desist
रमण *m.* a lover; a husband
रमा *f.* name of a woman
रवि *m.* the sun
रस *m.* juice
राक्षस *m.* a wicked person, an evil spirit
राज् *1st conj. Parasm. & Ātm. with* वि, to shine, to appear beautiful

राजद्वार *n.* (द्वार *n.* door) the door of a king, *i. e.*, of a king's house

राजन् *m.* a king

राजपुत्र *m.* a prince

राजपुरुष *m.* king's officer

राज्ञी *f.* a queen

राज्य *n.* a kingdom

राज्यकामाकृष्ट *adj. m.n.*(राज्य royalty, काम desire, आकृष्ट drawn) drawn by the desire of royalty

रात्रि *f.* night

राम *m.* name of a person

रावण *m.* king of Lañkā or Ceylon, the great enemy of Rāma

राशि *m.* a heap

राष्ट्र *n.* a country, a nation

रीति *f.* manner, way

रुच् *1st conj. Ātm.* to please, to be liked

रुद् to cry

रुध् *4th conj. Ātm. with* अनु, to obey

रुध् *with* नि *pass.* to be checked

रुह् *1st conj. Parasm.* to grow; *with* आ, to mount or ascend; *with* प्र, to grow

रे रे *inter.* O ! Oh !

रोदन *n.* crying

ल

लक्ष् *10th conj. with* सम्, to observe, to test, to prove

लक्ष्मण *m.* brother of Rāma

लक्ष्मी *f.* wife of Viṣṇu; goddess of wealth

लग्नवेला *f.* a (lucky) conjuncture

लघिमन् *m.* littleness

लघु *adj. m. n. f.* short

लङ्घ् *1st conj. Ātm.* to transgress, to overcome

लज्ज् *6th conj. Ātm.* to feel shame

लज्जा *f.* shame

लता *f.* a creeping plant

लतागृह *n.* a bower of creepers

लभ् *1st conj. Atm.* to get

लम्ब् *1st conj. Atm. with* अव, to resort to

ललना *f.* a woman

लव *m.* a particle

लव *m.* the name of a son of Rāma

लवण *adj. m. n.* salt; *s. n.*

लाङ्गूल *n.* the tail

लाभ *m.* acquisition, obtaining

लिङ्ग *n.* sex

लुठ् *4th conj. Parasm.* to wallow

लुभ् *4th & 6th conj. Parasm.* to covet, to be fascinated

लोक *m.* people, world

लोभ *m.* avarice

व.

वंश *m.* race

वक्तृ *adj. m. n.* a speaker

वक्षस् *n.* the breast

वचन *n.* saying, advice; request

वचनीय *adj. m. n* censurable; *n.* censure, anything censurable

वचस् *n.* speech

वञ्चक *m.* a cheat

वत्स *m.* a child

वद् *1st conj. Parasm.* to speak

वध *m.* killing

वधू *f.* a young woman; daughter-in-law

वन *n.* a forest

वनवासिन् *adj. m. n.* living in a forest

वनौकस् *m.* one dwelling in a forest

वन्द् *1st conj. Ātm.* to salute

वयस् *n.* age

वयस्य *m.* a companion, a friend

वर *m.* a boon

वरतनु *adj. m n. f.* one whose form is elegant, handsome, beautiful

वरम् *ind.* well

वराह *m.* a hog

वर्ण् *10th conj.* to extol or describe

वर्ण *m.* a caste, colour

वर्त्मन् *n.* a way

वल्लभ *m.* a lover, a husband

वशा *f.* a wife, a mate

वस् *1st conj. Parasm.* to dwell; *with* **अधि**, to sit upon, to rest upon

वसत् (*pr. part. of* **वस्** *Parasm.*) dwelling

वसति *f.* a place of residence

वसन *n.* cloth

वसन्त *m.* spring

वसु *n.* wealth

वसुदेव *m.* name of Kṛṣṇa's father

वसुधा *f.* the earth

वस्तु *n.* a thing, a real thing

वस्त्र *n.* cloth

वह् *1st conj. Parasm & Ātm.* to bear. to flow

वा *ind.* or

वाक्पटुता *f.* (पटुता *f.* cleverness) cleverness in speech

वाक्य *n.* sentence, words

वाच् *f.* }
वाचा *f.* } speech

वाञ्छ् *1st conj. Parasm.* to desire

वाणी *f.* speech

वात *m.* wind

वातायन *n.* a window

वाद् *10th conj. Ātm with* **अभि**, to salute, to respect

वापी *f.* a well

वायस *m.* a crow

वायु *m.* wind

वारि *n.* water

वार्ता *f.* intelligence, news, account

वास *m.* habitation, residence

वासस् *n.* cloth

वासित *adj m. n.* made fragrant

वासुदेव *m.* name of the god Kṛṣṇa

विकार *m.* a change of form, a transformation

विकास *m.* development

विग्रहसंधि *m.* (**विग्रह** *m.* hostility; war, **संधि** *m.* peace) war and peace

विघ्न *m.* an obstacle

विचित्र *adj. m. n.* curious, variegated

वित्त *n.* wealth

विद् [विन्द्] *6th conj Parasm. & Ātm.* to obtain

विद् *4th conj. Ātm.* to be

विद्या *f.* learning

विद्युत् *f.* lightning

विद्वत्त्व *n.* learning, learnedness

विद्वस् *adj.m. n.* learned

विधि *m.* fate; a sacred precept

विधृत *past pass. part.* of **धृ** *with* वि) upheld, supported

विधेय *adj. m. n.* what is to be done

विनय *m.* modesty

विना *ind.* without

विनाश *m.* destruction

विपत्ति *f.* adversity

विपद् *f.* misery, adversity

विप्रिय *adj. m. n.* disliked; *n.* an offence

विभव *m.* wealth, riches

विमार्ग *m.* a wrong path, evil conduct

विमुख *adj. m.* n. with the face turned away from

वियत् *n.* the sky

वियोग *m.* separation

विराव *n.* a cry

विरूप *adj. m. n.* deformed

विवर *n.* a cave

विवाह *m.* marriage

विविध *adj. m. n.* various

विश् *6th conj. Parasm.* to enter; *with* **उप**, to sit

विशुद्ध (*past pass. part* of **शुध्** *4th. conj. Parasm. with* **वि**) pure

विशुद्धि *f.* purity

विश्रामहेतोः *abl.* or *gen. sing.* of **विश्रामहेतु** *m.* (**विश्राम** *m.* rest, **हेतु** *m.* purpose) for the purpose of rest

विश्व *n.* the universe

विश्वकर्मन् *m.* the architect of the gods

विश्वामित्र *m.* name of a sage

विश्वास *m.* confidence

विश्वासकारण *n.* (**विश्वास** *m.* belief, **कारण** *n*, a reason) a reason for belief

विष *n.* poison

विष्णु *m.* the god Viṣṇu

विहग *m.* a bird

विहित (*past pass. part* of **धा** *with* **वि**) done, established, laid down

वीथि *f.* a road

वीर *m.* a warrior

वीर्य *n.* heroism, bravery, valour

वृ *with* **परि**, to surround

वृक्ष *m.* a tree

वृत् *1st conj. Ātm.* to be: *with* **नि**, to return: *with* **परा**, to bend back–**परावृत्य** having bent back; *with* **प्र**, to set about; *with* **प्रति** and **नि**, to return, to come back

वृत्ति *f.* profession, avocation

वृथा *ind.* in vain

वृद्धिमत् *adj. m. n.* lengthening

वृध् *1st conj. Ātm.* to increase; *with* **सम्** to in

crease, to flourish

वृन्त *n.* a stalk

वृष *m.* a bullock

वृषभध्वज *m.* Śiva

वेद *m.* Hindu sacred scriptures

वेधस् *m.* Brahmā

वेप् *1st conj. Ātm.* to tremble, to quake

वैकुण्ठ *n.* name of the celestial abode of the god Viṣṇu

वैयात्य *n.* rudeness, impudence

वैर *n.* enmity

व्यथा *f.* pain

व्यसन *n.* a difficulty; addictedness to anything

व्याख्येय *adj. m. n.* to be expounded

व्याघ्र *m.* a tiger

व्याध *m.* a hunter

व्याधि *m.* sickness or disease

व्याघ्री *f.* a tigress

व्रज् *1st conj. Parasm.* to go

व्रीहि *m.* rice of various kinds, or grain of it

श.

शंस् *1st conj. Parasm.* to praise or tell

शंस् *with* **आ** *1st conj. Ātm.* to hope for

शकुन्तला *f.* name of a woman

शङ्क् *1st conj. Ātm.* to suspect

शङ्का *f.* doubt

शठ *m.* a rogue

शत *n.* a hundred

शत्रु *m.* an enemy

शत्रुविग्रह *m.* hostility with an enemy

शनैस् *ind.* slowly

शम् [**शाम्**] *4th conj. Parasm.* to be or become calm, cool or tranquil

शम्बूक *m.* name of a person

शम्भु *m.* the god Śiva

शर *m.* an arrow

शरद् *f.* autumn

शरीर *n.* the body

शरीरस्थ *adj. m. n.* living in the body, bodily

शय्या *f.* a bed

शव *n.* a dead body

शस्त्र *n.* a weapon

शाखा *f.* a branch

शान्ता *f.* sister of Rāma

शान्ति *f.* peace

शाला *f.* an establishment; a place

शास् to rule

शासत् (*pr. part.* of **शास्** to rule) ruling

शासन *n.* an order.

शास्त्र *n.* a science

शिक्ष् *1st conj. Ātm.* to learn

शिखर *m. n.* the top, summit

शिखरिन् *m.* a mountain

शिरस् *n.* the head

शिला *f.* a stone

शिव *n.* welfare, happiness

शिवालय *n.* a temple of Śiva

शिशिर *m. n.* the cold season

शिशु *m.* an infant, a child

शिष्य *m* a pupil

शीर्ष *n.* the head

शुक *m.* a parrot

शुक्लपक्ष *m.* (**शुक्ल** *adj. m. n.* white, **पक्ष** *m.* a half of a lunar month) the bright half (of a month)

शुच् *1st conj. Parasm.* to bewail

शुभ् *1st conj. Ātm.*—to be splendid, to become, to behove

शुभ *adj. m. n.* good, virtuous

शुष् *1st conj. Parasm.* to dry

शूद्र *m.* a person of the lowest Hindu caste

शूद्रक *m.* name of a king

शूलिन् *m.* name of the god Śiva

शृगाल *m.* a jackal

शोभन *adj. m. n.* good

शोभा *f.* beauty

शौर्य *n.* valour

श्मशान *n.* a cemetery, a burning-place

श्याम *adj. m. n.* dark

श्यामिका *f.* impurity

श्रद्धा *f.* confidence

श्रद्धेय *adj. m. n.* credible

श्रम् [**श्राम्**] *4th conj. Parasm.* to be weary; *with* **वि**, to rest

श्रम *m.* labour

श्रवण *n.* hearing

श्रि *1st conj. Parasm.* & *Ātm. with* **आ**, to resort to, to depend upon

श्रीमत् *adj. m. n.* prosperous

श्रीषेण *m.* a proper name

श्रु to hear

श्रुति *f.* hearing; Hindu religious books, the *Vedas*

श्रुतिमत् *adj. m. n.* one who knows the *Vedas*

श्रेष्ठ *adj.m.n.* best, supreme

श्रेयस् *adj. m. n.* superior, prosperous

श्रोतृ *m.* a hearer; *adj. m n.*

श्लथ *adj. m. n.* loosened

श्लाघ् *1st conj. Ātm.* to panegyrize, to praise

श्लिष् *4th conj. Parasm.* to embrace; with **आ**, to embrace

श्लोक *m.* a verse

श्वश्रू *f.* mother-in-law

श्वस् *ind.* to-morrow

श्वापद *m.* a beast of prey

श्वेत *adj. m. n.* white

स

संकट *n.* difficulty, perplexity

संगत *n.* friendship, companionship

संगम *m.* confluence

संगीत *n.* a song, singing

संगमोत्सुक *adj. m. n.* eager for union

संघात *m.* a collection

संचलन *n.* moving to and fro

संतप्त (*past pass part.* of **तप्** *with* **सम्**) heated, oppressed by heat

संदेश *m.* a message

संदेह *m.* a doubt

संनिधि *m.* proximity, vicinity

संपद् *f.* wealth, prosperity

संपर्क *m.* touch, contact

संभार *m.* preparation

संमार्जन *n.* sweeping

संश्रय *m.* resting place

संसार *m.* the world, mundane existence, the series of the transmigrations of the soul

सखि *m.* a friend.

सखी *f.* a female friend

सगर *m.* name of a king of the solar race

सचिव *m.* minister

सत् (*pr. part.* of **अस्** to be) being, good; *m.* a good or virtuous man

सत्तत्त्व *n.* the real thing

सत्त्व *n.* truth; goodness

सत्य *adj. m. n.* true: *n.* truth

सत्यम् *adv.* truly

सत्वरम् *adv.* speedily

सद् [**सीद्**] *1st conj. Parasm, with* **अव**, to decline; *with* **नि** [**निषीद्**], to sit; *with* **प्र**, to favour, to be pleased

सदस् *f. n.* an assembly

सदा *ind.* always

सदाचार *m.* good conduct

सदैव (**सदा+एव**) *ind.* always

सद्मन् *n.* a house

सन् *nom.sing.masc.* of **सत्** *pres.part.* of **अस्** to be

सभा *f.*a court, an assembly

समचित्त *adj. m.n.* (**सम** *adj. m. n.* even, **चित्त** mind) even-minded, regarding all equally

समराङ्गण *n.* a field of battle

समर्थ *adj.m.n.*able,powerful

समाज *m.* an assembly

समुद्र *m.* the sea

समूह *m.* a multitude; a crowd

समृद्धि *f.* plenty, prosperity

सम्यक् *adv.* well

सरस् *n.* a lake

सर्प *m.* a serpent

सर्वत्र *ind.* everywhere

सर्वथा *ind.* wholly

सर्वदा *ind.* always

सवितृ *m.* the sun

सव्येष्टृ *m.* a charioteer

सह् *1stconj.Ātm.* to endure

सह *ind.* with

सहचरी *f.* a female companion or mate

सहसा *ind.* at once,suddenly

साक्षिन् *m.* a witness

साधयितव्य *adj. m. n.* what should be accomplished

साधु *m.* a sage, a man of piety; *adj.m.n.f.*good

साध्य *adj.m.n.* obtainable, possible to make

सान्त्व् *10th conj.*to appease

सामर्थ्य *n.* power

सारङ्ग *m.* a kind of bird

सारथि *m.* a charioteer

सारमेय *m.* a dog.

सार्थ *m.* a caravan, a crowd

साशङ्क *adj. m.n.* suspicious

साष्टाङ्गपातम् *comp. adv.* with prostration or falling on the eight bodily members

साहस *n.* an adventure

सिंह *m.* a lion

सिंहासन *n.* a throne

सिच् [**सिञ्च्**] *6th conj. Parasm. & Ātm.* to sprinkle

सीता *f.* Rāma's wife

सीमन् *f.*boundary, bounds

सु (*prefixed to nouns*) good

सुकृत *n.* } a virtuous or
सुकृति *f.* } good action

सुख *n.* happiness. ease

सुखभाज् *adj. m.n.f.* happy, one who enjoys happiness

सुखलेश *m.*(**लेश***m.* an atom) an atom of happiness

सुगन्धि *adj.m,n.f.* fragrant

सुचरित *n.* a virtuous or good action

सुजन *m.* a good person, a good man

सुमन्त्र *m.* name of Rāma's charioteer

सुरभि *adj. m.n.f.* fragrant

सुवर्ण *n.* gold

सुवर्णकार *m.* a goldsmith

सुवृत्त *adj. m. n.* virtuous, good

सुष्ठु *ind.* well

सुहृद् *m.* a friend

सूक्त *n.* a Vedic hymn

सूत्रधार *m.* the manager or chief actor in a play

सूद् *10th conj. with* नि [निषूद्] to destroy

सूद *m.* a cook

सूनु *m.* a son

सूर्य *m.* the sun

सृ *1st conj. Parasm.* to move: *with* अनु, to follow; *with* प्र, to spread

सृज् *5th conj. Parasm.* to abandon or create; *with* अति, to give

सृष्टि *f.* creation

सेना an army

सेनापति *m.* a general, commander of an army

सेव् *1st conj. Ātm.* to serve; *with* परि, to resort to

सैनिक *m.* a soldier

सोत्कण्ठ *adj. m. n.* anxious

सोम *m.* a plant used in sacrifices, or its juice

सोमवासर *m.* Monday

सोढ (*past pass. part.* of (सह्) endured

सौन्दर्य *n.* beauty

स्तुति *f.* praise

स्तेन *m.* thief

स्त्रीरत्न *n.* a jewel amongst women

स्था [तिष्ठ्] *1st conj. Parasm,* to stand—स्थी *passive, with* अनु, to carry out, to act according to; *with* उद्, to get up; *with* प्र, *Ātm.* to set out, to start

स्थान *n.* a place

स्निह् *4th conj. Parasm.* to feel affection for

स्निग्ध (*past pass. part.* of स्निह्) affectionate

स्नेह *m.* affection, friendship

स्पन्द् *1st conj. Ātm.* to throb

स्पर्ध् *1st conj. Ātm.* to rival

स्पृश् *6th conj. Parasm.* to touch

स्पृष्ट (*past pass. part.* of स्पृश्) touched

स्पृह् *10th conj.* to desire

स्फुर् *6th conj. Parasm.* to throb

स्मि *1st conj.Ātm.* to smile; *with* वि, to wonder, to be dismayed

स्मृ *1st conj. Parasm.* to remember; *with* वि, to forget

स्मृति *f.* rememberance; Hindu law-books

स्रंस् *1st conj. Ātm.* to drop down

स्रष्टृ *m.* the Creator; *adj. m. n.*

स्वकृत्य *n.* one's duty

स्वदेश m. (स्व one's own, देश country) one's one country

स्वप्न *m.* a dream

स्वर्ग *m.* Heaven

स्वविषय *m.* (स्व and विषय dominion) one's own dominion

स्वसृ *f.* a sister

स्वस्ति *ind.* hail !

स्वस्थ *adj. m. n.* patient tranquil

स्वाद् *1st conj. Ātm.* to taste

स्वादु *adj. m. n.f.* delicious

स्वामिगुणोपेत *adj m.n.* (स्वामिन् a lord, गुण a virtue and उपेत endowed or joined with) endowed with the virtues of a lord

स्वामिन् *m.* a lord

स्वास्थ्य *n.* tranquillity

स्वीय *adj. m. n.* one's own

ह.

हन् to kill; हन्ति ((*pres 3rd pers. sing.*) kills

हरण *n.* taking away

हरि *m.* the name of a man or the god Indra

हरिण *m.* a deer

हर्म्य *m.* a mansion

हलाहल *n.* a deadly poison

हविस् *n.* an offering

हस् *1st conj. Parasm. with* वि, to laugh in contempt

हस्त *m.* the hand

हि *with* प्र, to send

हित *adj. m. n.* beneficial: *n.* a benefit

हितकर *adj, m.n.* beneficial

हिम *n.* snow

हुतभुज् *m.* fire

हृ *1st. conj. Parasm & Ātm.* to carry away, to take away, to remove, to captivate; *with* **आ**, to eat, or perform a sacrifice; *with* **परि**, to dispel, to remove; *with* **प्र**, to strike; *with* **वि**, to divert one's self, to amuse, to play

हृदय *n.* the heart

हे *ind,* O!

हेमन् *n.* gold

होतृ *m.* a sacrificial priest

ह्यस् *ind.* yesterday

ह्लाद् *10th conj. with* **आ**, to delight

ह्वे *1st. conj. Parasm. & Ātm..* to call

A

Abandon *v.* त्यज् *1st conj. Parasm.*, सृज् *6th conj. Parasm. with* वि

Able *adj.* समर्थः to be—*v* क्लृप् *1st conj Ātm.*

Absolution *s.* मोक्ष *m*, मुक्ति *f.*

Abundance s. समृद्धि *f.*

Accomplished, what should be, साधयितव्य *adj.*

Account *s* वार्ता *f.*

Account, take into *v* ईक्ष् *1st coj. Ātm.*

Acquisition *s.* लाभ *m.*

Act (as in a dramatic play) *v.* नाट् *10th conj. Parasm. & Ātm.*

Act according to *v.* स्था *1st conj. Parasm. with* अनु

Action s. कृति *f.*, कर्मन् *n.*, कार्य *n.*

Action, good or virtuous, *s.* सुकृति *f.*, सुकृत *n.*, सुचरित *n.*; previous—s. प्रथम-सुकृत *n.*

Action, wicked, *s.* दुष्कृति *f.*, दुष्कृत *n.*

Actor, chief, in a play *s.* सूत्रधार *m.*

Actress *s.* नटी *f.*

Addictedness to anything *s.* व्यसन *n.*

Adopted as a son *p. p.* पुत्रीकृत

Adore *v.* पूज् *10th conj. Parasm. & Ātm.*

Adorn *v.* भूष् *10th conj. Parasm. & Atm.*, कृ [क्रि *pass.*] *with* अलम्

Adventure s. साहस *n.*

Adversity *s.* आपद् *f.*, विपत्ति *f*, विपद् *f.*

Advice *s.* वचन *n.*, उपदेश *m.*

Advise *v.* दिश् *6th conj. Parasm. & Ātm with* उप

Affection *s.* स्नेह *m.*, प्रीति *f.*, प्रेमन् *m. n.*

Affection, to feel, for *v.* स्निह् *4th conj. Parasm.*

Affectionate *adj.* स्निग्ध

Afflict *v.* पीड् *10th conj. Parasm. & Ātm.*

Afflicted *p. p.* दुःखित *adj.*

After *prep.* अनन्तरम् *adv.*

Afterwards *adv.* पश्चात् *ind.*, अनन्तरम् *adv.*

Again *adv.* पुनर् *ind.*

Age *s.* वयस् *n.*; old—जरा *f.*

Agitated *p. p.* पर्याकुल *adj.*

Agitated, to be, *v.* क्षुभ् *4th conj. Parasm.*

Agree to *v.* मन् *4th conj. Ātm. with* अनु

All *adj.* अखिल, सर्व *pron.*

Alms s. भिक्षा *f.*

Aloft *adv.* उच्चैस् *ind.*

Always *adv.* नित्यम् *adv.* सदा *ind.*, सदैव *ind.*, सर्वदा *ind.*

Amuse one's self *v.* रम् *1st conj. Parasm. & Ātm. with* वि

And *conj.* च *ind.*

Anger *s.* क्रोध *m.*

Angry, to be, become, *v.* कुप् *4th conj. Parasm.* क्रुध् *4th conj Parasm.*

Animal *s.* जीव *m.* प्राणिन् *m.*, भूत *n.*

Another's परकीय *adj.*

Anxiety *s.* चिन्ता *f.*, उत्कण्ठा *f.*

Anxious *adj.* सोत्कण्ठ

Apartment occupied by women in a house *s.* अंतःपुर *n.*

Appearance (coming to birth) *s.* उद्गम *m.*

Appease *v.* सान्त्व् *10th conj. Parasm. & Atm.*

Application *s* उद्योग *m.*

Architect of the gods त्वष्टृ *m.*, विश्वकर्मन् *m.*

Arm *s.* बाहु *m.*

Army *s.* सेना *f.*, बल *n.*

Arrange *v.* रच् *10th conj. Parasm & Atm.*

Arrived at *p. p.* प्राप्त

Arrogance *s.* मद *m.*

Arrow s. शर *m.*, बाण *m*, इषु m,

Art *s.* कला *f.*

As *adv.* इव *ind.*, यथा *ind.*

Ascend to *v.* रुह् *1st conj. Parasm. with* आ

Ascetic *s.* यति *m.*, योगिन् *m.*

Ascribing *s.* आरोप *m.*

Ascribing something not real *s.* अवस्त्वारोप *m.*

Ask *v.* प्रच्छ् [पृच्छ्] *6th conj. Parasm.*

Asked *p. p.* पृष्ट

Assemblage of clouds *s.* मेघजाल *n.*

Assembly *s.* सभा *f.*, संसद् *f. n.* समाज *m.*

Atom *s.* लेश *m.*;—of happiness *s.* सुखलेश *m.*

Attendant on the women's apartments *s.* कञ्चुकिन् *m.*

Austerity (religious) *s.* तपस् *n.*

Author *s.* कर्तृ *m. n.*

Authority *s.* प्रमाण *n.*

Authorize *v.* कृ *with* अधि

Autumn *s.* शरद् *f.*

Avarice *s.* लोभ *m.*

Avocation *s.* वृत्ति *f.*

Away with अलम् *ind.*

Axe *s.* परशु *m.*

B.

Bank *s.* तीर *n.*, पार *m.*

Bathe in *v.* गाह् *1st Conj. Ātm. with* अव

Battle *s.* युद्ध *n.*, युध *f.*

Be *v.* भू *1st Conj. Parasm.*; अस् *2nd Conj. Parasm.*, वृत् *1st Conj. Ātm.*, विद् *4th* Conj. *Ātm.*

Bear *v.* वह् *1st Conj. Parasm. & Ātm.*

Beast *s.* पशु *m.*;—of prey श्वापद *m.*

Beat *v.* तड् *10th Conj. Parasm. & Ātm.*

Beating *s.* ताडन *n.*

Beautiful *adj.* वरतनु, चारु

Beautiful, to appear, *v.* राज् *1st Conj. Parasm. & Ātm. with* वि

Beautify *v.* कृ [क्रि *pass.*] *with* अलम्

Beauty *s.* सौन्दर्य *n.* शोभा *f.*

Become *v.* भू *1st Conj. Parasm.*; (behove) शुभ् *1st Conj. Ātm.*

Bed *s.* शय्या *f.*

Bee *s.* अलि *m.*, मधुकर *m.*, भ्रमर *m.*

Before (space) *adv.* पुरः *ind.*

Beg *v.* याच् *1st Conj. Parasm.: & Ātm.*, भिक्ष् *1st Conj. Ātm*, अर्थ् *10th Conj. Ātm.*, *with* अभि

Beggar *s.* भिक्षुक *m.*

Begin *v.* रभ् *1st Conj. Ātm. with* आ

Beginning *s.* आरम्भ *m.*

Behove *v.* शुभ् *1st Conj. Ātm.*

Being *pr. part.* सत्

Belief *s.* प्रत्यय *m.*, विश्वास *m.*; reason for—विश्वासकारण *n.*

Beloved *adj.* प्रिय, प्रियतम

Bend back *v.* वृत् *1st Conj. Ātm. with* परा; having bent back परावृत्य

Bend down *v.* नम् *1st Conj. Parasm. with* अव

Beneficial *adj.* हित *p. p.*, हितकर *adj.*

Benefit *s.* हित *n.*, भद्र *n.*

Bent, to become, *v.* नम् *1st Conj. Parasm. with* अव

Best *adj.* श्रेष्ठ

Bewail *v.* शुच् *1st Conj. Parasm.*

Bewildered *p. p.* पर्याकुल *adj.* भ्रान्त *p. p.*

Bird *s.* विहग *m.*, पक्षिन् *m.*

Birth *s.* जन्मन् *m.*, उद्भव *m.*

Blessing *s.* आशीर्वाद *m.*

Blow *v.* वह् *1st Conj. Parasm. & Ātm.*

Blush *v.* लज्ज् *6th Conj. Ātm.*

Boat *s.* नौ *f.*;—in the shape of the body *s.* कायनौ

Bodily members, with prostration of the eight. साष्टाङ्गपातम् *adv. comp.*

Body *s.* देह *m*, शरीर *n.*; dead—*s.* शव *n.*

Body, living in the, *adj.* शरीरस्थ

Bold *adj.* धीर

Book *s.* पुस्तक *n.*, ग्रन्थ *m.*; Hindu religious—s *s.* श्रुति *f.*

Boon *s.* वर *m.*

Bought *p. p* क्रीत

Boundary, bounds *s.* सीमन् *f.*

Bow *s.* चाप *m.*, धनुस् *n.*

Bow *interj.* नमस् *ind.*

Bow to *v.* नम् *1st Conj Parasm.*

Bower *s.* मण्डप *m.*

Boy *s.* कुमार *m.*

Braid of hair *s.* कबरी *f.*

Branch *s.* शाखा *f.*

Bravery *s.* वीर्य *n.*

Break *v.* भिद्

Breaking *s.* भङ्ग *m.*

Breast *s.* वक्षस् *n.*

Brightly *adv.* उज्ज्वलम्

Bring *v.* नी *1st Conj. Parasm. & Ātm. with* आ

Brother *s.* भ्रातृ *m.*, बान्धव *m*

Buffalo *s.* महिष *m.*

Bullock *s.* वृष *m.*

Burden *s.* भार *m.*

Burn *v.* दह् *1st Conj. Parasm.*

But *Conj.* किंतु *ind.*, परम् *ind.*, तु *ind.*

C

Cage s. पञ्जर *m.*

Calamity s. अनिष्ट *n.*

Call *v.* ह्वे *1st Conj. Parasm. & Ātm.*; (name) ख्या [ख्यी *pass.*] *with* अभि

Calm, to be, *v.* शम् [शाम्] *4th Conj. Parasm.*

Captivate *v.* हृ *1st Conj. Parasm. & Ātm.*

Capture *s.* ग्रहण *n.*

Caravan *s.* सार्थ *m.*

Care for *v.* गण् *10th Conj. Parasm. & Ātm.*, ईक्ष् *1st Conj. Ātm.*

Care of, to take, *v.* तन्त्र् *10th Conj. Ātm.*

Carry *v.* नी *1st Conj. Parasm. & Ātm.*

Carry out *v.* स्था *1st Conj. Parasm. with* अनु

Cases, in many, बहुशस् *ind.*

Caste *s.* वर्ण *m.*; जाति *f*;

Cat s. बिडाल *m.*

Cause *s.* कारण *n.*

Cave *s.* बिवर *n.*

Celebrate *v.* प्रथ् *10th Conj. Parasm. & Ātm.*

Censurable *adj.* गर्ह्य, वचनीय

Censurable anything, *s.* वचनीय *n.*

Censure *v.* निन्द् *1st. Conj. Parasm.*

Censure *s.* निन्दा *f.*, वचनीय [*n.*

Certain *adj.* ध्रुव

Chamberlain *s.* कञ्चुकिन् *m*,

Chariot *s.* रथ *m.*

Charioteer *s.* सारथि *m.*, सव्येष्टृ *m.*

Cheat *s.* वञ्चक *m.*

Checked, be, रुध् *with* नि [*pass.*

Cheek *s.* कपोल *m.*

Cheerfulness *s.* उत्साह *m.*

Chief *adj.* मुख्य, प्रधानतम

Child *s.* बाल *m.*, शिशु *m.*, वत्स *m.*, डिम्भ *m.*

Citizen *s.* पौर *m.*

City *s.* नगरी *f.*, पुरी *f.*

Civility *s.* प्रश्रय *m.*

Cleverness *s.* पटुता *f.*,—in speech वाक्पटुता *f.*

Closely *adv.* दृढम्

Cloth *s.* वस्त्र *n.*, वासस् *n.*, वसन *n.*

Cloud *s.* मेघ *m.*

Coin, gold, *s.* निष्क *m.*

Cold season *s.* शिशिर *m. n.*

Collecting, collection *s.* अवचय *m.*

Collection *s.* संघात *m.*

Colour *s.* वर्ण *m.* [and आ

Come *v.* या *with* आ or सम्

Come back *v.* वृत् *1st Conj. Ātm. with* प्रति and नि

Come to *p. p.* प्राप्त

Command *v.* दिश् *6th Conj. Parasm.& Ātm. with* आ

Command *s.* आदेश *m.* आज्ञा *f.*

Commander of an army *s.* सेनापति *m.*

Companion *s,* वयस्य *m.*; female—*s.* सहचरी *f.*

Companionship *s.* संगत *n.*

Company *s.* मेल *m.*

Compassion *s.* कारुण्य *n.*

Compose *v.* नी *1st Conj. Parasm. & Ātm. with* प्र

Concealed *p. p.* छन्न

Conduct *s.* आचार *m.*; bad—*s.* दुराचार *m.*; good—*s.* सदाचार *m.*; proper—*s.* आचार *m.*

Confidence *s.* विश्वास *m.*, श्रद्धा *f.*

Confluence *s.* संगम *m.*

Conjuncture (lucky) *s.* लग्न वेला *f.*

Conquer *v.* जि *1st Conj Parasm., with* वि, *1st Conj. Ātm.*

Conquering *pr. p.* जयत्

Conqueror *s.* जेतृ *m. n.*

Consent to *v.* मन् *4th Conj. Ātm. with* अनु

Contact *s.* संपर्क *m.*

Contemplate *v.* चिन्त् *10th Conj. Parasm. & Ātm.*

Contemplation *s.* ध्यान *n.*

Continent *s.* द्वीप *m. n.*

Conviction *s.* प्रत्यय *m.*

Cook *v.* पच् *1st. Conj. Parasm. & Ātm.*

Cook *s.* सूद *m.*

Cool, to be or become, *v.* शम् [शाम्] *4th Conj. Parasm.*

Copy *s.* प्रतिकृति *f.*

Corn *s.* धान्य *n.*

Coronation *s.* अभिषेक *m.*

Cotton *s.* तूल *m.*

Counsel *s.* उपदेश *m.*

Counsellor *s.* अमात्य *m.*, धीसचिव *m.*

Count *v.* गण् *10th Conj. Parasm. & Ātm.*

Country *s.* देश *m.*, राष्ट्र *n.*, जनपद *m.* one's own— स्वदेश *m.*

Courage *s.* धृति *f.*

Court *s.* सभा *f.*

Courtesy *s.* प्रश्रय *m.*

Cover *v.* आप् *with* वि

Covered *p. p.* छन्न

Covering *s.* आवरण *n.*

Covet *v.* लुभ् *4th Conj. Parasm.*

Cow *s.* धेनु *f.*

Cowpen *s.* गोष्ठ *m.* *n.*

Create *v.* सृज् *6th Conj. Parasm.*, मा *with* निर्.

Creation *s.* सृष्टि *f.*

Creator *s.* धातृ *m.*, स्रष्टृ *m.*, ब्रह्मन् *m.*:—of the world s. जगत्कर्तृ *m.*

Creature *s.* भूत *n.*

Credible *adj.* श्रद्धेय

Creeper *s.* लता *f.*; bower of—s. *s.* लतागृह *n.*

Cross *v.* तॄ *1st Conj. Parasm.*

Crow *s.* वायस *m.*

Crowed *s.* सार्थ *m.*, समूह *m.*

Crown, to अभिषेक्तुम् *inf.*

Cry *v.* रुद्

Cry *s.* विराव *m.*

Crying *s.* रोदन *n.*

Curious *adj.* विचित्र

Current *s.* प्रवाह *m.*

Cut off, be, छिद् *pass.*

D.

Dance *v.* नृत् *4th Conj. Parasm.*

Dance / Dancing } s. नृत्य *n.*

Danger *s.* भीति *f.*

Dark *adj*, श्याम

Darkness *s.* तमस् *n.*

Daughter *s.* कन्या *f.*, दुहितृ *f.*, आत्मजा *f.*

Daughter-in-law *s.* वधू *f.*

Day *s.* दिन *n.*

Day, by, दिवा *ind.*

Dear, very, / Dearer } *adj.* प्रेयस्

Dearest *adj.* प्रियतम

Dearth *s.* दुर्भिक्ष *n.*

Death *s.* मृत्यु *m.*

Debtor *s.* अधमर्ण *m.*

Deceit *s.* कपट *n.*

Decline *v.* सद् [सीद्] *1st Conj. Parasm. with* अव

Decreasing *pr.p.* क्षयिन् *adj.*

Deed *s.* कृति *f.*, चरित *n*; good—*s.* शुभा कृतिः, शुभं चरितम्, पराक्रम *m.*, विक्रम *m.*

Deer *s* हरिण *m*, मृग *m.*

Defeat *v.* जि *with* परा *1st Conj. Ātm.*

Defence *s.* रक्षण *n.*

Defender *s.* रक्षितृ *m.*

Deformed *adj.* विरूप

Deity *s.* देवता *f.*

Delicious *adj.* स्वादु

Delight *v.* ह्लाद् *10th Conj. Parasm. & Ātm. with* आ

Delight, giving, to *s.* अनुरञ्जन *n.*

Delighted, be, *v.* मुद् *1st Conj Ātm. with* प्र

Delighting *adj.* आह्लादक

Demon *s.* असुर *m.*

Depart *v.* गम् *1st Conj. Parasm. with* निर्

Departure *s.* गमन *n.*

Depend upon *v.* श्रि *1st Conj. Parasm. & Ātm with* आ

Dependent *adj.* परवत्

Derive *v.* गम् *1st Conj. Parasm. with* अधि, लभ् *1st Conj. Ātm.*

Descend *v.* तॄ *1st Conj. Parasm. with* अव

Descending *pr. p.* अवसरत्

Describe *v.* वर्ण् *10th Conj. Parasm. & Ātm.*

Deserve *v.* अर्ह् *1st Conj. Parasm.*

Deserving person or thing *s.* पात्र *n.*

Desire *v.* स्पृह् *10th Conj. Parasm. & Ātm.*, वाञ्छ् *1st Conj. Parasm.*, अर्थ् *10th Conj. Ātm. with* प्र

Desire *s.* अभिलाष *m.*, लोभ *m*, काम *m.*

Desired *p. p.* इष्ट

Desist *v.* रम् *with* वि *1st Conj. Parasm.*

Despise *v.* धीर् *10th Conj. Parasm. & Ātm. with* अव

Destroy *v.* सूद् *10th Conj. Parasm. & Ātm. with* नि [निषूद्]

Destruction *s.* अत्यय *m.*

Development *s.* विकास *m.*

Devotee *s.* भक्त *m.*

Devotion *s.* भक्ति *f.*

Devour *v.* अद् *2nd Conj. Parasm.*, भक्ष् *10th Conj. Parasm & Ātm.*

Die *v.* मृ *6th Conj. Ātm.*

Difficulty *s.* संकट *n.*, दुर्ग *n.*, व्यसन *n.*

Dig *v.* खन् *1st Conj. Parasm. & Ātm. with* उद्

Diligent *adj.* दक्ष

Dinner *s.* भोजन *n.*

Direct *v.* दिश् *6th Conj.parasm.& Ātm.with* आ

Direction *s.* निर्देश *m.*; (quarter) दिश् *f.*

Disadvantage *s.* अनर्थ *m.*

Disc *s.* बिम्ब *n.*

Discharge *a.* अस् *4th Conj Parasm.*, क्षिप् *6th Conj. Parasm. & Ātm.*, मुच् [मुञ्च्] *6th Conj. Parasm. & Ātm.*

Disease *s.* व्याधि *m.*

Disliked *p.p.* विप्रिय *adj.*, अप्रिय *adj.*

Dismayed, be, *a.* स्मि *1st Conj. Ātm. with* वि

Dispel *v.* हृ *1st Conj. Parasm. & Ātm. with* परि

Disposition *s* प्रकृति *f.*

Disregard *v.* धीर् *10th Conj. Parasm & Ātm. with* अव

Distant *adj.* दूर

Distress *s.* क्लेश *m.*

Divert oneself *v.* हृ *1st Conj. Parasm. & Ātm. with* वि

Diverted, be, *v.* रम् *1st Conj. Ātm.*

Divine *adj.* भगवत्

Do *v.* कृ, पद् *4th Con. Ātm. with* प्रति

Doer *s* कर्तृ *m. n.*

Dog *s.* सारमेय *m.*

Doing *pr.p.* कुर्वत् *Parasm.*, कुर्वाण *Ātm.*

Dominion *s.* विषय *m.*, one's own—s. स्वविषय *m.*

Done *p.p.* विहित [विधेय

Done, what is to be, *adj.*

Done, what should be, *adj.* कर्तव्य

Donor *s.* दातृ *m. n.*

Door *s.* द्वार *n.*; a king's–s. राजद्वार *n.*

Doubt *s.* शङ्का *f.*, संदेह *m.*

Drama *s.* नाटक *n.*

Drawn *p.p.* आकृष्ट

Dreadful *adj.* दारुण

Drink *v.* पा [पिब्] *1st Conj. Parasm.*

Driving *pr p.* चोदयत्

Drop *v.* गल् *1st Conj. Parasm.*

Drop down *v.* स्रंस् *1st Conj. Ātm.*

Drop *s.* बिन्दु *m.*

Dry *v.* शुष् *4th Conj. Parasm.*

Dug *p. p.* उत्खात

Dust *s.* पांसु *m.*, रजस् *n.*

Duty *s.* धर्म *m.*,one's—*s.* स्वकृत्य *n.*

Dwell *v.* वस् *1st Conj. Parasm.*

Dwelling *pr. p.* वसत्

Dwelt *p.p.* अभ्यूषिवस् *perf. part.*

E

Eager for union *adj.* संगमोत्सुक

Earth *s.* मृद् *s.*, the—*s.* मही *f.*, पृथ्वी *f.*, वसुधा *f.*, भूमि *f.*, मेदिनी *f.*

Ease *s.* सुख *n.*

East *s.* प्राची *f.*

Eat *v.* अद् *2nd Conj Parasm*, भक्ष् *10th Conj. Parasm. & Ātm.*, ह *1st Conj. Parasm. & Ātm. with* आ

Educate *v.* नी *1st Conj.Parasm. & Ātm. with* वि

Effort *s.* यत्न *m.*, आयास *m.*

Elder *adj.* ज्यायस्

Elephant *s.* गज *m.*, नाग *m.*

Elephant, the young of an *s.* करभक *m.*

Embrace *v.* श्लिष् *4th Conj. Parasm.*, श्लिष् *with* आ, कुल् *4th Conj. Parasm.*

Endowed *p. p.* उपेत;—with the virtues of a lord स्वामिगुणोपेत *adj.*

Endure *v.* सह् *1st Conj. Ātm.*

Endured *p. p.* सोढ

Enemy *s.* अरि *m.* शत्रु *m.*, रिपु *m.*; great—*s.* महारिपु *m.*,—of the gods *s.* असुर *m.*

Energy *s.* उत्साह *m.*

Engaged, be, *v.* रभ् *1st Conj. Ātm. with* आ

England *s.* अङ्गलभूमि *f.*

Englishman *s.* अङ्गल *m.*, आङ्गलभौम *m.* [*m.*

Enjoyment(sensual) *s.* भोग

Enmity *s.* वैर *n.*

Enough *interj.* अलम् *ind.*

Enter *v* विश् *6th Conj. Parasm.*

Entered *p. p.* प्रविष्ट

Equal *adj.* तुल्य

Err *v.* मद् [माद्] *4th Conj. Parasm. with* प्र

Established *p. p.* विहित

Establishing *s.* प्रवर्तन *n.*, प्रतिष्ठापन *n.*

Establishment *s.* शाला *f.*

Even *adv.* अपि *ind.*

Even *adj.* सम

Even-minded *adj.* समचित्त

Event *s.* अर्थ *m.*

Everywhere *adv.* सर्वत्र *ind.*

Evidence *s.* प्रमाण *n.*

Evil *s.* अनर्थ *m.*, अनिष्ट *n.*

Examine *v.* ईक्ष् *1st Conj. Ātm. with* परि, मृश् *6th Conj. Parasm. with* वि

Examiner *s.* प्राश्निक *m.*

Excavate *v.* खन् *1 st Conj. Parasm. & Ātm. with* उद्

Exchange *v.* दा [यच्छ्] *1st Conj. Parasm. with* प्रति

Execution (performance) *s.* अनुष्ठान *n.*

Exertion *s.* उद्यम *m.* उद्योग *m.*; like—*adj.* उद्यमसम

Expect *v.* ईक्ष् *1st Conj Ātm. with* अप

Experience *v.* भू *1st Conj. Parasm with* अनु

Exploit *s.* पराक्रम *m.*

Expose *v.* क्षि [क्षि *pass.*] *with* आक्षिप्

Expounded, to be, *adj.* व्याख्येय

Extol. *v.* वर्ण् *10th Conj. Parasm. & Ātm.* श्लाघ् *1st Conj. Ātm.*

Eye *s.* नेत्र *n.*, नयन *n.*, चक्षुस् *n.*

F.

Face, with the turned away from *adj.* विमुख

Faint *v.* मुह् *4th Conj. Parasm.*

Faint away *v.* मूर्छ् *1st Conj. Parasm.*

Faithless *adj.* अविश्वास्य

Fall *v.* पत् *1st Conj. Parasm.*

Fall, falling *s.* पात *m.*

Fall off *v.* मद् [माद्] *4th Conj. Parasm. with* प्र

Fallen *p. p.* पतित

Falling *s.* पतन *n.*
Falsehood *s.* असत्य *n.*, अनृत *n.*
Fame *s.* कीर्ति *f.*, यशस् *n.*
Family *s.* गोत्र *n.*, born of a good—*adj.* कुलीन
Family-man *s.* कुटुम्बिन् *m.*
Famine *s.* दुर्भिक्ष *n.*
Famous *adj.* यशस्वत्
Far *adv.* दूरम्
Fate *s.* विधि *m.*
Father *s.* जनक *m.*, पितृ *m.*
Fatigue of a journey *s.* अध्वखेद *m.*
Fault *s.* अपराध *m.*; small—*s.* अपराधलव *m.*
Favour *v.* सद् [सीद्] *1st Conj. Parasm. with* प्र
Favour *s.* प्रसाद *m.*, कृपा *f.*;—of seeing दृष्टिप्रसाद *m.*
Fear *s.* भय *n.*, भीति *f.*
Fear,·causing, *adj.* भयंकर
Feel *v.* भू *1st Conj.Parasm with* अनु (*Imp. sing.*) *2nd pers. sing. imp. of the causal form of* भू, भावय
Feeling (view) *s.* मति *f.*
Female beloved *s.* कान्ता *f.*
Festival *s.* महोत्सव *m.*
Festive occasion *s.* उत्सव *m.*
Field *s.* क्षेत्र *n.*
Field of battle *s.* समराङ्गण *n.*
Fierce *adj.* चण्ड
Fight *v* युध् *4th Conj. Ātm.*
Fill *v.* भृ *1st Conj. Parasm. & Ātm.*, पूर् *10th Conj. Parasm & Ātm.*
Fire *s* अग्नि *m.*, हुतभुज् *m*, अनल *m.*
Firmly *adv.* दृढम्
First *adj.* प्रथम ;—day of a lunar fortnight *s.* प्रतिपद् *f.*
First, at, पुरा *ind.*
Fish *s.* मत्स्य *m.*
Flatter *v.* कत्थ् *1st Conj. Ātm.*
Flesh *s.* मांस *n.*
Flourish (increase) *v.* वृध् *1st Conj. Ātm. with* सम्
Flow *v.* वह् *1st Conj. Parasm. & Ātm.*
Flow *s.* प्रवाह *m.*
Flow together *v.* गम् *with* सम् *1st Conj. Ātm.*
Flower *s* कुसुम *n.*; having —*s. adj.* पुष्पधारिन्
Flowered *p p.* पुष्पित *adj.*
Fly *v.* डी *1st Conj. Ātm.*
Fly up *v.* पत् *1st Conj. Parasm. with* उद्

Follow *v.* सृ *1st Conj. Parasm with* अनु, गम् *1st Conj. Parasm. with* अनु

Follower of the *Nyāya s.* नैयायिक *m.*

Food *s.* अन्न *n.*

Fool s. मूर्ख *m.*; a hundred —*s.* मूर्खशत *n.*

Foot *s.* पाद *m.*

Foot of a tree *s.* मूल *n.*

Foot-soldier *s.* पत्ति *m.*

For *prep.* कृते *ind.*

Forest *s.* अरण्य *n.*, वन *n*, अटवी *f.*; living in-*adj.* वनवासिन्; one dwelling in a—*s.* वनौकस् *m.*

Forget *v.* स्मृ *1st Conj. Parasm. with* वि

Forgive *v.* क्षम् *1st Conj. Ātm.* क्षम् [क्षाम्] *4th Conj. Parasm.*

Forgiveness *s.* क्षमा *f.*

Form, change of, *s* विकार *m.*

Form, having, *adj.* मूर्तिमत्

Formerly *adv.* पुरा *ind.*

Fortune *s* दैव *n.*

Found out *p.p.* निरूपित. [*n.*

Four, collection of, *s.* चतुष्टय

Fragrant *adj.* सुरभि, सुगन्धि

Fragrant, made, *p p.* वासित

Fraud *s.* कपट *n*,

Frequently *adv.* अनेकशस् *ind.*

Friend *s.* मित्र *n.* वयस्य *m*, सुहृद् *m.*, सखि *m.* female—*s.* सखी *f.*

Friendship *s.* स्नेह *m.*, संगत *n.*, मित्रता *f.*

Frightful *adj.* भयंकर

Front, in *adv.* पुरतस् *ind.*

Fructify *v.* फल् *1st Conj. Parasm.*

Fruit *s.* फल *n*-

Fruit-eater *adj* फलाशिन्

Fruitless *adj.* निष्फल

Fuel *s.* इन्धन *n.*

Fulfilled, be *v.* फल् *1st Conj. Parasm.*

Future *adj.* भाविन्

G.

Gallop *v.* पत् *1st conj. Parasm. with* उद्

Gandharva *s.* गन्धर्व *m.*

Ganges *s.* गङ्गा *f.* भागीरथी *f*,

Garden *s.* उद्यान *n.* उपवन *n.*

Garland *s.* माला *f.*

Gathering *s.* अवचय *m.*

General *s.* सेनापति *m.*

Generally *adv.* प्रायस् *ind.*
Get *v.* लभ् *1st Conj. Ātm.*
Get up *v.* स्था [तिष्ठ] *1st Conj. Parasm. with* उद्
Ghee *s.* घृत *n.* [कुमारी] *f.*
Girl *s.* कन्या *f.*, नन्दिनी *f.*
Give *v.* दा [यच्छ] *1st Conj. Parasm.* दा *with* प्र, सृज् *6th Conj. Parasm. with* अति
Given, to be, or to be given in marriage *adj.* प्रदेय
Giver *s.* दातृ *m. n.*
Glean *v.* उञ्छ् *6th Conj. Parasm.*
Glory *s.* यशस् *n.*
Go *v.* गम् [गच्छ] *1st Conj. Parasm.*, चर् *1st Conj. Parasm.*, चल् *1st Conj. Parasm.*, व्रज् *1st Conj. Parasm.*
Go after *v.* गम् [गच्छ] *1st Conj. Parasm. with* अनु
Go together *v.* गम् [गच्छ] *with* सम् *1st Conj. Ātm.*
Goat *s.* अज *m.*
God *s.* ईश्वर *m.*, देव *m.*; a god दिवौकस् *m.* देव *m.*—of wealth *s.* कुबेर *m.*;—of love *s.* मदन *m.*; wife of Madana *s.* रति *f.*
Goddess *s.* देवी *f.*
Goer *s.* गन्तृ *m. n.*
Going *pr. p.* गच्छत् ;—to a holy place *adj.* क्षेत्रगामिन्
Going *s.* गति *f.*
Gold *s.* सुवर्ण *n.*, काञ्चन *n.* हेमन् *n.*
Goldsmith *s.* सुवर्णकार *m.*
Gone *p. p.* गत, यात
Good *s.* कल्याण *n.*; *adj.* शोभन
Good man or person *s.* सत् *m.*, सुजन *m.*
Goodness *s.* सत्त्व *n.*
Grace *s.* प्रसाद *m.*
Gradually *adv.* क्रमेण *instr. sing.* of क्रम
Grandson *s.* नप्तृ *m.*
Grass *s.* तृण *n.*
Gratitude *s.* कृतज्ञता *f.*
Great *adj.* महत्, पर ; very-*adj.* परम, भूयस् ;—king महाराज *m.*
Greater *adj.* भूयस्
Greatest *adj.* पर
Greatly *adv.* अतीव *ind.*

Greatness *s.* प्रकर्ष *m.*, महिमन् *m.*

Greed *s.* तृष्णा *f.*

Ground *s.* भूमि *f.*

Grow *s.* रुह् *1st Conj. Parasm.* रुह् *with* प्र

Guest *s.* अतिथि *m.*

Guide *s.* मार्गोपदेष्टृ *m.*, मार्गदर्शक *m.*

Guilty *adj.* अपराधिन्

H.

Habitation *s.* वास *m.*

Hail *interj.* स्वस्ति *ind.*

Hampered *p. p.* कुण्ठित

Hand *s.* कर *m.*, पाणि *m.*, हस्त *m.*

Handful *s.* मुष्टि *m.*

Handsome *adj.* दर्शनीय, वरतनु

Happen *v.* पत् *1st Conj. Parasm. with* आ ;—ed *p. p.* आपतित

Happiness *s.* सुख *n.*, उत्साह *m.*, शिव *n.*; he who enjoys—*adj.* सुखभाज्

Happy *adj.* सुखभाज्, कुशलिन्, निर्वृतिमत्

Happy, feel, *v.* रम् *1st Conj. Ātm.*

Harm *s.* अपाय *m.*, अहित *n.*

Hasten *v.* त्वर् *1st Conj. Ātm.*

Hater *s.* द्वेष्टृ *m.*, *n.*

Head *s.* शीर्ष *n.*, शिरस् *n.*, मूर्धन् *m.*

Heap *s.* राशि *m.*

Hear *v.* श्रु

Hearer *s.* श्रोतृ *m.*, *n.*

Hearing *s.* श्रुति *f.*

Heart *s.* हृदय *n.*, अन्तरात्मन् *m.*, अन्तःकरण *n.*

Heaven *s.* स्वर्ग *m.*

Helpless *adj.* अशरण

Hence *adv.* अतः *ind.*

Herd *s.* यूथ *n.*

Herdsman *s.* गोप *m.*

Here *adv.* अत्र *ind.*, इह *ind.*

Hermitage *s.* आश्रम *m.*

Heroism *s.* वीर्य *n.*

Hog *s.* वराह *m.*

Hold *v.* धृ *10th Conj. Parasm. & Ātm.*

Holding *s.* अवलम्बन *n.*

Holy *adj.* पूत *p. p.*, पुण्य

Home *s.* गृह *n.*

Honey *s.* मधु *n.*

Honour, your, भवत् *pron.*

Hope *v.* कांस् *with* आ *1st Conj. Ātm.*

Hope *s.* आशा *f.*

Horse *s.* अश्व *m.*, रथ्य *m.*

Hostility *s.* विग्रह *m.*,—with an enemy *s* शत्रुविग्रह *m.*

Hot *adj.* चण्ड ; to be—*v.* तप् *1st Conj. Parasm.*

Hotṛ *s.* होतृ *m.* sacrificial priest

House *s.* गृह *n.* सद्मन् *n.*

However *Conj.* परम् *ind*, तु *ind.*

Human being *s.* मानव *m.*

Hundred *s.* शत *n.*

Hungry *adj.* क्षुधित

Hunter *s.* व्याध *m.*

Husband *s.* वल्लभ *m.*, रमण *m.*, भर्तृ *m.*;—'s brother *s.* देवृ *m.*;—'s brother's wife *s.* यातृ *f.*;—'s sister *s.* ननान्दृ *f.*

Husbandman *s.* कृषीवल *m.*

Hut *s.* उटज *m.*

Hymn, Vedic, *s.* सूक्त *n.*

I.

I *pron.* अस्मद्

Idol *s.* मूर्ति *f.*

If *Conj.* यदि *ind.*

Ignorance *s.* अज्ञान *n.*

Illiterate person *s.* अपण्डित *m.*

Image *s.* मूर्ति *f.*, प्रतिकृति *f.*

Immersed *p. p.* निमग्न

Immutable *adj.* अक्षर

Impatient, be, *v.* त्वर् *1st. Conj. Ātm.*

Impeded *p. p.* कुण्ठित

Importunity *s.* निर्बन्ध *m.*

Impudence *s.* वैयात्य *n.*

Impurity *s.* श्यामिका *f.*

Inciting *s.* प्रवर्तन *n.*

Increase *v.* वृध् *1st Conj. Ātm.*, वृध् *with* सम्

India, native of, *s.* भारतवर्षीय *m.*

Indicate *v.* दिश् *6th Conj. Parasm.*&*Ātm.* *with* निर्

Industry *s.* उद्यम *m.*

Infant *s.* शिशु *m.*

Injury *s.* अहित *n.*

Innumerable *adj.* असंख्येय

Insignificant *adj.* क्षुद्र

Insolence *s.* मद *m.*

Intellect *s.* मति *f.* बुद्धि *f.*

Intelligence *s.* वार्ता *f.*;—about one's beloved *s.* प्रियाप्रवृत्ति *f.*

Intelligent *adj.* मेधाविन्

Intensity *s.* प्रकर्ष *m.*

Intoxication *s.* मद *m.*

Invite *v.* मन्त्र् *10th Conj. Ātm. with* नि

Invoke *v.* ह्वे *1st Conj. Parasm. & Ātm. with* आ

Island *s.* द्वीप *m. n.*

J.

Jar *s.* घट *m.*

Jackal *s.* शृगाल *m.*, जम्बूक *m.*

Jealousy *s.* अक्षमा *f.*

Jewel *s.* मणि *m.*, रत्न *n.*;—amongst women *s.* स्त्रीरत्न *n.*

Jeweller *s.* मणिकार *m.*

Join *v.* गम् *with* सम् *1st Conj. Ātm.*

Joined *p. p* युक्त

Joined, having, मिलित्वा *ind. past. part.*

Joined with *p. p.* प्रपन्न, उपेत

Juice *s.* रस *m.*

Justice, court of, *s.* न्यायसभा *f.*

K.

Karpūratilaka, near, कर्पूरतिलकसमीपम् *adv.*

Kill *v.* हन्

Killing *s.* वध *m.*

Kind *s.* जाति *f.*

Kindness *s.* कारुण्य *n.*

King *s.* नृप *m.*, नृपति *m.*, पार्थिव *m*, भूप *m.*, भूभृत् *m.*, राजन् *m.*

Kingdom *s.* राज्य *n.*

Know *v.* बुध् *1st Conj. Parasm. & Ātm.*, गम् *1st Conj. Parasm. with* अव, ज्ञा

Knowing the *Brahman adj.* ब्रह्मविद्

Knowledge *s.* ज्ञान *n.*

L.

Labour *s.* श्रम *m.*

Laid down *p. p.* विहित

Lake *s.* कासार *m.*, सरस् *n.*

Lame *adj.* खञ्ज

Lamp *s.* दीप *m.*

Land *s.* भूमि *f.*

Laugh in contempt *v.* हस् *1st Conj. Parasm. with* वि

Lawbook, Hindu, *s.* स्मृति *f.*

Lead *v.* नी *1st Conj. Parasm & Ātm.*

Leader *s.* नायक *m.*

Leaf *s.* पर्ण *n.*

Learn *v.* शिक्ष् *1st. Conj. Ātm.*, पठ् *1st Conj. Parasm.*

Learned *adj.* विद्वस्

Learnedness *s.* विद्वत्त्व *n.*

Learning *s* विद्या *f.*, विद्वत्त्व *n.*

Leather *s.* चर्मन् *n.*

Leave, leave off *v.* मुच् [मुञ्च्] *6th Conj. Parasm. & Ātm.*, त्यज् *1st Conj. Parasm.*

Leave, to take, (as at the time of departure) *v.* प्रच्छ् [पृच्छ्] *with* आ *6th Conj. Ātm.*

Leaving *s.* त्याग *m.*

Left *p. p.* मुक्त

Lengthening *pr. p.* वृद्धिमत् *adj.*

Lessening *pr. p.* क्षयिन् *adj.*

Lesson *s.* पाठ *m.*

Lie *s.* असत्य *n.*

Life *s.* जीव *m*, जीवित *n.* प्राण *m. plur.*

Lift up *s.* हृ *1st Conj. Parasm. & Ātm. with* उद्

Light *s.* प्रकाश *m.*, प्रभा *f.*, कान्ति *f.*, तेजस् *n.*

Lightning *s.* विद्युत् *f.*

Like *v.* नन्द् *1st Conj. Parasm. with* अभि

Liked, be, *v.* रुच् *1st Conj. Ātm.*

Liking अभिरुचि *f.*

Limb *s.* गात्र *n.*

Lion *s* सिंह *m.*

Little *adj.* अल्प, प्रतनु

Littleness *s.* लघिमन् *m.*

Live *v.* जीव् *1st Conj. Parasm.*: वस् *1st Conj. Parasm.*

Livelihood *s.* जीविका *f.*

Load *s.* भार *m.*

Long *adj.* दीर्घ, गुरु

Long (time) *adj.* चिर; *adv.* चिरम् *ind*; as—as *adv.* यावत् *ing.*

Longing *s.* उत्कण्ठा *f.*

Long-lived *adj.* आयुष्मत्

Loosened *p. p.* श्लथ *adj.*

Lord *s.* प्रभु *m.*, स्वामिन् *m.*

Lotus *s.* कमल *n.*, पद्म *n.*

Love *s.* प्रीति *f.*, स्नेह *m*, प्रेमन् *m.n.*, अनुराग *m.*, अनुरक्ति *f.*

Lover *s.* रमण *m.*, वल्लभ. *m.*

M.

Machine *s.* यन्त्र *n.*

Mad, to be, *v.* मद् [माद्] *4th Conj. Parasm.*

Made *p. p.* कृत, निर्मित

Magnanimons person *s.* महात्मन् *m.*

Maid / Maid-servant } *s.* दासी *f.*

Maintain *v.* मन् *4th Conj. Ātm.*

Majestic *ad.* भगवत्

Make *v.* *2nd pres. sing. imp.* भावय

Make, possible to, *adj.* साध्य

Man *s.* जन *m.*, नर *m.*, पुरुष *m.*, नृ *m.*, मानव *m.*; learned—*s.* पण्डित *m.*; old—*s.* जठर *m.*, वृद्ध *m.*; —of piety *s.* साधु *m.*; rich —*s.* धनिक *m.*; wise—*s.* प्रज्ञ *m.*, बुध *m.*

Manager in a play *s.* सूत्रधार *m.*

Mango (fruit) *s.* आम्र *n.*

Manifest *v.* कृ *with* आविस्

Manner *s.* रीति *f.*

Manner, in that, *adv.* तथा *ind.*; in this—*adv* इत्थम् *ind.*; in what—*adv.* कथम् *ind.*; in which—(relative) *adv.* यथा *ind.*; —of leading life *s.* चरित [*n.*

Mansian *s.* हर्म्य *n.*

Many *adj.* बहु

Marked out *p. p.* निरूपित

Marriage *s.* विवाह *m.*

Marry *v.* नी *1st Conj. Parasm. & Ātm. with* परि

Master *s.* अधिपति *m.*, भर्तृ *m.*

Mat *s.* कट *m.*

Mate *s.* सहचरी *f.*

Mean *adj.* क्षुद्र

Medicine *s.* अगद *m.*, औषध *n.*

Meditation *s.* ध्यान *n.*, आध्यान *n.*

Mendicant *s* याचक *m.*

Merciful *adj.* कारुणिक

Merit *s.* पुण्य *n.*, गुण *m.* one who appreciates —*adj.* गुणज्ञ

Meritorious *adj.* गुणवत्, गुणिन्

Message *s.* संदेश *m.*

Messenger *s.* दूत *m.*

Miles, two, *s.* क्रोश *m.*; eight—*s.* योजन *n.*

Mind *v.* गण् *10th Conj. Parasm. & Ātm.*

Mind *s.* चित्त *n.*, मनस् *n.*

Minister *s.* सचिव *m.*

Ministry *s.* प्रकृति *f.*

Misdeed *s.* दुष्कृति *f.*

Miser *s.* कदर्य *m.*

Misery *s.* दुःख *n.*, विपद् *f.*

Modesty *s.* विनय *m.*

Monday *s.* सोमवासर *m.*

Money *s.* द्रव्य *n* ,—given to *Brāhmaṇas s.* दक्षिणा *f.*

Monkey *s.* कपि *m.*

Month *s.* मास *m.*; four—s or fourfold month मासचतुष्टय *n.*

Month, bright half of a, *s.* शुक्लपक्ष *m.*

Moon *s.* चन्द्र *m.*, चन्द्रमस *m.*, इन्दु *m.*

Moonlight *s.* कौमुदी *f.*, ज्योत्स्ना *f.*

Morning, in the, *adv.* प्रातर् *ind.*

Mother *s.* जननी *f.*, मातृ *f.*

Mother-in law *s.* श्वश्रू *f.*

Motionless *adj.* निश्चेष्ट

Mount *v.* रुह् *1st Conj. Parasm. with* आ

Mountain *s.* गिरि *m.*, पर्वत *m.*, शिखरिन् *m.*

Mouth *s.* मुख *n.*

Move *v. i.* सृ *1st Conj., Parasm.*; चल् *1st Conj. Parasm.*

Moving to and fro *s.* संचलन *n.*

Mud *s.* पङ्क *m.*

Multiplicity *s.* बाहुल्य *n.*

Multitude *s.* समूह *m.*

Music *s.* संगीत *n.*

N.

Nail *s.* नख *n.*

Name *v.* धा [धी *pass.*] *with* अभि

Name *s.* अभिधान *n.*, नामन् *n.*

Name, by, namely, नाम *ind.*

Nation *s.* राष्ट्र *n.*

Natural *adj.* प्रकृतिसिद्ध

Nature *s.* प्रकृति *f.*

Neck *s.* कण्ठ *m.*

Nectar *s.* अमृत *n.*;—in the form of knowledge *s.* ज्ञानामृत *n.*

Neglect. *v.* ईक्ष् *1st Conj. Ātm. with* उप

Net *s.* जाल *n.*

New *adj.* नव

News *s.* वार्ता *f.*

Nichais, called, *adj.* नीचैराख्य

Night *s.* रजनी *f.*, निशा *f.*, रात्रि *f.*, तमिस्रा *f.*

Noble *adj.* अवदात *p. p.*

Nobly *adv.* उच्चैस् *ind.*

Not *adv.* न *ind.*; (prohibitive) मा *ind.*

Not ground *s.* अभूमि *f.*

Nourish *v.* पुष् *4th Conj. Parasm.*

Nyāya follower of, *s.* नैयायिक *m.*

O.

O *interj.* हे *ind.*, रेरे *ind.*

Obey *v.* रुध् *4th Conj. Ātm. with* अनु

Oblation (food) *s.* बलि *m.*

Observe *v.* लक्ष् *10th Conj, Parasm. & Ātm. with.* सम्

Obstacle *s.* विघ्न *m.*

Obstructed *p. p.* प्रतिहत

Obstruction *s.* आवरण *n.*

Obtain *v.* गम् *1st Conj. Parasm. with* अभि, विद् [विन्द्] *6th Conj. Parasm. & Ātm.*, लभ् *1st Conj. Ātm.*, आप्, आप् *with* अव or प्र

Obtain, difficult to *adj.* दुराप

Obtainable *adj.* साध्य

Obtaining *s.* लाभ *m.*

Occurrence (event) *s.* अर्थ *m.*

Ocean *s.* उदधि *m.*

Offence *s.* विप्रिय *n.*

Offending *adj.* अपराधिन्

Offer *v.* दा [यच्छ्] *1st Conj Parasm.*

Offering *s.* हविस् *n.*, बलि *m.*

Officer, king's राजपुरुष *m.*

Often *adv.* बहुशस् *ind.*

Oh *interj.* हे *ind.*, रेरे *ind.*

Old *adj.* वृद्ध (man)

Once, at, *adv.* सहसा *ind.*

One *adj.* एक *pron.*

Only *adv.* एव *ind.*

Or *Conj.* अथवा *ind.*, वा *ind*, उत *ind.*

Order *v.* दिश् *6th Conj. Parasm. & Ātm. with* आ

Order *s.* शासन *n.*, आज्ञा *f.*

Ornament *s.* अलंकार *m.*, भूषण *n.*

Out of *prep.* बहिस् *ind.*

Overcome *v.* लङ्घ् *1st Conj. Ātm.*

Overcome, Overpowered *p.p.* अभिभूत

Owe *v.* धृ *10th Conj. Parasm. & Ātm.*

Own, one's *adj.* स्वीय, आत्मिय, स्व *pron.*

P.

Pain *s.* क्लेश *m.*, व्यथा *f.*, पीडा *f.*; to give—to *v.*

पीड् *10th Conj.Parasm. & Ātm.*; to inflict—on *v.* तुद् *6th Conj. Parasm.*

Palace *s.* प्रासाद *m.*

Palate *s.* तालु *n.*

Pardon *v.* क्षम् [क्षाम्] *4th Conj. Parasm.*

Pardon *s.* क्षमा *f.*

Parents *s.* पितरौ *du.* of पितृ *m.*

Parrot *s.* शुक *m.*

Part, the first, *s.* पूर्वार्धं *m.*; the second or latter—*s.* परार्धं *m.*

Particle *s.* लव *m.*

Passing away *s.* अत्यय *m.*

Path, wrong, *s.* विमार्ग *m.*

Patient *adj.* स्वस्थ

Peace *s.* स्वास्थ्य *n.*, शान्ति *f.*

Peacock *s.* मयूर *m.*

Pearl *s.* मुक्ता *f.*, मौक्तिक *n.*

People *s.* जन *m.*. लोक *m.*

Perfect *adj.* निरतिशय

Performance *s.* अनुष्ठान *n.*

Peril *v.* भय *n.*, संकट *n.*

Perish *v.* नश् *4th Conj. Parasm.* ध्वंस् *1st Conj. Ātm.*

Perished *p. p.* नष्ट

Permission *s.* अनुज्ञा *f.*

Perplexity *s.* संकट *n.*

Person *s.* जन *m.*; respectable—*s.* आर्य *m.*, wicked—*s.* निशाचर *m.*, राक्षस *m.*;—who is a slave *s.* दासजन *m.*

Philosopher, metaphysical, *s.* ब्रह्मविद् *adj.*

Pilgrim *s.* यात्रिक *m.*

Pit *s.* गर्ता *f.*

Place *v.* धा [*pass* धी] *with* नि

Place *s.* स्थान *n.*; (establishment) *s.* शाला *f.*

Place, in another, *adv.* अन्यत्र *ind.*

Place of residence *s.* वसति *f.*

Placed *p. p.* निवेशित

Plant, creeping, *s.* लता *f.*

Planting *s.* आरोपण *n.*

Play *v.* क्रीड् *1st Conj. Parasm.*, हृ *1st Conj. Parasm. & Ātm. with* वि

Play *s.* क्रीडा *f.*; (drama) *s.* नाटक *n.*

Please *v.* प्री [प्रीण्] *10th Conj. Parasm. & Ātm.*, रुच् *1st Conj. Ātm.*

Pleased *p. p.* प्रसन्न ; be—*v.* तुष् *4th Conj. Parasm.*, सद् [सीद्] *1st Conj. Parasm. with* प्र

Pleasing *s.* अनुरञ्जन *n.*, आराधन *n.*

Pleasure *s.* रति *f.*, सुख *n.*

Plentiful *adj.* प्रभूत

Plenty *s.* समृद्धि *f.*

Plough *v.* कृष् 1*st Conj. Parasm.* & 6*th Conj.Parasm.* & *Ātm.*

Plunged in *p. p.* निमग्न

Poet *s.* कवि *m.* lord of–s, chief of—s *s.* कवीश *m.*

Poison *s.* विष *n*

Poison, deadly, *s.* हलाहल *n.*

Politics *s.* नीति *f.*

Pollen *s.* रजस् *n.*

Polluted *p. p.* दूषित

Pond, small, *s.* पल्वल *m. n.*

Poor *adj.* दरिद्र

Potter *s.* कुम्भकार *m.*

Poverty *s.* दारिद्र्य *n.*

Power *s.* प्रभाव *m.* सामर्थ्य *n.*

Powerful *adj.* समर्थ

Practise *v.* चर् 1*st Conj. Parasm. with* आ

Praise *v.* शंस् 1*st. Conj. Parasm.*, कत्थ् 1*st* Conj. *Ātm.* श्लाघ् 1*st Conj.Ātm.*

Praise *s.* स्तुति *f.*

Praiseworthy *ad.* प्रशस्य

Prate / Prattle } जल्प् 1*st Conj. Parasm.*

Precept, sacred, *s.* विधि *m*

Preceptor *s.* आचार्य *m.*, गुरु *m.*

Predilection *s.* प्रवृत्ति *f.*

Preparation *s.* संभार *m.*

Prepared *adj.* उद्यत *p. p.*

Presence, in the, (of) पुरतस् *ind.*

Present *s.* उपहार *m.*

Price *s.* पण्य *n.*; religious merit as the—पुण्यपण्य *n.*

Pride *s.* मद *m.*

Priest at the Soma sacrifice *s.* मैत्रावरुण *m.*

Priest, sacrificial, *s.* ऋत्विज् *m.*, होतृ *m.*

Prince *s.* राजपुत्र *m.*

Prison *s.* कारागृह *n.*

Proclaim *v.* घुष् 10*th Conj. Parasm.* & *Ātm.* [भी]

Produce *v.* मा *with* निर् *pass.*

Produced *p. p.* जात

Produced, be, *v.* भू 1*st Conj. Parasm. with* उद्, जन् [जा] 4*th Conj. Ātm.*, पद् 4*th Conj. Ātm.*, *with* उद्

Profession *s.* वृत्ति *f.*

Proficiency *s.* प्रावीण्य *n.*

Proficient *adj.* निपुण

Progeny *s.* प्रजा *f.*

Promised *p. p.* प्रतिज्ञात

Proper *adj.* उचित

Propitiation *s.* आराधन *n.*

Prosper *v.* ऋध् *4th Conj. Parasm. with* सम्

Prosperity *s.* अभ्युदय *m.*, भूति *f.*, संपद् *f.*

Prosperous *adj.* श्रीमत्, श्रेयस्

Protect *v.* रक्ष् *1st Conj. Parasm.*, अव् *1st Conj. Parasm.*

Protected *p. p.* रक्षित

Protection *s.* रक्षा *f.*

Protector *s.* पालक *m. n.*, रक्षितृ *m. n.*

Proud *adj.* उद्धत *p. p.*

Prove *v.* लक्ष् *10th Conj. Parasm. & Ātm. with* सम्

Proximity *s.* संनिधि *m.*

Publish *v.* प्रथ् *10th Conj. Parasm. & Ātm.*

Puddle *s.* पल्वल *m. n.*

Punish *v.* दण्ड् *10th Conj. Parasm. & Ātm.*

Punishment *s.* दण्ड *m.*

Pupil *s.* शिष्य *m.*, छात्र *m.*

Pure *adj.* अवदात *p. p.*, विशुद्ध *p. p.*

Purity *s.* विशुद्धि *f.*

Purified *p. p.* पूत

Q.

Quality *s.* गुण *m.*

Quarrel *s.* कलि *m.* कलह *m.*

Quarter *s.* दिश् *f.*

Queen *s.* राज्ञी *f.*; crowned —*s.* महिषी *f.*

Quickly *adv.* द्रुतम्

R.

Race *s.* गोत्र *n.*, वंश *m.*

Ramble *v.* अट् *1st Conj. Parasm.*

Rascal *s.* जाल्म *m.*

Reach *v.* आप् *with* अव or प्र

Ready *adj.* उद्यत *p. p.*, सिद्ध *p. p.*

Reality *s.* तत्त्व *n.*, भूतार्थ *m.*

Reason *s.* कारण *n.*, निमित्त *n.*

Recourse, have, to *v.* भज् *1st Conj. Parasm. & Ātm.*

Red *adj.* रक्त *p. p.*

Regard *v.* मन् *4th Conj. Ātm.*

Regarding all equally *adj.* समचित्त

Rejoice *v.* मुद् *1st Conj. Ātm.*, नन्द् *1st Conj. Parasm. with* अभि

Relation *s.* बन्धु *m.* ज्ञाति *m.* बान्धव *m.*

Release *v.* मुच् [मुञ्च] *6th Conj. Parasm* & *Ātm,* घ *1st* & *10th Conj. Parasm.* &*Ātm. with* उद्

Released *p. p.* मुक्त

Remedy *s.* उपाय *m.*

Remember *v.* स्मृ *1st Conj. Parasm.*

Remembrance *s.* स्मृति *f.*

Remove *v.* हृ *1st Conj.Parasm* &*Ātm.,* हृ *with* परि, नी *1st Conj. Parasm.* & *Ātm. with* अप

Reply *v.*भाष् *1st Conj. Ātm. with* प्रति

Repulse, Repulsion *s.* अवधीरणा *f.*

Request *v.* अर्थ् *10th Conj. Ātm. with* प्र or अभि

Request *s.* वचन *n.*

Requisites *s..* संभार *m. pl.*

Reside *v.* वस् *1st Conj. Parasm. with* नि

Residence *s.* वास *m.*

Resort to *v.* भज् *1st Conj. Parasm.* & *Ātm.,* लम्ब् *1st Conj. Ātm. with* अव, सेव् *1st Conj. Ātm. with* परि

Respect *s.* आदर *m.*

Rest.*v.* श्रम् [श्राम्] *4th Conj. Parasm. with* वि

Rest upon *v.* वस् *1st Conj Parasm. with* अधि

Rest, for the purpose of, विश्रामहेतोः *abl.* or *gen. sing.* विश्रामहेतु *m.*

Resting place *s.* संश्रय *m.*

Restraining of the mind *s.* मनःसंयम *m.*

Restraint *s.* सयंम *m.*

Result *v.* भू *1st Conj. Parasm. with* उद्, जन् [जा] *4th Conj. Ātm.,* पद् *4th Conj. Ātm. with* उद् or निस्

Results.परिणाम *m.*

Resulted *p. p.* जात

Retaliation *s.* प्रतिक्रिया *f.*

Return *v.* वेत् *1st Conj. Ātm.with* नि, or *with* प्रति and नि, गम् [गच्छ] *1st Conj. Parasm. with* प्रति and आ

Returned *p. p.* निवृत्त

Revenge, the way to revenge *s.* प्रतिक्रिया *f.*

Revere *v.* पूज् *10th Conj. Parasm. & Ātm.*

Reverence, object of, *s.* पूजास्थान *n.*

Reward *s.* पारितोषिक *n.*

Rice *s.* तण्डुल *m.*; ball of—given to the dead *s.* पिण्ड *m.*; cooked—*s.* ओदन *m.*; —of various kinds (a grain of) *s.* व्रीहि *m.*

Riches *s.* विभव *m.*

Rise *v.* स्था [तिष्ठ] *1st Conj. Parasm. with* उद्

Rise *s.* अभ्युदय *m.*

Rise up (fly up) *v.* पत् *1st Conj. Parasm with* उद्

Rising *pr.p.* उद्यत्

Rival *v.* स्पर्ध् *1st Conj.Ātm.*

Rivalry *s.* अक्षमा *f.*

River *s.* नद *m.*, नदी *f.*

Road *s.* मार्ग *m.*, वीथि *f.*

Rogue शठ *m.*

Room (space) *s.* अवकाश *m.*

Root *s.* मूल *n.*

Rope *s.* रज्जु *f.*

Royalty *s.* नृपत्व *n.*, राज्य *n.*; drawn by the desire of—*adj.* राज्यलोभाकृष्ट

Rudeness *s.* वैयात्य *n.*

Ruin *s.* नाश *m.*

Rule *v.* शास्

Ruling *pr.p* शासत्

Run *v.* धाव् *1st Conj. Parasm.*

S.

Sacrifice, belonging to a *adj.* यज्ञिय; to perform a—*v.* हु *1st Conj.Parasm. & Ātm. with* आ

Sacrificer *s.* यजमान *m.*

Sad *adj.* दुःखित, विषण्ण *p.p.*

Sage *s.* ऋषि *m.*, साधु *m.*

Sailor *s.* नाविक *m.*

Sake, for the, (of) कृते *ind.*

Salt *adj.* लवण ; *s.* लवण *n.*

Salute *v.* नम् *1st Conj. Parasm.*, वाद् *10th Conj. Parasm. & Ātm. with* अभि (*i. e.* the causal of वद् *1st Conj. Parasm with* अभि), वन्द् *1st Conj. Ātm.*

Sat *p. p.* तस्थिवस् *perf. p. act.*

Satisfaction *s.* प्रीति *f.*

Satisfied, be, *v.* तुष् *4thConj. Parasm.*, तृप् *4th Conj. Parasm.*

Save *v.* घ *1st* and *10th Conj. Parasm. & Ātm. with* उद्, रक्ष् *1st Conj. Parasm. with* परि

Saying *s.* वचन *n.*

Says *pres. tense 3rd pers. sing.* ब्रूते

Scarcity *s.* दुर्भिक्ष *n.*

Scatter *v.* अस् *4th Conj. Parasm. with* निर्

Scattered *p. p.* निरस्त

Scholar *s.* छात्र *m.*

School *s.* पाठशाला *f.*

Science *s.* शास्त्र *n.*

Sea *s.* समुद्र *m.*

Search for *v.* इष् *4th Conj Parasm with* अनु

Seat *s.* आसन *n.*

Seated *p. p* निषण्ण

See *v.* ईक्ष् *1st Conj Ātm.*, ईक्ष् *with* प्र, दृश् [पश्य्] *1st Conj. Parasm.*

Seed *s.* बीज *n.*

Seeing *pr. p.* पश्यत्

Seeing *s.* दृष्टि *f.*

Seek *v.* मार्ग् *10th Conj. Parasm. & Ātm.*, मृग् *10th Conj. Ātm.*, अर्थ् *10th Conj. Ātm. with* प्र

See *p. p.* दृष्ट

Seen, having, अवलोक्य *ind. past part.*

Seer *s.* द्रष्टृ *m. n.*

Seize *v* धृ *1st Conj. Parasm. & Ātm.*

Self *s.* आत्मन् *m.*

Send *v.* हि *with* प्र

Sense,lose, *v* मुह् *4th Conj. Parasm.*

Sensible *adj.* धीमत्

Sent *p. p* प्रस्थापित

Sentence *s.* वाक्य *n.*

Separation *s.* वियोग *m.*

Serpent *s.* सर्प *m.*

Servant *s.* किंकर *m*, भृत्य *m.*, अनुजीविन् *m.*

Serve *v* सेव् *1st Conj. Ātm.*

Sesamum *s.* तिल *m.*

Set about *v* वृत् *1st Conj. Ātm. with* प्र

Set out *v.* स्था *with* प्र *1st Conj. Ātm.*

Sex *s* लिङ्ग *n.*

Shade *s* छाया *f.*

Shake *v* कम्प् *1st Conj Ātm.*

Shame *s.* लज्जा *f.*; to feel— *v.* लज्ज् *6th Conj. Ātm.*

Sharp *adj* निशित *p. p.*

Shine *v.* काश् *1st Conj. Ātm. with* प्र द्युत् *1st Conj. Ātm.*, तप् *1st Conj. Parasm*, राज् *1st Conj Parasm. & Ātm. with* वि

Ship *s.* नौ *f.*

Shoe s. उपानह् *f.*

Shore s. तीर *n.*

Short *adj.* लघु

Show v दिश् *6th Conj. Parasm. & Ātm.*, कृ [क्रि *pass.*] *with* आविस्

Shunned, what should be, *adj.* परिहर्तव्य

Sickness s. व्याधि *m.*

Side, the other, s पार *m.*

Sight s. दर्शन *n.*

Silence s. मौन *n.*

Silent *adj.* मूक

Silent, silently *adv.* तूष्णीम् *ind.*

Silly, to be, *v.* मुह् *4th Conj. Parasm.*

Sin s. पाप *n.*, अधर्म *m.*

Sinful *adj.* पाप

Sing *v.* गै *1st Conj. Parasm.*

Singing s. संगीत *n.*, गान *n.*

Sinner s. पाप *m.*

Sister s. स्वसृ *f.*

Sit *v.* विश् *6th Conj. Parasm. with* उप, सद् [सीद्] *1st Conj. Parasm with* नि [निषीद्] ;—upon *v.* वस् *1st. Conj. Parasm. with* अधि

Sitting *pr. p.* निषण्ण *p. p.*

Śiva s. शूलिन् *m.*

Skill s. चातुर्य *n.*

Sky s. आकाश *m. n.*, अम्बर *n.*, नभस् *n.*, वियत् *n.*

Sky, the, and the earth s. द्यावापृथिवी *f. du.*

Slow *adj.* मन्द

Slowly *adv.* शनैस् *ind.*

Sluggishness s. जाड्य *n.*

Small *adj.* प्रतनु, अल्प, तनु

Smile *v.* स्मि *1st Conj. Ātm.*

Snow s. हिम *n.*

So *adv.* इति *ind.*

Soft *adj.* मृदु

Soldier s. सैनिक *m.*

Solely *adv.* केवलम्

Solicit *v.* अर्थ् *10th Conj. Ātm. with* अभि

Son s. पुत्र *m.*, तनय *m.*, आत्मज *m.*, सूनु *m.*

Son, like the birth of a, *adj.* पुत्रजन्मसम

Song s. संगीत *n.*, गीत *n.*

Songster s. गायक *m.*

Son-in-law s. जामातृ *m.*

Soon *adv.* द्रुतम्, अचिरात् *ind.*

Sorry *adj.* दुःखित

Sort, of this, *adj.* एतादृश

Soul *s.* आत्मन् *m.*; great—*s.* महात्मन् *m.*

Soul, the internal, *s.* अन्तरात्मन् *m.*

Sound *s.* ध्वनि *m.*

Source *s.* प्रभव. *m.*

Sowing *s.* आरोपण *n.*

Space *s.* अवकाश *m.*

Spade *s.* खनित्र *n.*

Speak *v* वद् *1st Conj. Parasm*, भाष् *1st Conj. Ātm.*

Speaker *s.* वक्तृ *m. n.*

Speech *s.* वाचा *f.*, वाणी *f.*, वाच् *f.*, वचस् *n.*

Speed *s.* जव *m.*

Speedily *adv.* सत्वरम्

Spirit, evil, *s.* निशाचर *m.*, राक्षस *m.*, रक्षस् *n.*

Spiritual *adj.* आध्यात्मिक

Splendid, be *v.* शुभ् *1st Conj. Ātm.*

Splendour *s.* कान्ति *f.*

Spoken, spoken to *p. p.* उक्त

Sport *s* क्रीडा *f.*

Sport *v.* रम् *1st Conj. Ātm.*

Spot *s.* कलङ्क *m.*

Spread *v.* सृ *1st Conj. Parasm. with* प्र

Spring *s.* वसन्त *m.*

Sprinkle *v.* सिच् [सिञ्च्] *6th Conj. Parasm. & Ātm.*

Sprout *s.* पल्लव *m. n.*

Stain *s.* कलङ्क *m.*

Stalk *s.* वृन्त *n.*

Stalk abroad *v.* चर् *1st Conj. Parasm*

Stand *v.* स्था [तिष्ठ] *1st Conj. Parasm*

Star *s.* तारक *n.*, तारा *f.*; cluster of—*s. s.* तारागण *m.*

Start *v.* स्था *with* प्र *1st Conj. Ātm.*

State, bad, *s.* दुर्दशा *f.*

Steady *adj.* अविचालित

Steal *v* चुर् *10th Conj. Parasm. & Ātm.*

Step *s.* पद *n.*

Step towards *v.* पद् *4th Conj. Ātm. with* प्रति

Stick *s.* दण्ड *m.*, यष्टि *f.*

Stone *s.* शिला *f.* दृशद् *f.*, अश्मन् *m.*

Stood up, having उत्थाय *ind.*, *p. p.*

Stop *v.* रम् *with* वि *1st Conj. Parasm.*
Store *s.* निधि *m.*
Story *s.* कथा *f.*
Straightforwardness *s.* ऋजुता
Street *s.* रथ्या *f.*
Strength *s.* बल *n.*
Strife *s.* कलि *m.*, कलह *m.*
Strike *v.* हृ *1st Conj. Parasm. & Ātm. with* प्र
Strive *v.* यत् *1st Conj. Ātm.*
Strong *adj.* प्रबल
Study *s.* अध्ययन *n.*
Subjects *s.* प्रजा *f.*
Submit *v.* गम् *1st Conj. Parasm. with acc. sing of* शरण or वश
Success *s.* जय *m.*, विजय *m.*, सिद्धि *f.*
Suddenly *adv.* सहसा *ind.*
Summer *s.* ग्रीष्म *m.*
Summit *s* शिखर *m. n.* [*m.*
Sun *s.* सूर्य *m.*, रवि *m.* सवितृ
Sun (Sunshine) *s.* आतप *m.*
Superior *adj.* श्रेष्ठ श्रेयस्
Supported *p. p.* विधृत
Surface, upper, of a palace *s.* प्रासादतल *n.*
Surmount *v.* तॄ *1st Conj. Parasm. with* सम् or शद्, पार् *10th Conj. Parasm. & Ātm.*
Surround *v.* वृ *with* परि
Suspect *v.* शङ्क् *1st Conj. Ātm.*
Suspicious *adj.* साशङ्क
Swagger *v.* गल्भ् *1st Conj. Ātm. with* प्र
Sweeping *s.* संमार्जन *n.*
Sweetly *adv.* मधुरम्
Sweetmeat *s.* मोदक *m.*
Sweetness *s.* माधुर्य *n.*
Swoon *v.* मूर्च्छ् *1st Conj. Parasm.*
Sword *s.* असि *m.*, खड्ग *m.*

T.

Tail *s.* लाङ्गूल *n.* पुच्छक *n.*; holding the—*s.* पुच्छकावलम्बन *n.*
Take away *v.* हृ *1st Conj. Parasm. & Ātm.*, नी *1st Conj. Parasm. & Ātm. with* अप
Taking away *s.* हरण *n.*
Talent *s.* बुद्धि *f.*; power of—*s* बुद्धिप्रभाव *m.*
Talented *adj.* धीमत्, मेधाविन्
Tank *s* तडाग *m.*
Taste *v.* स्वाद् *1st Conj. Ātm.*
Taunt *s.* उपालम्भ *m.*
Teach *v.* दिश् *6th Conj. Parasm. & Ātm. with* उप
Tear *s.* अश्रु *n.*
Tear दॄ *10th conj. Parasm. & Ātm*

Tell *v.* कथ् *10th Conj. Parasm & Ātm.*, शंस् *1st conj Parasm.*

Temple *s* देवकुल *n*, देवायतन *n.*;—of Śiva *s.* शिवालय *n.*

Tend *v.* तन्त्र् *10th Conj. Ātm.*

Terrace of a palace *s.* प्रासादतल *n.*

Test *v.* मृश् *6th Conj Parasm. with* वि, लक्ष् *10th Conj Parasm. & Ātm. with* सम्

That *pron* तद्, अदस्

Theft *s* चौर्य *n.*

Then *adv.* तदा *ind.*

Thence *adv* ततः *ind.*

There *adv.* तत्र *ind.*

Thief *s.* स्तेन *m*, चोर *m.*

Thing *s.* वस्तु *n.* अर्थ *m*; real—*s* वस्तु *n.*, सत्तत्त्व *n.*; not a—*s.* अवस्तु *n.*; unreal —*s.* अवस्तु *n.*

Think *v.* मन् *4th Conj. Ātm.*

Thirst *s.* तृष्णा *f.*

This *pron.* एतद्, इदम्, अदस्

Thorn *s.* कण्टक *m. n.*

Thou *pron.* युष्मद्

Thought *p. p* चिन्तित; *s.* मति *f.*

Throb *v.* स्फुर् *6th Conj Parasm.*, स्पन्द् *1st Conj Ātm.*

Throne *s.* सिंहासन *n.*

Throw अस् *v. 4th Conj. Parasm.* अस् *with* प्र, क्षिप् *6th Conj. Parasm & Ātm.*

Thunderbolt, Indra's *s.* पवि *m.*

Thus *adv.* इति *ind.*, एवम् *ind.*

Tiger *s.* व्याघ्र *m.*

Tigress *s* व्याघ्री *f.*

Time *s* काल *m.*; proper—*s.* काल *m.*; improper—*s.* अकाल *m.*

Timid *adj.* भीरु; भीरू *f.*

Tip *s* अग्र *n.*

To-day *adv* अद्य *ind.*

Token *s.* चिह्न *n.*

To-morrow *adv.* श्वस् *ind.*

Tongue *s* जिह्वा *f.*; tip of the—*s.* जिह्वाग्र *n.*

Top *s* शिखर *m. n.*

Tortoise *s.* कूर्म *m.*

Touch *v* स्पृश् *6th Conj. Parasm.*

Touch *s.* संपर्क *m.*

Touched *p. p* स्पृष्ट

Town *s.* नगर *n.*, पुरी *f.* नगरी *f.*

Traitor, act the, *v.* द्रुह् *4th Conj. Parasm.*

Tranquil *adj.* स्वस्थ

Tranquil, be, *v* शम् [शाम्] *4th Conj. Parasm.*

Tranquillity *s* स्वास्थ्य *n.*, शान्ति *f.*

Transformation *s.* विकार *m.*

Transgress *v.* लङ्घ् *1st Conj. Ātm.*
Transgressed, that cannot be, *adj* अलङ्घनीय
Transitory *adj.* चञ्चल
Treasure *s* कोश. *m.*
Tree *s.* वृक्ष *m.*, तरु *m.*, पादप *m.*
Tremble *v.* वेप् *1st Conj. Ātm.*
Trouble *s.* आयास *m.*
True *adj.* सत्य
Truly *adv.* सत्यम्
Truth *s.* सत्त्व *n.*, सत्य *n.* भूतार्थ *m.*
Tutor *s.* आचार्य *m.*

U

Uncertain *adj* अध्रुव
Uncle, paternal, *s* पितृव्य *m.*
Understand *v.* बुध् *1st Conj. Parasm. & Ātm.*
Union *s.* मेल *m.*
Union, eager for, *adj.* संगमोत्सुक
Universe *s.* विश्व *n.*
Unpalatable *adj.* अप्रिय
Unsurpassed *adj.* निरतिशय
Untruth *s.* अनृत *n.*
Upheld *p. p.* विधृत

V.

Valour *s.* वीर्य *n*, शौर्य *n.*
Variegated *adj.* विचित्र
Various *adj* विविध
Venerable person *s.* गुरु *m.*
Verily *adv.* किल *ind.*
Verul *s.* एलापुर *n.*
Very *adv* अतीव *ind.*
Verse *s* श्लोक *m.*; Vedic— *s.* मन्त्र *m.* [*m.*
Vicinity *s.* संनिधि *m.*, सकाश
Victory *s.* विजय *m.*
View *s.* मति *f.*
Village *s.* ग्राम *m.*
Villain *s.* खल *m.*
Violation *s.* भङ्ग *m.*
Virgin *s* कुमारी *f.*
Virtue *s.* धर्म *m.*, गुण *m.*
Virtuous *adj.* पुण्यवत्, सुवृत्त
Virtuous man *s.* सत् *m.*
Visnu, celestial abode of, *s.* वैकुण्ठ *n.*
Visible *adj* दृश्य
Vowed *p. p.* प्रतिज्ञात
Vultures, lord of, *s.* गृध्रराज *m.*

W.

Wait upon *v.* चर् *1st Conj. Parasm. with* परि, सेव् *1st Conj. Ātm.*
Walk *v.* चर् *1st Conj. Parasm.*
Walking, mode of, *s* गति *f.*
Wallow *v.* लुट् *4th Conj. Parasm.*
Wander *v.* अट् *1st Conj. Parasm.*
War *s.* युध् *f*, विग्रह *m.*:—and peace विग्रहसंधि *m.*

Warrior *s.* योध *m.*, वीर *m.*

Wash / Wash off *v.* क्षल *10th Conj. Parasm* & *Ātm.* *with* प्र

Waste away *v.* क्षि *1st Conj. Parasm.*

Water *s.* जल *n.*, वारि *n.*, उदक *n.*, पयस् *n.*

Water *v. i.* स्रु *1st Conj. Parasm.*

Way *s.* वर्त्मन् *n.*; (manner) रीति *f.*

We *pron.* अस्मद्

Wealth *s.* धन *n.*, वसु *n.*, संपद् *f.*, वित्त *n.*, अर्थ *m.*, विभव *m.*

Wealth, goddess of, *s.* लक्ष्मी *f.*

Wealth, possessor of, *s.* धनभाज् *adj.*

Weapon *s.* शस्त्र *n.*

Weapon, miraculous, *s.* अस्त्र *n.*

Wear *v. t.* धृ *10th Conj. Parasm.* & *Ātm.*

Weary, to be, *v.* श्रम् [श्राम्] *4th Conj. Parasm.*

Weigh *v.* तुल *10th Conj. Parasm.* & *Ātm.*

Weight *s.* भर *m.*

Welfare *s.* कल्याण *n.*, शिव *n.*

Well *adj.* कुशलिन्

Well *adv.* सुष्ठु *ind.*, सम्यक्; (preferably) वरम्

Well *s.* वापी *f.*, कूप *m.*

Well-being *s.* भद्र *n.*

Well-versed *adj.* निष्णात

Wet, be, *v.* स्नु *1st Conj. Parasm.*

What *interr. pron* किम्

What is to be *adj.* भाविन्

Wheel *s.* चक्र *n.*

When *interr. adv.* कदा *ind.*

When *relat. adv.* यदा *ind.*

Whence *interr. adv.* कुतः *ind.*

Whence *relat. adv.* यतः *ind.*

Where *interr. adv.* कुत्र *ind.*, क्व *ind.*

Where *relat. adv.* यत्र *ind.*

Which *interr. pron.* किम्

Which *relat. pron.* यद्

White *adj.* श्वेत; brilliant —*adj.* भास्वर शुक्ल

Who *interr. pron.* किम्

Who *relat. pron.* यद्

Whole *adj.* अखिल

Wholesome thing, what is wholesome *s.* पथ्य *n.*

Wholly *adv.* सर्वथा *ind.*

Wicked *adj.* नृशंस

Wife *s.* भार्या *f.*, पत्नी *f.*, कान्ता *f.*, गेहिनी *f.*,—and husband *s.* जायापती *m. du.*

Wilderness *s.* अरण्य *n.*, अटवी *f.*

Wind *s.* पवन *m.*, मारुत *m.* वायु *m.*, मरुत् *m.*, वात *m.*

Window *s.* वातायन *n.*

Wine s. मदिरा *f.*

Wise *adj* धीर

Wish *v* इष् [इच्छ्] *6th Conj. Parasm.*

Wish *s.* इच्छा *f.*

Wished *p. p.* इष्ट

With *prep.* सह *ind.*

Without *prep* विना *ind.*

Witness s. साक्षिन् *m.*

Woman s. नारी *f.*, ललना *f.*; —of distinction *s* देवी *f.*; proud—*s* मानिनी *f.*; venerable—s. आर्या *f.*; young —प्रमदा *f.*, वधू *f.*

Wonder *v.* स्मि *1st Conj. Ātm. with* वि

Wood *s.* काष्ठ *n*, (forest) वन *n.*

Words *s.* वाक्य *n.*

Work *s.* कार्य *n.*

Work (book) s. ग्रन्थ *m.*

World s. लोक *m.*, जगत् *n.*

Worn *p p.* परिहित

Worn out *p. p.* जीर्ण

Worship *v.* पूज् *10th Conj. Parasm.& Ātm.*, पूज् *1st Conj. Parasm. & Ātm.*, यज् *1st Conj. Parasm. & Ātm.*

Worship *s.* पूजा *f.*, अर्चन *n.*, materials of—*s* अर्घ्य *n.*, object of—*s* पूजास्थान *n.*

Worthlessness *s.* असारता *f.*

Worthy of honour *adj.* पूज्य

Wreath *s.* माला *f.*

Wreathing *s.* प्रथन *n.*

Wretch *s.* जाल्म *m.*

Write *v.* लिख् *6th Conj. Parasm.*

Write (a book) *v.* नी *1st Conj. Parasm. & Ātm. with* प्र

Written *p. p.* प्रणीत, लिखित

Y

Yesterday *adv.* ह्यस् *ind.*

You *pron.* युष्मद्

Younger *adj.* कनीयस्